Dear Reade

The book yo
the St. Mart
York Times
Crime Libr
latest, most sensational crimes that have captured the
national attention. St. Martin's is the publisher of John
Glatt's riveting and horrifying SECRETS IN THE CELLAR,
which shines a light on the man who shocked the world
when it was revealed that he had kept his daughter locked
in his hidden basement for 24 years. In the Edgar-
nominated WRITTEN IN BLOOD, Diane Fanning looks at
Michael Petersen, a Marine-turned-novelist found guilty
of beating his wife to death and pushing her down the
stairs of their home—only to reveal another similar death
from his past. In the book you now hold, THE BLACK
WIDOWER, Michael Fleeman examines a case in which a
seemingly perfect marriage went terribly wrong.

St. Martin's True Crime Library gives you the stories
behind the headlines. Our authors take you right to the
scene of the crime and into the minds of the most no-
torious murderers to show you what really makes them
tick. St. Martin's True Crime Library paperbacks are better than the most terrifying thriller, because it's all true!
The next time you want a crackling good read, make sure
it's got the St. Martin's True Crime Library logo on the
spine—you'll be up all night!

Charles E. Spicer

Charles E. Spicer, Jr.
Executive Editor, St. Martin's True Crime Library

ALSO BY MICHAEL FLEEMAN

CRAZY FOR YOU
LOVE YOU MADLY
KILLER BODIES
THE OFFICER'S WIFE
DEADLY MISTRESS
OVER THE EDGE
LACI
THE STRANGER IN MY BED
IF I DIE . . .

THE **BLACK WIDOWER**

MICHAEL FLEEMAN

St. Martin's Paperbacks

THE BLACK WIDOWER

Copyright © 2017 by Michael Fleeman.

All rights reserved.

For information address St. Martin's Press, 175 Fifth Avenue, New York, NY 10010.

ISBN: 978-1-250-07886-5

Our books may be purchased in bulk for promotional, educational, or business use. Please contact your local bookseller or the Macmillan Corporate and Premium Sales Department at 1-800-221-7945, ext. 5442, or by e-mail at MacmillanSpecialMarkets@macmillan.com.

Printed in the United States of America

St. Martin's Paperbacks edition / August 2017

St. Martin's Paperbacks are published by St. Martin's Press, 175 Fifth Avenue, New York, NY 10010.

10 9 8 7 6 5 4 3 2 1

FOREWORD

It was a glorious fall day. The aspens blazed yellow in the bright afternoon sun. The air was thin and warm enough for short-sleeves and smelled of pine and dust from the trail. Harold and Toni Henthorn looked like any other middle-aged couple on the trail to the summit of Deer Mountain. Toni wore jeans and hiking boots and a pink polo shirt and carried a purple backpack. That morning she had carefully combed and styled her shoulder-length light reddish blond hair, taking a curling iron to the ends so it turned up on either side of her face. She applied red lipstick and wore big amber tinted sunglasses. Harold wore jeans and a white T-shirt with a long-sleeved denim shirt over it and a gray baseball cap on which was written "2000 U.S. Open" beneath an embroidered American flag. He was a few inches taller than his wife, had brown hair and a good smile and a slight middle-aged paunch. His backpack was gray.

They had spent the night at the $300-a-night Stanley Hotel in Estes Park, Colorado, the historic and (supposedly) haunted inspiration for Stephen King's *The Shining,* posing for photos in front of the stately white-painted Georgian structure with a red roof and a wide porch with white columns and a row of American flags fluttering in the mountain air. They'd made dinner reservations at the nicest place in Estes Park, Nicky's Steakhouse, for later that evening. A handwritten entry in the reservation book had them down for 7 P.M., though their name was misspelled "Henchorn."

It was a Saturday, September 29, 2012, their twelfth wedding anniversary.

The couple set out at about 1:30 P.M. from the Deer Mountain trailhead marked by a wooden National Park Service kiosk warning them of all the things they shouldn't do and all the dangers that could await them on the trail. The trek begins at 8,930 feet above sea level and rises another 1,210 feet, for the next three miles, to a final elevation, at the mountain's summit, of 10,013 feet. The guidebooks list the Trail Difficulty Rating as "moderate," owing to the altitude and round-trip length and for sections of the trail that rise steeply on narrow switchbacks strewn with rocks and boulders and fallen branches and marked by little arroyos and tiny rock piles from mini-avalanches along the trail wall.

Anyone who has hiked the six-mile trek can attest that the experience is sublime. The trail cuts through meadows and stands of pine and reaches an apex that is not a craggy peak but a broad plateau from which, two miles high, one can see everything worth seeing. In one direction looms a row of mountains dominated by the famous Longs Peak. In another direction rises a series of gray peaks, aligned in formation, over Mills Valley and, to the east, the "sylvan paradise," as one nineteenth-century writer called it, claimed by Kentuckian Joel Estes for his log cabins and cattle.

The Rocky Mountains have always inspired awe, the earliest writings about them filled with dreamlike wonder. In 1820, during an expedition across the continent, Capt. John R. Bell described seeing "a blue stripe, close in with the horizon to the west—which was by some pronounced to be no more than a cloud—by others, to be the Rocky Mountains." Here, where the continent divides and the rivers run to different seas, the scenery overwhelms the senses. "This is a glorious region," the English traveler Isabella Bird wrote to her sister in 1873, "and the air and life are intoxicating."

Perhaps that is one reason why some people act the way they do in Rocky Mountain National Park. Intoxicated by the wilderness, they feed the wild animals and toss their cigarettes out of car windows. They leave their trash on the ground and lose track of their kids and lock their keys in their rental Kias in the visitor center parking lots.

And, if they're Harold and Toni Henthorn, they leave the trail. They ventured off a clearly marked long-established heavily traversed pathway and plunged into an ever-darker forest of ponderosas. They made their way to a rocky outcropping on the side of the mountain and ate lunch and posed for pictures that they took with their camera and their cell phone. Then as the day drew later and the temperatures became cooler and the sun started to set behind the Rockies, they ventured even farther. They went down a rocky incline so steep that experienced climbers have to shimmy on their backsides to traverse it, and then they reached another rocky outcropping on the side of a cliff of dizzying heights where they posed for more pictures, one of which shows a fair redhaired Toni Henthorn, her pale arms freckled, holding binoculars, looking at something in the distance.

Around that moment—maybe at that moment—fifty-year-old Toni Henthorn was gone.

ONE

"911, what's the address of the emergency?"

"Hello, my name is Harold Henthorn. I'm in the Rocky Mountain National Park. I need an Alpine mountain rescue team immediately."

"What is your exact location?"

"My exact location is Deer Mountain near the summit about one mile south of the visitor center."

Harold's voice was urgent, but not hysterical. The cell phone reception came through crisp and clear.

It was 5:54 P.M. Mountain Time. He had reached the main Estes Park emergency dispatch center.

"I'm going to transfer you to the Park so hang on the line," the operator said. "You're going to hear some clicking. Right now, I'm calling on my phone here."

As the sound of dial tones could be heard, Harold said, "I'll tell you where I am," but the operator instructed, "I'll introduce who we are when they pick up the phone."

She could then be heard telling another operator: "This is Estes and we have a gentleman on Deer Mountain. Go ahead, sir."

"Thank you," said Harold. "My wife has fallen from a rock on the north summit of Deer Mountain on the Deer Mountain trail. She's in really critical condition. She's had a bad fall."

"How far did she fall, sir?" asked the new operator.

"Thirty, forty feet. Thirty feet."

"Thirty, forty feet?"

"I think thirty feet."

"Are you with her now?"

"I am," said Harold. "Let me be sure you know my location first. I have really bad cell coverage. I'm on Deer Mountain near the summit. Not the normal regular northern summit, on the southern outcrop."

"The southern outcrop?"

"If you look up south from the visitor center, there are two very large outcrops. We are not on either one of those two. We are between the two. Between the two outcrops that you can see from Fall River," he repeated, then gave his location in latitude and longitude coordinates.

"Hold on for one second," said the operator, who began talking to somebody else in the background. Harold's breathing could be heard, slow and steady.

A different Park Service operator came on the line.

"OK, who am I talking to?"

This operator had a sharper, more businesslike tone. It was a busy night in the emergency dispatch center. The Park Service had waived the entrance fee this weekend and the crowds were large.

"My name is Harold Hill Henthorn," he repeated.

"Are you with the patient?"

"Yes, I am, yes."

"I already have rangers getting ready to come up there," she said, and then tried to pin down his location further. "So you're looking at Deer Mountain, you're looking at two outcrops, and this person is between two outcrops?"

"Yes," said Harold. "If you're looking from the visitor center directly south, magnetic south, you'll see two large outcrops about 9,000 feet. We are not on those two. We are between the two. About 200 feet off the crest of the hill."

"And tell me some things about the patient," she asked.

"She is a white female fifty years old, great health," he said. "She had respiration approximately five to eight beats a minute, her pulse is about between sixty and eighty beats a minute."

"And what's her main injury?"

"Head injury. Concussion."

"OK, any other injuries?"

"Could be internal—I don't—."

"Is she conscious, breathing?"

"No, she's not. She has not been conscious. She is breathing. Anywhere between five and eight beats a minute now."

"OK, hold on just a second."

There was a pause, dead space for a few seconds.

Harold asked, "Can you hear me?"

"Yes," said the operator.

"She is going to be evacuated from here," Harold said. It came out as a statement, not a question. "Is there any way you can bring a helicopter in? A Flight for Life? There is a clearing about 200 meters south of me. There is this clearing where you could easily, easily—"

"Hold on," the operator interrupted. "I'm on the radio."

In muffled tones, the operator could be heard saying, "White female . . . not conscious . . . She is breathing."

To Harold, she asked, "Are you a paramedic?" There was a touch of something that sounded like suspicion in her voice.

"No, I'm not, no," he said, then mumbled something about being "with Civil Air Patrol."

Harold appeared to grow impatient. "Let me be sure you know exactly where I am," he said, his voice sharper, "because trying to get a ranger here is going to take you at least an hour on the AT trail."

"Hold on, hold on, sir!" the operator interrupted again. "They're talking to me on the radio." She then asked Harold if he and his wife were engaged in "technical rock climbing."

"We were not climbing," Harold answered, "but you're going to need an Alpine mountain rescue team from where we are right now. Let me ask you a question: There is a clearing about 200 meters south of me."

"Hold on," said the operator again, still on the radio.

"You could easily—" Harold started, but the first operator came back.

"Sir, I'm sorry, there are only two of us here today, and we're kind of switching you back and forth, but I know what's going on."

"Here's the thing," said Harold. "I will pay any and all expenses for a helicopter. I don't care if it's private, I don't care if it's commercial. It wouldn't matter if it was Medevac. I will pay any and all expenses right now if you drop a paramedic down here."

"I understand that, sir. It's really on the safety of everybody involved. So that will be up to the ranger in charge."

"Weather's good. There's no wind whatsoever right now. Weather is excellent. Visibility is at least five to eight miles. There's definitely—I'm not a paramedic, but you could safely drop a paramedic from a ten-foot rope. Easily, you could do that."

"I understand, but they definitely need to probably get on scene," said the operator. "They do have Hasty teams and those are the teams that are going to run up there if that's possible and get to your location."

"OK, our car is parked at the intersection of 34 [and] 36, our green Jeep," he said, referring to the intersection of two mountain roads near the trailhead to Deer Mountain trail. "But it's going to take an hour, a full hour to get here."

"We definitely have people who are really fast on the trail and they're in very great shape. Now talk me through—how did you get to that location?"

"We were just having lunch on the outcropping," Harold said. "Not the two really steep ones, but a really nice outcropping. We come down a little further and, uh, she was trying to get a perfect picture, I think, and fell, and I came around, and she was unconscious. I came down and—"

"You were at Deer Ridge Junction, right, that's where you parked?"

"Deer Ridge Junction, the intersection of 34 and 36."

"And how far on the trail do you think you went?"

"We went to the actual summit."

"The actual summit?"

"Not the summit on the south side—9,012-foot summit. We crested around there, came around the switchbacks, came up to where the Deer Mountain Trail levels off."

"OK, so you went to the switchbacks where Deer Mountain Trail levels off?"

"We turned directly north."

"Turned north, OK."

"Went about maybe, you know, several hundred yards, and there you reach the north outcrops. We didn't go to the really steep one that you can see from the visitor center or the one to the west of that. We were between the two."

This meant that Harold and his wife had gone off the trail about 2.2 miles into the hike after making a steady incline as they passed meadows with views of Longs Peak and the mountains of the Continental Divide before reaching a junction where a series of steep sharp switchbacks led to the summit.

"How far from the top of the peak do you think you are?" asked the operator.

"We didn't actually go to the peak. We were not at that area. We were in the saddle between those two and we came on down."

"And if you look up at the peak, how far do you think you are from the peak?"

"I can see the top, maybe two hundred feet from the top."

"Two hundred feet from the peak?"

That placed them somewhere before those switchbacks on the north side of the mountain overlooking the Fall River Valley and the Park Service's Fall River Visitor Center and, to the right, the town of Estes Park.

"Yeah. They're not going to see me from where the pine trees are grown out," Harold said. "I'm not sure how long the cell coverage is going to be."

"How much battery power do you have left, sir?"

"It's not great," he said. "What I can do is—I can't imagine them being within an hour if they're hiking from Deer Ridge. Worst case scenario, if we lose complete contact here, I've got a whistle someplace, I'll blow that whistle every 15 minutes from the top of the hour, starting at 7 o'clock."

It was now after 6 P.M. The almanac had sunset for 6:46 P.M. but the trees and high peaks would make it darker earlier.

"There's no way you'll be here before seven if you walk in," Harold continued. "Again, if there's any chance I can persuade you to think about a chopper, in this light wind. Normally in the park it's just blowing like crazy. I will pay any expense."

"They're asking you to put as many bright items out as possible to see if they can't see you," said the operator. "Is anybody near you, sir?"

Harold didn't answer. Instead, he said, "OK, I'm looking at the visitor center right now, and I'm flashing a mirror, but I can't see the sun, so there's minimal chance you can see this."

"You're in some pine trees there?"

"Pine trees, yeah. You're not going to see anything. It's too dark. I'm definitely now in view of the visitor center, to the magnetic north. Is there somebody at the visitor center?"

"You know, I'm not sure," said the operator.

"I've got a purple bag. I'm moving a purple bag right now. I'm in the shadow." There was now the sound of rummaging around.

Harold asked if the rescuers were driving to the highway junction where he parked.

"What's that, sir?"

"They're driving to the junction?"

A change had come to Harold's voice. Annoyance crept in.

"I'm not sure if they're there yet because I'm working on a different side of the Park," the operator said. "Are you back with your wife right now?"

For several minutes now, Harold had not mentioned his wife or her condition.

"I'm right here," he said. "I'm right with her."

"How is she doing?"

"Her respiration is weaker," he said.

"Her respiration is weaker?"

"Yeah, five beats a minute."

It was the second time he made reference to "beats." The operator didn't seem to know what he meant.

"Five beats a minute?"

"Yeah."

Then she asked, "Do you know how to perform CPR?"

"I do, I do," he said.

Trying to assess the woman's condition, the operator asked, "More about this fall, sir. Was it like a sliding fall or did she fall directly?"

"I didn't see it exactly. I was messing with one camera, she was messing with the other one."

"You didn't see her fall?"

"I didn't actually see. I saw the motion but I—"

"Do you have any flashlights?"

"Yes, I do. I do have one."

"You have a flashlight. And how much battery power do you have on your cell phone?"

"Not much, half power."

"I'm going to give you another number just in case we do get disconnected. Do you have something to write with or will you remember? Or you can call 911, and they'll transfer you back to us"

"I'll do that. That will be the fastest way."

"Let me get your cell phone number, sir."

He read it off to her. A 303 area code—Denver area. "And your name, please?" he asked.

"My name is Kelly."

"Kelly. Thank you. Appreciate your help."

"And there's also an Elizabeth in here."

"OK."

The operator now explained why a helicopter couldn't be dispatched. "I want to let you know, most of our helicopters are Medevac helicopters."

"I understand."

"They're not really trained to do technical type things. They do land in certain areas."

"You would not need technical to get to me," Harold said.

"They can't like drop somebody from the helicopter."

"From a ten-foot rope?"

"No, sir, that's not been done in my experience. But we do have EMT-qualified rangers."

"I understand, yeah. It's—She needs to get out of here. She needs to get to the hospital."

What the operator didn't tell him was that no civilian could order up a rescue helicopter. The risks to the crew were too high. Only a rescuer on scene could make that determination.

"And what is your name, sir?"

"My name is Harold Henthorn." She asked him to spell it, he did.

"And your wife's name?"

"Her name is Toni. T-O-N-I."

"OK, and does she have any other health issues?"

"None at all. We were staying at the Stanley Hotel. She has no health issues at all. I'd better save the cell battery here."

"Why don't we do this," said the operator. "I'm going to hang up with you and check with the ranger first to see if there's any information that we need. We're going to hang up, and you're going to turn off your phone. I don't know if it causes more battery power to turn it off and turn it on."

"It'll save the battery."

"If you want to try to call us back in twenty minutes, if we set a time frame."

"OK."

"OK, so hold on line a second and we're going to see if there's any additional information that we may need."

"All right, Kelly, thank you."

"OK, so I'm going to hang up with you. If you want to leave your phone off, if that makes you feel better, definitely do that option. Call us if anything changes with her."

"I will call you at exactly 6:30."

"At exactly 6:30?"

"Yeah, at exactly 6:30."

"And like I said you can always call 911, and they'll transfer it over."

"OK, thanks so much. Thanks, Kelly."

But Harold Henthorn didn't wait until 6:30. At ten after 6, he called 911 again, his voice more frantic.

"Respiration is really getting shallow," he said.

"Did you do CPR?" asked the operator.

"I haven't started."

"But they're getting shallower?"

"What do you recommend?" Harold sounded a little out of breath. "She had no respirations."

"I'm not quite sure," said the operator. "I'm going to check with somebody else on that. Were you waving at all? We have a ranger that's parked on a road that he thinks he may have visibility of someone. He wanted to make sure it's you. Can you see a vehicle with lights on?"

"Yes, I can. Yes, absolutely."

"Were you waving at him?"

Again, he didn't answer. Instead, he said, "Let me give you a compass heading on that. Hang on a second. I've got a light on looking for a compass. It's a very small light. I've got it."

Harold was breathing heavily. The operator told him to relax.

"I'm just looking for the compass headings," he said. "It's hard to get level." He said he was 10 to 15 degrees off of magnetic north. "I have started a small fire in a completely enclosed rock enclosure with wet moss on it thinking he can see the smoke."

"Sir, there might be some climbers in your area. Are you sitting right on the edge looking over a 150-foot fall line?"

"Probably."

"Can you hold for a moment, I have another emergency call, OK?"

She put Harold on hold. "Dispatch, this is Kelly, what's your emergency," she said, answering the other call.

A man came on the line. "Hi, Kelly, this is just a concern from one of our tour guides, people getting too close to the elk in upper Sheep Lakes. They got out there too close and kind of ended up driving them—."

"I'm sorry, sir," she interrupted, "we have an emergency going on, but I'll let them know."

Another call came in from a ranger responding to a car that wouldn't start. She disposed of that and said, "Harold, are you still there?"

He said, "You said you have climbers in my area?"

The operator said a ranger was trying to find him. "He's seeing other people. He wants to make sure which one you were. He's trying to get that down. Looks like there's people above you and people below you."

"Shoot, this phone is cutting out."

"Sir?"

But Harold had disconnected. He called back and got another dispatcher, the one named Elizabeth. He told her, too, he'd started a fire. "Did they see smoke?"

"Did you light something?" asked Elizabeth, not privy to the previous conversation. A fire in the park after a long dry summer could provide yet-another complication.

"I'm burning moss," he said.

In between speaking with the dispatcher, Harold reached out to somebody else via text message.

"Barry . . . Urgent . . . Toni is injured . . . in estes park . . . Fall from rock. Critical . . . requested flight for life. Emt rangers on way. Please come to Denver next flight. Low cell batt. Please return message."

Barry Bertolet was Toni Henthorn's brother. He was also a cardiologist in Mississippi.

When Barry didn't immediately respond to the text, Harold left a voicemail message: "Check your phone. I have a low cell battery and can't talk."

Barry responded with a text asking Harold if he needed help. Harold replied with "H," which Barry took to mean that he did need help with a capital H.

Barry then called the National Park Service dispatchers while more texts poured in from Harold. One of them came at 8:25 P.M. Eastern Time—which meant it was sent at 6:25 P.M. Denver Time—and read: "Pulse 60 Resp 5."

"What is status?" Barry texted to Harold at 6:39 P.M. Denver time.

"No min pulse," Harold ominously replied.

Barry's fears deepened when Harold texted at 7:12 P.M.: "CPR critt."

"Is ranger there?" Barry texted back.

"No," texted Harold.

At about 7:30 P.M. Harold texted, "Can't find pulse."

"Maybe still there," Barry texted of her pulse. "Keep on with CPR."

"Y," replied Harold.

At 7:55 P.M., Harold texted Barry: "Cpr . . . Help 10 min out."

Back at the dispatch center, the phone lines were lighting up. While Elizabeth talked to Harold, Kelly reached out on another line to another unidentified law-enforcement official, a man, who sounded like a supervisor, seeking help for Harold.

"Going crazy over here," said Kelly. "We have a rescue; a woman took a forty-foot fall on Deer Mountain. She's unconscious but breathing. He's starting to ask questions like when to start CPR, and I didn't know how to answer him."

"She's breathing, she's just unconscious, right?" the man asked.

"Respiration is slowing."

"Shit," he said. He suggested having Harold call 911 again and connecting him to a police officer who could run Harold through "the protocol"—the series of chest compressions and blowing into a patients' mouth to try to revive her.

Kelly repeated how busy it was in the operations center. "It's all backed up, just so you know," she said—and asked if he could come in and help. He said something about needing childcare and would do the best he could.

It took a few minutes, but somebody knowledgeable in CPR at the Estes Park Police Department was tracked down and given Harold's phone number. Harold's phone lit up and he answered.

"Hi, is this Harold? This is Julia from the Estes Park Police Department. They tell me you need some assistance doing CPR."

"Any help you could give me," Harold said.

Julia asked about the injured woman. "Is she awake?"

"No, unconscious."

"I'm going through my questions really fast with you. Is she breathing?"

"Her breathing has gone from ten to five to nothing, to zero."

Things were buzzing down in Estes Park, too, and Julia urged Harold to have patience. "I've got an officer who's going to help me answer the other line so I can work with you directly," she said. "What we're going to do—let me let my officer through the door here, hang on—Is anybody else there with you?"

"No, just me."

"What we're going to do is, we're going to start some compressions. What have you been doing so far?"

"Compressions. Compressions and stop."

"When you do your compressions, I want you to press down firmly, two inches, with only the heel of your lower hand touching the chest."

"I'm doing that, yes."

"I want you to pump the chest hard and fast thirty times at least twice per second."

"I did that."

"Let the chest come up all the way up between pumps and tell me when you're done with that."

After a couple of seconds, he said, "OK."

"I want you to check her mouth for an object and remove anything that you may find, if she has anything in her mouth."

"She has no object in mouth."

"With your hand under her neck, pinch her nose closed, tilt her head back again, give two more regular breaths and then pump thirty more times."

"That's exactly what I've been doing."

"Just keep on doing that routine and make sure you're doing at least twice per second. Make sure the heel of your hand is on the breastbone in the center of her chest right between her nipples. Have you removed any outer clothing so you can tell exactly where you need to be?"

"Yes, yes."

"That's definitely what we want to do," said Julia. After a few seconds, she asked, "And tell me when you start with the two breaths."

"You're telling me exactly what I've been doing," said Harold.

"What I'm going to do now is I'm going to count for you as you go through the breaths. I've got my computer on and I can count so we can make sure we're getting that blood flow."

But Harold didn't do that. He spoke over her, saying something about his "cell battery" and that "I've got to turn off."

Exasperation in her voice, the dispatcher said, "Okay, call 911 any time and you'll get me. Keep on checking her mouth."

"Thank you, do you know the ETA of the rangers?"

"No," she said brusquely.

"Could somebody find that out and text that to me, please?"

"I will, definitely," she said.

It was now 7:30 P.M., darkness enveloping Rocky Mountain National Park, temperatures plunging into the 40s. It had been more than an hour and a half since Harold Henthorn had initially called 911. He dialed the dispatch center directly and got operator Kelly again.

"You guys have an ETA on the rangers?" asked Harold.

"We actually have a ranger in the area," she said. "If you can start using your whistle, he's trying to find you."

"OK, great, thanks a lot. OK, bye."

After a couple of minutes, Harold called the dispatch center again.

"It's Harold."

"Oh, hi, Harold." It was another operator, this one a man named Chris.

"You guys have my location yet?" Harold asked.

"We think Ranger Faherty is close," said Chris. "He gave the other rangers his coordinates, and they're trying to figure out how close he is to you. He's been yelling for you. Do you hear him at all?"

"If he tells you where he is, I can direct him exactly to me," said Harold.

"I don't think he knows exactly where he is in the dark now. He was just reading his coordinates off of a GPS. Do you have your specific GPS coordinates?"

"No," said Harold. He said he had gotten his coordinates off a map.

In the background, the dispatcher could be heard talking on the radio to the rescue ranger, who was trudging through the darkness with a heavy pack full of medical equipment somewhere near Harold.

Faherty could be heard asking the dispatcher, "He's in the valley between the rock outcroppings?"

"You know where that is?" the operator asked Faherty.

"Yeah, makes total sense," said the ranger. "I didn't see him in there, I scanned that."

About a half hour later, Harold called the dispatcher one last time. It was 8:01 P.M., and the ranger was just a few feet away, carefully going down the steep slope toward Harold.

Within minutes, he was there.

Guided by the light of a small fire, U.S. Park Service Ranger Mark Faherty found Harold Henthorn at the base of a cliff. From the moment Faherty arrived, it was a scene unlike anything he'd encountered before. The first thing Harold did when the ranger emerged from the woods was go over to the woman, who was lying on her back on the hard ground, her head wrapped in some kind of cloth, and start pushing down on her chest.

Faherty told Harold to stop, saying he'd handle it now.

The woman appeared to be of middle age and dressed for a day hike in blue jeans, pink shirt, brown boots over gray socks. Blood soaked her light red hair from what appeared to be a severe head wound. She didn't move.

Faherty checked her vital signs. Her pupils were fixed, she had no pulse and she wasn't breathing.

At 8:12 P.M., Faherty called the Rocky Mountain National Park's Incident Command Post to report that Toni Henthorn was dead.

TWO

"Woman Dies in Fall at Rocky Mountain National Park," read the headline on the *Denver Post* website the morning of Sept. 30, 2012. Lifted almost verbatim from a National Park Service press release, the article said rangers and a rescue unit were in the process of recovering the body of a fifty-year-old woman "who fell to her death" forty to fifty feet on Saturday while hiking near Deer Mountain. The *Post* reported that "a caller" alerted rangers to her fall at 5:50 P.M., and that rangers reached her at 8:10 p.m., by which time she was dead, and stayed with the body overnight. The early versions of the story said the woman's name was being withheld until next of kin could be notified; later posts identified her as Toni Henthorn of Highlands Ranch, Colorado, a suburb of Denver.

A nearly identical version of the story from the same press release appeared on the website of the *Estes Park News* and other news sites, with updates by Sunday evening that the body had been transferred to the Larimer County Coroner's office for autopsy. Soon, the death made news across the country and in Mississippi, where the *Natchez Democrat* played the local angle. "Mountain Fall Kills Native," read the headline, and the story noted that Toni Henthorn was the daughter of Bob and Yvonne Bertolet. The Bertolets were a prominent family from their successful oil business.

A paid obituary that later appeared in local papers filled in more gaps. Toni was a "faithful Christian, loving wife, devoted mother, thoughtful daughter and sister, and an incredibly skilled physician." A 1980 graduate of Trinity Episcopal Day School in Natchez, Mississippi, this "Southern Daughter" ran track, helped lead the girl's championship basketball team as a guard, played the piano beautifully and sang in a perfectly pitched alto. She went to Ole Miss, graduating magna cum laude, before getting her degree at University Medical Center. She practiced as an ophthalmologist, first in Mississippi, then in Denver and made the Consumer Research Council's list of America's Top Ophthalmologists. For a time, she served as the team eye doctor for the Colorado Avalanche of the National Hockey League.

After those first-and second-day news reports and the obituary, Toni's death received no more coverage in Colorado and Mississippi. There were no follow up news stories identifying who the "caller" was who alerted rangers or the fact that Toni had been hiking with her husband. In fact, nothing was said at all about Harold Henthorn, save for a passing mention in the official obituary that he shared Toni's love for "travel, hiking, snowshoeing and golfing." As for the cause of death, the reports mirrored what was said in the obituary: Toni Henthorn "passed away as the result of a tragic accident while hiking."

Behind the scenes, however, much was being said and done. From the moment he saw Harold and Toni Henthorn in the light of the little moss fire, Ranger Mark Faherty felt something was amiss. It wasn't that a visitor perished in an accident. Toni Henthorn was one of 143 people who had died in America's national parks that year from everything from slips and falls to drownings. Over a six-year span, four people also were killed by grizzly bears, one by a snakebite, and one by a goat. As the heavy phone traffic at the 911 center in Rocky Mountain National Park showed, rangers are kept busy. In 2012, Grand Canyon National Park alone had 348 search-and-rescue operations and notched twenty-one fatalities, a grim statistic that led the national park system.

But factoring the vast size of the parks and the crowds of visitors who pour in each year, the death toll is extremely low. From 2007 to 2013, 1,025 died in national parks. But with 2 billion visitors during that period, that works out to a tiny dent and well below even the nation's mortality rate in the general population of 821.5 deaths for 100,000 population, according to the Centers for Disease Control. A person has a better chance of dying in their kitchen than in a national park, and in deaths by accident Rocky Mountain National Park was among the safest of all. In 2012, it didn't even make *Backpacker* magazine's top six most dangerous parks (they were, in order, Grand Canyon, Lake Meade, Yosemite, Mount Rainier, Denali, and Yellowstone).

Those who do get hurt or killed come from a common demographic. More than half of the search-and-rescue missions target people in their twenties; the largest number of those killed in 2012 were between the ages of twenty and twenty-nine—considerably younger than the Henthorns. The one key category that fit the couple was the fact they were on a day hike. Usually day hikers are novices to the forests and mountains, failing to bring adequate food and water, wearing improper clothing, and miscalculating the weather or sunset. Day hikers made up 43 percent of all search-and-rescue missions in 2102, according to *Backpacker.*

Indeed, the Henthorns seemed ill-prepared for the trek ahead. They had set off in the afternoon for a six-mile round-trip hike over steep and rocky terrain that would challenge any hiker and could be particularly taxing on somebody over fifty. In the best of circumstances their return trip would have been a race to beat sundown, yet the only flashlight that Faherty could find appeared to be the small keychain penlight Harold carried. The couple then acted like dumb kids, leaving the trail to go through the forest to the edge of a precipice—*then* going down a harrowing steep slope to the edge of another cliff. All as night was approaching and miles of trail grew between them and their car parked near the trailhead.

Then there was Harold. It was odd enough that he'd scurry over to his wife and start chest compressions just as Faherty arrived. Harold had claimed he'd been trying to revive Toni all evening. But as an experienced emergency medical technician, Faherty knew this probably wasn't true. Toni had been wearing lipstick, which would have transferred to Harold's face when he was doing mouth-to-mouth resuscitation. But a close look showed Harold's face clean.

After declaring Toni dead, he told Harold that they would have to leave her body overnight, guarded by other Park Service rescuers who were now arriving. Harold "mildly protested," court papers later said, and the pair hiked back in the dark toward the trailhead. It took them two and a half hours to get there. Faherty drove

Harold to the Incident Command Post where two of Harold's friends, Jack Barker and Steve Tokarski, where waiting to take him home to Highland Park, where he would have to break the news to his seven-year-old daughter that her mother was dead. Harold gave permission to have his Jeep kept in a Park Service impound lot; he'd pick it up later.

The next morning, Ranger Faherty trudged back to the fall site where the other rangers had kept a grim vigil to keep predators away and preserve the scene. With the benefit of daylight, Faherty took a more detailed inventory and had pictures taken. Toni's body remained as Faherty had found her, lying amid pine needs, broken twigs, and granite rocks with sharp edges. A pink blanket covered her legs, her light blue fleece jacket over her torso. A white T-shirt was wrapped around her head, stained in blood from a gaping wound to her scalp. Her head rested on a rock and her matted hair took on a sickening bright-pink hue from the blood.

This was, daylight revealed, not where she had landed. Looking up, Faherty estimated she had plunged more than 100 feet—Harold had greatly underestimated the distance in the 911 call—and crashed through pine trees, severing a big branch, and landing in or near a tree. A trail of blood spots showed that she had then been moved several feet to where she now rested. Her hands showed no scrapes or lacerations to her palms; apparently, she never had a chance to grab at branches on her way down.

Next to her lay a purple daypack from which somebody had removed the blue fleece jacket, white T-shirt and blanket now covering her. There remained an extra pair of boots inside. Faherty found no flashlight or lamp of the sort one would take for a hike that would stretch into the late afternoon or early evening. A camera was next to her body, but it oddly showed little damage.

Rangers strapped Toni Henthorn's body to a gurney and carried it three miles to the trailhead. It was transported to McKee Medical Center in Loveland, Colorado, thirty miles to the east, for an autopsy. Faherty then set up an appointment to speak with Harold.

The ranger had a long list of questions.

THREE

The Henthorns lived on the 9000 block of South Sand Hill Street in Highlands Ranch, a suburb of strip malls and housing tracts, twelve miles from Denver, built by the same company that developed Mission Viejo in California's southern Orange County. Ranger Mark Faherty had wanted to speak with Harold in a Park office the day after Toni's death. But a friend of Harold's called, saying that Harold didn't want to leave his daughter after her mother had been killed. The friend asked that the interview be delayed, and Faherty arranged to talk to Harold at his home the next day.

Faherty arrived the morning of Monday, October 1. Harold answered the door. Just as he had that night on the mountain, Harold made a strange first impression. He led Faherty to a room and the first thing he did was turn on the computer and display a photo slide show. The pictures were of Harold, Toni, and a girl Faherty presumed to be their daughter.

Only after the slide show finished did Harold begin answering questions, according to Faherty's account of the interview, detailed later in a search-warrant affidavit and in the ranger's trial testimony. Harold described the hike as a part of a carefully planned celebration of their twelfth wedding anniversary, which was on Sept. 30. Two to three months earlier, Harold said, he had gone to Rocky Mountain National Park for a "scouting trip," looking for the best place to take her. He originally planned to go to Bear Lake, a spectacularly beautiful alpine location that sits, mirror-like, reflecting snow-covered Hallett Peak. A popular trailhead, the lake area is accessible by car on a small road open nearly all year, and much of the trail itself is relatively flat and paved. Harold opted not to go there because, he said, he thought too many people would be around—he wanted a quiet, private, romantic setting free of any crowds.

Harold instead decided to take Toni on the Deer Mountain trail, still popular but not as much as Bear Lake. He charted their itinerary, he told Faherty, on a topographical map, not a regular Park Service map. It was this topographical map from which he had established his latitude and longitude coordinates that he had relayed to the emergency operator.

The weekend trip was intended to be a surprise. Harold secretly worked with Toni's coworkers to have her patient list cleared and then drafted a fake patient list to throw Toni off. That Friday, he arrived at her clinic and hid in an examination room, then surprised her with news of the trip. They packed up the Jeep and made the ninety-minute drive northwest into the Rockies to Estes Park. He arranged for a friend to pick up Toni's car at the clinic.

On Friday evening, the couple checked into the Stanley Hotel, a historic, elegant grand hotel of Georgian architecture known for its majestic location against the mountain crags and amazing views of Estes Park. Legend also has it that the hotel is haunted. The Stanley inspired the setting for Steven King's *The Shining,* a fact of which it is quite proud, even offering ghost tours.

The next day, Saturday, Harold said the couple drove to the trailhead, parked the Jeep on the street, and set off on the hike between 1:30 P.M. and 1:45 P.M. They traversed the first three miles or so through the meadows, up the switchbacks, and into the pine forest. Rather than make the last leg up to the summit of Deer Mountain, they veered off on what he called a "use trail" looking for a romantic spot for views. At about 3:30 P.M., he said, they reached a rocky nob atop a ridge and had lunch for about an hour.

According to Harold, they had planned to leave at about 4:45 P.M. so they could get back to Estes Park in time for an anniversary dinner. Harold had made 8 P.M. reservations at Nicky's Steakhouse, where dinner for two, with wine and desert, could top $200. But they spent more time on the mountain after Toni spotted through her binoculars what she thought were wild turkeys and deer. They hiked down to a second rocky nob to take pictures and to enjoy what Harold called "romantic time." He explained that this second spot afforded them even more privacy than the spot above.

The pair took turns using the camera, passing it back and forth. As Toni told Harold where to stand for a photo, he received a text from their babysitter, Katy Carvill. The message said their daughter Haley's soccer team had won, 5 to 1.

Out of the corner of his eye Harold caught a blur. When he looked up, Toni was gone.

Harold peered over the edge of the cliff. He saw her

lying on the rocks below. It took him forty-five minutes to negotiate his way to the bottom to find his wife. She was unconscious but still alive. He then dragged her from the rocks to a flatter area where she would be more comfortable and so he could do CPR. But in doing this, he said, her head and shoulders bounced against the rocks, leaving the blood trail. He then called 911.

Harold gave his account in a calm, businesslike way. The ranger was struck by what he perceived to be a lack of emotion. There were no tears. His voice never wavered. When Faherty asked Harold if his wife had any life insurance, she said she did. It was for $1.5 million, payable to a trust. Harold was the trustee, but the money went to their daughter.

Finally, Faherty showed Harold something. A search of Harold's Jeep had turned up a map in the glove compartment. It was a standard Park Service map given to all visitors at Rocky Mountain National Park showing the roads, campgrounds, hiking trails, and surrounding area.

In the upper right-hand corner, a circle in pink highlighter was drawn around Nicky's Steakhouse in Estes Park. Inside the Park, the Deer Mountain trail was highlighted. And in the area where Toni plunged, written in pink highlighter, was an "X."

Ranger Faherty asked about this. Harold suddenly became "at a loss for words," the ranger would later recall in court testimony. Harold "hemmed and hawed" before saying that "he wasn't sure why there was an X." Then Harold said the map probably was intended for a hike that had nothing to do with their anniversary weekend.

More details came out the next day. Park Service rescuers had to carry her body back to the trailhead, then transferred it to the morgue at McKee Medical Center in Loveland, forty miles away. On Monday, Oct. 1, 2012, Dr. James A. Wilkerson IV, the medical examiner for Larimer County, conducted the examination.

He stripped the body and inventoried the clothing, then measured and weighed her. She was five foot five, 141 pounds. His report noted that she "appears compatible with the reported age of 50." She had blue eyes and fingernails painted pink and "intact." He found two old injuries that predated the fall. Both knees featured what he called "well-healed" scars from surgery years earlier.

As expected, the fall had wreaked havoc on her body. She hit the ground so hard one of her breast implants ruptured, her chest flattened and her liver had a two-inch cut. Two of her vertebrae cracked, several of her ribs shattered, and there were injuries to her chest, abdomen, thighs, one ankle and foot, and pelvis. She suffered abrasions to her forehead and a gash on the top of the head with internal bleeding around her brain. Scratches covered her shoulders, back, hips, right shin, buttocks, and arms. There was a particularly deep scratch on her right side, another on her left.

In all, the pathologist listed twenty-seven injuries, and he noted in his report that Toni had bled so much that "blood samples are very difficult to obtain due to a lack of blood in the circulatory system."

But it was what he didn't find that raised questions. Often when somebody receives CPR they're left with a broken sternum from the chest compressions. Even experienced rescuers will break the chest bone. Toni may have suffered more than a dozen broken bones, but her sternum remained intact.

An inventory of her belongings turned up something else peculiar. The pathologist noted that Toni was wearing a wedding ring set—but the diamond on the engagement ring was missing.

Pathologists are tasked with determining two things: the cause of death—the medical reasons a person expires—and the manner of the death, which are the circumstances that led to a person's demise. From his examination of the body, Dr. James Wilkerson could determine one but not the other.

"It is my opinion that Toni Henthorn, a 50-year-old white female, died as the result of multiple blunt force injuries when she fell or was pushed down a cliff while hiking in Rocky Mountain National Park," he wrote in his final report. "The manner of death is undetermined. The circumstances of death are under investigation at the time of this report. Homicide cannot be excluded."

FOUR

One day in 1999, Toni came upon a photo of a handsome man with a full head of real-looking hair. He described himself as being in his forties, standing about six feet tall with a "toned" physique, wavy brown hair and brown eyes. "My vision is perfect. I have no eyewear," read Toni, the ophthalmologist.

The man seemed to possess every quality she admired. A Presbyterian who served as a deacon in the church, he enjoyed contemporary Christian music and going to the movies, rarely drank alcohol, didn't smoke, resided in a house in the "Midwest/Central USA" and owned a dog. He listed his job description as "Executive & Managerial."

"I love telling jokes," he wrote, and described himself as "rather fashionable" and "Romantic and loving" and said green was his favorite color. "I plan most things," he wrote, "but am flexible." He had a sock drawer and drove an SUV.

"I'm an outgoing, fun, caring, sincere, growing man of God, one who is very young at heart, is passionate about life, has a great sense of humor, and who communicates well," he wrote. "Friends would also probably add that I'm an active, adventurous, trustworthy, sensitive man, who has a heart for others, especially children and is a good listener. Even though I've never had any children, I'm a dedicated uncle to my many (15, yes can you believe it?) nieces and nephews! I'm also usually described as being tall, dark, athletic and attractive . . . and then back when I was 15, I was an eagle scout . . . ☺"

ChristianMingle.com's motto comes from Psalms: "Delight yourself in the Lord and He will give you the desires of the heart." The website is run by Spark Networks, which specializes in "niche" online dating services. There are sites for Jews (Jdate.com), Catholics (CatholicMingle.com), Mormons (LDSSingles.com), African-Americans (BlackSingles.com) and older folks (SilverSingles.com). On any of the sites, punch in gender, age range, zip code, country of origin, and email address and you can "Browse FREE now!" for the man or woman of your dreams. On ChristianMingle.com that means you will "Meet Christian singles."

Even by the standards of dating websites, his description was a little much but it didn't stop. He said he worked for the last decade for a "national firm as a development consultant for not-for-profit organizations" including "churches, ministries and hospitals." Based in Denver, he had a "little" travel each week but added, "I pretty much have the world's best job and I definitely don't let work interfere with me having a quality life. ☺"

Sometime in late the 1990s Toni Henthorn registered for ChristianMingle. Her family had no idea.

An intelligent woman with a thriving career as an

opthmalogist, Toni seemed to have it all. "She was a beautiful blond Southern belle," says her father, Robert Bertolet. The middle child of three, born between two brothers, Toni grew up in Mississippi in a family that did well in the oil and gas business. "Being sandwiched between two brothers can be an advantage and not so much an advantage," recalls her brother Todd Bertolet. "She was kind of left out hanging when it came to playing and everything. We're not going to sit around and play girl games. She had to conform to whatever her brothers wanted to do. Her entire life, she was a very easygoing. She never got into any girl drama. You go back to grade school up, you'll never find anybody she got into an argument with. She just kind of went with the flow."

Behind that dwelled a certain toughness from growing up with two brothers. Toni could hold her own on the playground and became a talented athlete, excelling in basketball. School came easily to her. "She could just do whatever she put her mind to," says Todd. "She had a photographic memory. She took Latin in high school and knew it so well that by the time she got to college she didn't even go to class. In high school, one of the musicals needed someone who could play the guitar. She said, 'I'll do it.' She had never picked up a guitar in her entire life. And one week later she was playing it like she was playing it for years."

The Bertolet children all knew what they wanted to be when they grew up. For Todd, it was to become a geologist like his father. For Barry and Toni, it was medicine. They each succeeded, Todd going into the family oil business, and Barry and Toni heading to medical school. Barry, two years Toni's senior, would specialize in cardiology. Barry would say that she chose ophthalmology "because looking into one's eyes draws a dedication and a commitment to the person observed." Her father says, "She was deeply religious, teaching Sunday school, singing in both college and church choirs. Her greatest asset was her ability to feel what others were feeling. She had a passion to console and give advice to those who were in need of direction and comfort."

After medical school, Toni set up her own practice in Mississippi. Her mother kept her books. She cared deeply for her patients, and they in turn would describe her in the most glowing terms, as an angel or a godsend. But she came to learn the costs of practicing medicine. "Remarkable deeds didn't always shield Toni from heartaches and losses seen in the practice of medicine," said her brother Barry, who as a heart doctor was in a position to know it all too well. "But those heartaches and losses defined and elevated her compassion and care."

Early in her career, she got a call for emergency care for a five-year-old boy critically injured in a car accident. As the child lay on the ER table, he pointed to his head and moaned, "Hurt, hurt." Toni did everything she could, but the boy died.

"Overwhelmed by the loss of the child, Toni never wanted to see the hurt in another person's eyes, much less a child's eyes," her brother Barry would recall. "Toni always carried the pain of the loss, which you know those tragic moments taught her as a person. Every great doctor has seen loss, has seen suffering, has seen life struggles, but all had discovered a purpose in their own lives to rebound in the purpose of tragedy."

As devoted to her career as Toni was, she sought work-life balance. Ophthalmology appealed to her because it didn't come with the same punishing hours she saw Barry keep. "Not only is he working but he is on call," says Todd. "That keeps you basically working the entire

twenty-four hours of the day. I think Toni liked oph-
thamology because she felt like it wouldn't be as de-
manding time-wise. She wanted more of a nine-to-five
job."

She wanted that time and flexibility because she always planned on scaling back her work to start a family.
She married her college sweetheart, a dentist named
Charles Richardson, and settled in Meridian, Mississippi.
But any dreams of having children collapsed along with
the marriage. The divorce weighed on Toni for the rest
of her life. A rare failure in her life, the divorce so traumatized her that she promised never to go through it
again. Still, she yearned to have children—and to have
children, she wanted to be married. By her late thirties,
Toni feared time was running out.

"I pretty much enjoy most things, including sports and
outdoor activities, especially if they involve connecting
with others," the man had written on the dating site's
section listing his favorite "sports, hobbies, musical abil-
ities, and pets." He liked to spend time with friends in
"great conversation" and "traveling to interesting places
to explore new areas and do fun things such as snorkeling, scuba diving, jeeping through the mountains and
camping." He also listed enjoying "working out, playing tennis."

"I grew up on the East Coast near the ocean, I really
love anything that involves the water, including swim-
ming, canoeing and especially sailing!" Among his
favorite movies were Sleepless in Seattle and *Sabrina*.
"Am I a diehard romantic or what?"

"My dream vacation would likely involve walking
barefoot, hand in hand with someone very special
through the warm surf on some secluded sandy beach,"
he wrote. "We would take in the smell of the salt air,

listen to the roar of the ocean and feel the warm wind on our faces & blowing through our hair. Our trip might include some sailing, snorkeling, scuba diving, biking or even just exploring the area, but we would definitely enjoy some casual as well as elegant dining followed by dancing until late in the evening."

The only thing tempering his boundless self-confidence and relentless efforts to impress was a flash of self-deprecating humor. "Aside from improving my very average ability at golf, I'd love to be able to multi-task in my regular life better than I do," he wrote. "It's no problem for me at work, but in my personal life I find that the women I know are far better at it than I am. ☺"

He also appeared open and comfortable with his faith. He listed the Bible as one of his favorite books (the others are mysteries by Tim LaHaye and military adventures by Tom Clancy) and the faith-themed TV shows *Touched by an Angel* and *Promised Land.*

"I became a Christian during high school through the ministry of young life," he wrote, "but it was during my college years and involvement in Inter-Varsity Christian Fellowship that I matured in Christ. Over the past 20+ years I've been extremely involved in many aspects of ministry, including leadership of small group Bible studies, mentoring, Promise Keepers and Focus on the Family."

Devotion to Jesus dominated his life. "I'd like to meet and connect with women of similar faith, values and interests, to develop supportive relationships where we would encourage one another in our walks with Christ," he wrote. "Whether we become great friends or further connect in a remarkable way and share the rest of our lives together would be in His trustworthy hands."

And, he said, he was a widower, though his profile contained nothing about his late wife. The only previous relationship he mentioned was with a woman still very much alive who broke things off for no reasons involving him. "After going out for a little while, the previous woman in my life decided she needed to move back out of state for a few years, so she could process the recent loss of her mom and be there to support her family."

Another woman may have recoiled at the boundless self-promotion and what could be seen as transparent attempts at modesty and spirituality. Toni wasn't that woman. By all accounts, she was smitten at first click. All in secret. Although Toni came from a close-knit family, and her mother felt that Toni confided in her, Toni never told her mother or anyone else in her family about looking for a date on the Internet.

The Bertolets' introduction to Harold Henthorn came on New Year's Eve 1999.

"He came to Mississippi and we met him," Toni's mother Yvonne says. It took place at Toni's Natchez condominium, and the meeting brought several surprises to her parents. One, they had no idea that Harold and Toni had been dating for several weeks, on the Internet no less. Second, they announced they were going to be married. And they were going to move to Denver where Harold worked.

"Frankly, I was fairly impressed with him," said Toni's father Robert. "He was very personable, he was well-mannered. He seemed humble in a way because he was asking our permission to marry our daughter. From his conversation, he said that he wanted to take care of our daughter. One of the thigs that impressed me—and my wife is going to kick me in the butt for saying this— was what Harold said. He said, 'When your daughter comes to Denver, I'm going to build her a million-dollar house.' Well, to a father that shows this man is really going to take care of my daughter. I was impressed, and I think the boys were impressed. "

A dinner was arranged for Harold to meet the rest of the Bertolets, including brothers Todd and Barry. "He was on his best behavior," said Toni's mother. "Felt like he was a nice person. We took him to dinner, and he was very nice and polite, opening the doors for us, seating us. He seemed to love Toni."

The brothers cast a more skeptical eye. "When they lined up the dinner, this was the first time I heard about him," says Todd. "It was basically for Harold to meet the family. My first impression—I wouldn't say it was overwhelmingly positive. I was certainly happy that my sister had met somebody. That void in her life was being filled. I wouldn't describe him as somebody I would normally want to be friends with. He was outgoing, supposedly he had this great career, supposedly he was wealthy and everything. I thought they're probably compatible. I gave him a pass."

Harold talked about his background studying and working briefly as a geologist. "That was another reason I gave him a pass," Todd recalls. "She's marrying a geologist like her brother and dad. You quickly find out he knew about geology and supposedly worked for Chevron. He couldn't basically talk about the industry the way that dad and I could, living it every day. But that was understandable. From all indications, he basically only worked one year as a geologist, and that was as an apprentice."

Harold told the Bertolets his career path instead took him to fundraising for nonprofit organizations and churches. "That just rang a bell for me," said Toni's father. "I had been involved in church building projects and we had a professional fundraiser come in, and it's a tough job. I understood where he was at. I think he even mentioned some projects that he had going."

Todd, too, related, "When he gave that line, I thought: that's interesting. At the time, we were doing business with Texaco, and Texaco had a geologist I knew real well whose wife was a nonprofit fundraiser. It just so happened I knew somebody who was a nonprofit fundraiser so I knew that's a legitimate business."

Harold told them that he was a widower, and the family didn't press the sensitive subject. Beyond that, they knew little more about him—except that Toni wanted to marry him as quickly as possible. She set a date for September—nine months away. "It was fast," says Todd. "But my parents met and were married within six months, so it could happen. You would like to think that both of them had been married before, both were professionals, both knew what they wanted out of life. They're telling us they're compatible with each other. Would I say I was concerned? No. But there were some things that just started irking me."

First came the matter of the wedding announcements. He wanted his name to go first and he also didn't want Toni identified as a doctor. "He did not want to use Dr. Bertolet and Mr. Harold Henthorn," says Toni's mother. "He thought that was derogatory." Traditionally the bride's name appears first, and everybody knew Toni in town as Dr. Bertolet. "I even showed him Emily Post," says her mother. "I said: I'm doing this by the book."

Then there was the rehearsal dinner. "It was going to be at the clubhouse in my neighborhood and Harold said, 'Hey, could you set this up for me? I'll write you a check,'" recalls Todd. "I said, sure. So I lined it up, rented the clubhouse, lined up the band, the caterer, everything, and lo and behold, guess who didn't pay for it? Traditionally the groom pays for the rehearsal dinner. But it's not like you're going to chase down a bill from your new brother-in-law. Right off the bat he stiffed the family. For somebody who is supposedly extremely wealthy, why would he not pay the bill?"

Finally, the night before the wedding, Harold dropped by Toni's house. At the time, Toni and her mother were scrambling to make final arrangements for the ceremony the next day and Toni was packing for the honeymoon. "I told Harold, 'I don't think you're supposed to come over the night before the wedding," recalls Toni's mother. "Harold had brought by some shirts and he wanted me to iron them. This was 11:30 at night. It was really up-setting Toni. She went into the bathroom and cried. I told her, 'Look, it's never too late. If you don't want to go through this, I will stop it right then and there.'"

On September 30, 2000, Toni and Harold married in a big formal Southern wedding in Jackson, Mississippi. The ceremony was at noon at the First Baptist Church, and the reception was held in the afternoon at an ante-bellum home. Toni's parents paid for it though not without knocking heads with Harold. "He thought he was an expert in everything," says her father. "He tried to direct the wedding. He picked out the songs, picked out the girl to do the singing. I allowed the girl, but said that I'm going to pick out the music. The music he chose was not like formal music." Traditionally, the groom's side arranges and pays for the photos; Harold did none of that. "The only reason any pictures of the wedding exist is because my parents paid for them," says brother Todd.

Harold also made Toni's brothers ushers, not grooms-men. "I'm participating in this, but I'm kind of on the fringe," recalls Todd. "That was kind of strange to us." The scope and formality also struck the brothers as a little excessive. "It was full-blown," Todd said. "This was the second go-round for both of them. We already went through the first one." But the Bertolets had to admit that Toni never looked happier. "I would say that was the best I had ever seen her," says Todd. "She was very pretty, almost like saying: Hey, I'm blossoming in this situation."

After their Hawaiian honeymoon, the new Mr. and Mrs. Henthorn began married life, though the family would still see much of Toni. "It took her two years to sell her practice and make sure it went to the right person," her bother Todd says. Harold became a frequent and long-term visitor to Mississippi. "The commuting was more Harold," says Todd. "She would also go back and forth, Jackson to Denver. I wouldn't say they spent that much time apart. Harold would come to town, he would stay here." Her parents were in no hurry to see her go. "Of course, I didn't like the idea," her mother says. "She was my best friend. I did all of her shopping, and most of the time I did her bookkeeping. I knew everything going on in her life. We would come up and help her with her spring cleaning and things like that. Almost every Mother's Day, we spent working on one or more of her offices. It was a pleasure to me to be able to help her out."

"She couldn't just leave and walk out of a practice," her father adds. "It took her that length of time to sell her practice. That practice that she started now is a flourishing multimillion-dollar practice. I would say to myself: And she's going to leave this and go to Denver? But Harold said he needed to be in Denver for his job."

"Harold from the start said, 'I'm an extremely wealthy man, I've got this thriving business in Denver, that's where I need to be located,' Todd recalls. "He said that Toni doesn't have to work at all and just be a mother. He said, 'What she makes is insignificant from what I make.' From the start, that was the game plan: move to Denver."

In 2002, the practice in good hands, Toni left Mississippi for good. After moving into Harold's home in Highlands Ranch, she plunged into the business, social, and religious communities. She got a job at Associates in Eyecare in Cherry Creek and became active at the Cherry Hills Community Church, not far from her house. It broke her parents' hearts, but her family admitted that Denver suited her, particularly outdoor activities like hiking. "I was extraordinarily happy for my sister," Barry Bertolet would tell *48 Hours*. "It appeared that she found her true love. And if she was happy, I was happy. Her comments were that he was very kind, he was very romantic, he was very smart."

In 2005, the last part of her life plan came to be. She gave birth to a daughter, Haley. "That was a monumental moment for her," says Todd. "Her main focus was to be a mother. My wife was pregnant at the same time Toni was. So Toni became a mother and her little brother became a father at about the same time. She was on Cloud Nine. Everything was coming together."

Or so it seemed. It was a difficult birth. Toni was forty-three years old and her blood pressure was so high, and the labor was progressing so slowly, that the doctors recommended a C-section. Toni's parents, who had come out to welcome their grandchild, were in the waiting room with Harold when the doctor emerged with the word. "I had to wake Harold up and tell him to go in for the C-section," says Toni's mother. "When he came out, you would have thought he had delivered that baby himself. He came out bragging about what all they did. We went in and watched them examine the baby. We watched Haley touch the stethoscope, and we said,

'Yes, she's going to be a doctor like her mom.' And Harold looked at us with beady eyes and said, 'She will NOT be a doctor.'"

Yvonne Bertolet thought to herself: "Well, my goodness."

Todd Bertolet got the first call from his brother Barry at about 7 P.M. "I had sat down to watch the game on TV. Ole Miss was playing Alabama. I think they were just kicking off or something when my brother calls. I saw his name on the caller ID and told myself I'll call back in a minute," recalls Todd. "Then I thought: Oh, I'd better pick it up. My brother said that Toni had been in an accident and had fallen from a rock and he said that from what he's hearing, the vital signs and everything, he doesn't think that she's going to make it."

Todd went to his parents' home. "I thought I really should go down and talk to mom and dad and prepare them because I don't think the news is going to be good," says Todd. "I went down to tell my parents and I told them that Toni had been in an accident and she had fallen from a rock, that supposedly there's going to be a rescue but that Barry doesn't think she's going to make it."

The news had the Bertolets plunging into a nightmare that they would come to see as years in the making as they looked more critically at Harold—and at themselves. It all began and, they would come to believe, ended with money. "When Toni went out to Denver, Harold was telling her that he didn't want her working," said Todd Bertolet. "She was going to work part-time at most, do enough to keep her license up. She got out there thinking she would work three days a week at most. It quickly went to full-time. So we really didn't understand that."

The Bertolets had no direct information about Toni and Harold's finances since Yvonne Bertolet's handling of her daughter's books ended when Toni moved to Denver. They did know that Toni had a 4 percent interest in the family's oil and gas business that produced a monthly dividend of between $2,000 and $24,000, payable annually. And eighteen months before she died, Toni received $320,000 from a lawsuit payout involving litigation over oil wells.

As for Harold, it began to dawn on the Bertolets that they never knew anything about his business. They never met his coworkers or clients. All information about his deals came from him and him alone. Whatever he did, it appeared to them to fail to generate enough income to cut back on Toni's hours. Her full-time employment advanced to a partner position with presumably additional responsibilities.

Toni refrained from discussing their finances, dodging questions about her workload, and her family didn't pry. "But she made a comment to me one time," said Todd, "that she was the big earner in the family and that Harold basically wasn't pulling his weight. I think she was convinced he was just at a low point and that there was not a whole lot going on, that he didn't have projects that were producing." She said this when Todd had sent her a sizeable check from the oil business. "She was pretty grateful that she got the money," he said. "She said it was coming at a good time because Harold wasn't making any money."

Finances became so tight that Toni began taking on-call shifts at a hospital to make extra money, something she had once said she wanted to avoid. "Harold kept pushing the money situation," his mother said. "He said, 'You need to make more. They're not paying you enough. She would say, 'Harold, I'm doing okay.' But he kept pushing and pushing and pushing." Toni finally told her parents. "I'm the breadwinner. If Harold is making any money, I never see any of it."

That Toni would say this was out of character. She rarely complained about Harold or said anything negative about her home life. "I always go back to when she was in high school and messed up one of her knees playing basketball," said Todd. "She didn't want anybody to know about it. So when she came home that night, she walked back to her bedroom in front of my parents, smiling, grinning, acting like everything was perfectly fine. She walked without a limp or anything else. When she got back to her bedroom, she fell on the bed and started crying because of the pain," said Todd. "If Toni gave you any inkling that there was something wrong, it's a lot bigger than what she's letting on."

But while Toni seemed to be bringing in most, if not all, of the money, Harold still threw his weight around. He touted himself as a financial wizard and never hesitated to offer advice. He took over the accounting duties from Toni's mother. He sat in with Toni on the partner Associates in Eyecare, the only spouse to do so, one of many behaviors that irritated people.

"I would say for the first two or three years we had a good relationship with Harold. We went on vacations together. We thought things were well," said Toni's father. "Then it started. He just couldn't control himself, his mannerisms." Harold began to involve himself in more than finances.

"Harold was controlling," said Todd. "At first it was strange things like you couldn't have the TV on any time Haley was in the house. You're talking an infant at this point. The infant isn't going to be concerned about the content of the news, but you couldn't have it on. Little things like that started creeping in."

In time, Toni's calls to family and friends became less frequent. When family members called for her, Harold would always answer and take a message. During a visit to Denver, her mother asked Toni why she stop calling home. "She said, 'Well, nobody has called me. Harold never mentioned it to me,'" Yvonne recalled. "I said to Harold, 'I know for a fact that [the brothers] have called.' He grinned. That was my first indication of what was going on. He was playing a game.

Toni's personality seemed to change, and the Bertolets blamed Harold. "As a father, there were little things Harold did that would irritate me," said Robert Bertolet. "One of the things was when on my birthday, Harold would call and he would talk and wish me a happy birthday and everything, and I would finally say, 'Is Toni there?' And he'd say, 'Yes, she's here,' and she would get on the phone and maybe say a couple of words. This is not like Toni. She is so independent and strong-willed, and yet she's acting like she was beat down. I told my wife, 'I really want to go out to Denver and thrash him.' My wife said, 'If you do that, Bob, he'll take it out on Toni.' So I never dressed him down."

Nor did they say anything to Toni on another occasion. Once her parents visited Denver while Toni was undergoing another round of knee surgery, the continued fallout from high school sports injuries. Toni didn't want a knee replacement, and each surgery took a toll on her.

"I went out to take care of her," her mother said. "One night I couldn't sleep because there was some type of bird outside my window. I got up and walked in the hallway. As I was walking, like two o'clock in the morning, I heard all of this noise. I said, 'What is that?' I listened some more, and it was coming from Toni and Harold's room. They were arguing. Harold said, 'If you tell your parents this, I will divorce you.' I was embarrassed that I heard it. I went back in the room and shut the door. I never did ask her about it. I wish I had."

But aside from the one time expressing frustration about money, Toni remained mum about Harold. Her father believed it went back to her divorce. "Her mother and I have been married fifty-six years, and I think our children looked at divorce as a failure of sorts," said Robert Bertolet. "Sometimes there are good reasons for it. I think—this is only my opinion—I think Toni just did not want to malign her marriage and she didn't want to face a divorce. Especially when Haley came along, divorce became in her mind an impossibility."

Her brother also felt her attitude toward Harold's behavior related to her Christian faith. "She was extremely religious," Todd said. "Faith was extra-large in her life. Our mother's father was a preacher. And I think there is a certain vulnerably with people with faith. They don't seem to have that vigilance in their eyes. They just go through life with the goodness in their heart."

The Henthorns owned a cabin in Grand Lake, a fishing and boating resort on the southeastern border of Rocky Mountain National Park in the Arapaho National Forest. They had spent Memorial Day weekend of 2011 there, bringing Haley. At about 10 P.M. on the night of May 28, while the couple was outside around the back deck, a large piece of wood fell and struck Toni in the back of the neck.

"I did not find out about it from Harold," said Todd Bertolet. "And neither did mom and dad. They found out from Toni, two or three weeks after it happened. Harold always said it was no big deal, a scratch, a bump, but when you got the whole story it was bigger."

Pain had shot through her entire body and she fell

to the ground, everything numb but for tingling in her fingers. A 911 call summoned paramedics. The Grand County Emergency Medical Services ambulance brought her to the emergency room in the little hospital in Granby. Fearing she had suffered a broken back, doctors ordered her transported to the better-equipped Swedish Medical Center, down the mountain in Denver, ninety miles to the southeast. She didn't suffer a broken vertebra, but still had severe pain. Toni underwent therapy but aching and tingling to her fingers lingered for months.

"Toni told us that Harold called her out of the cabin, and when she walked through the threshold of the door she saw something on the deck and looked down," said Todd. "When she bent down and picked it up, that's when the beam hit her on the back of the neck. Had she not bent down it would have hit her on the head. She told it to my parents and my mother told me right after."

Toni, in fact, seemed to think her parents had already known about it. "Toni had just mentioned it casually, and she said, 'Well, didn't Harold call you? And I said, 'No, nobody called me about that.'"

In December 2011, Toni visited her parents without Harold. "We had the opportunity to talk freely," her mother recalled. "I said, 'Toni, I don't feel that was an accident. She listened carefully, and usually with Toni, if she didn't agree with you, she would tell you. She'd say, 'Oh, mama, you just feel that way about everybody. You're suspicious or you make something up.' This time she didn't say anything. And she just looked at me in the eye. I told her, 'I don't think that you should go anywhere alone with him.' She ignored that advice. I don't know if Toni really believed me or whether she thought: This is my husband and I trust him. I don't know how she was thinking."

Yvonne was so concerned she asked her husband to hire a private investigator to look into Harold. He said, no, he thought it would be wrong to do that to Toni's husband.

"I regret not listening to my wife," Robert Bertolet said. "That might have saved her life. There are so many what-ifs in the world, and that's a big one."

And so on that night in September 2012, Robert and Yvonne Bertolet and their son Todd awaited a call from Barry, who had been receiving the text messages from Harold from Rocky Mountain National Park.

The call finally came. "She is gone," Barry told his brother, who related the news to his parents.

"My blood pressure went to zero," Robert Bertolet said. "And without thinking, I said, 'He pushed her.'"

FIVE

The Bertolets packed for Denver, Toni's parents and brothers joined by other relatives. "It was a gang," said Robert Bertolet. They were to attend the memorial, the first of two for Toni. Another was set for Mississippi. They also had another agenda. The Bertolets' concerns about Harold focused on more than his behavior over the years. Toni's brother Barry reviewed the information Harold had texted him about Toni's condition after the fall. As a physician, Barry knew the vital signs Harold reported didn't seem to make sense. The declining respiration and heartbeat that Harold so worried about struck Barry as a good sign; it meant that Toni had not gone into shock. "We were fact-finding," said Todd Bertolet. "We were there to let Harold give us his version. We were not there to ask questions. We were going to let Harold do the talking. We were not going to ask questions. We didn't want him to be tipped off and clam up." The family drove to Memphis and boarded a plane.

Before they arrived, activity swarmed around the Henthorn house. Ranger Mark Faherty was still interviewing Harold when Tamara Gordon, a family friend and photographer, arrived. Somebody else let her in and she waited in another room for fifteen minutes. She saw Harold walk the ranger out the door before Harold asked her to wait a few minutes more. He came back and led her downstairs.

Tamara's photography business handled high school portraits, family photos, and weddings. She'd never worked a funeral before, but that's what Harold had hired her for. He wanted a slide show displayed at the memorial. She took a seat in the basement, which had been set up as a home office. From previous experience, Tamara braced herself. She had first met him in the summer of 2008 when he had called to set up an appointment for a family portrait. It was taken at the Gordon studio, which she and her then-husband operated out of their home. Harold came with his wife and daughter.

"It was a little unusual in that Harold came to the session knowing exactly what he wanted," Gordon would recall. "He kind of orchestrated what photos he wanted and what poses he wanted. He was clearly in charge." Toni was "very easy-going. She was very quiet. I don't remember her having any input."

Gordon would describe her as physically "very fragile" from obvious problems with her knees. "Harold wanted a lot of poses in the grass outside, laying down, on their backs, with hands under their chin, and she just seemed a little frail, a little fragile," recalled Gordon. "I thought she had a hard time getting into those poses, getting up and down."

Harold decided what photos to order. "Harold orchestrated everything," she said. "Toni didn't have anything to do with actually choosing any of the photos." One of the shots he wanted for his business was his headshot; he wanted her to crop out the rest of his family.

He told her he was a fundraiser for churches. "I remember him talking about a particular church in South Dakota, that he was trying to raise money for," she said. With his repeated calls, Harold was "one of the most high-maintenance clients we ever had," she said.

But nothing prepared her for what would happen next. Harold walked in and told her, in uncomfortable detail, how Toni had died.

"Toni was taking a picture, and he had turned around for some reason and when he turned back around Toni had stepped back and fallen off the cliff," Tamara later recalled, recounting Harold's statements. "It was a beautiful lookout and she was taking a photo, and . . . when he turned back around she was gone." He told her he never saw her fall. He said it took a long time to get down to where she landed. He thanked God that Haley wasn't with them.

By the time Harold finished, Tamara was in tears. But Harold remained dry-eyed. "It was like he was telling a story," Tamara said. "I thought he was in denial because he was able to articulate all of this to me. It was very uncomfortable. I felt like it was very raw, intimate information. And even though we had spent a lot of time with the Henthorns, I was just uncomfortable with hearing all of that."

On his computer, he showed her photos from the hike—Tamara didn't know if they had been taken from a camera or a cellphone—and Harold spoke of how beautiful the day had been. Of one picture, he said, "This is one of the last pictures that we had together." It was a selfie that appeared to have been taken by Harold, the smiling couple in their sunglasses, behind them the snow-topped peaks of the Rocky Mountains.

The pictures came up on his computer—60 or 70 photos, all on a flash drive. "I didn't understand how in the world he had the wherewithal to put all of those together," she said, thinking he would have been too grief-stricken.

Calmly, he went through the photos one-by-one, telling her he wanted to make sure that all her family members were represented in the memorial slide show. If one of Toni's brothers was in one picture he wanted to make sure another relative was in another. He had also chosen the music for the slide show, giving her the titles of the songs, which she wrote down. Finally, he had her make one large blowup of Toni for the church and a smaller one for the program.

"He didn't appear sad. He appeared shaken but he wasn't crying," she said. "He didn't strike me as somebody who had just lost his wife."

She returned to his house a day or two later with the finished slide show, which she previewed for him. "It was very uncomfortable because he wanted me to watch it with him," she recalled. "I just wanted to leave it for him so he could watch it in private. But he wanted me to view it with him."

A similar experience awaited the Bertolet family. Toni's relatives arrived at the house and also were escorted into the basement office. It was a little after 4 P.M. on the Monday after Toni's weekend death, the same day Harold had spoken to Faherty and met the first time with the photographer.

"Harold was over by his computer, and he came up and met us," Toni's mother recalled. "He was just—well, he was acting like: We can get on with our lives now. There was no sadness. I was kind of shocked." Then

Harold launched into the memorial plans. He told them he had the program ready and asked if they wanted to see it. He had also already picked out the photographs for the memorial slide show.

Harold had still said nothing about how Toni had died. When her family asked him, he told them that she had been about ten feet from the edge of the cliff taking pictures of wild turkeys when she fell. Although the family had intended not to press him, they couldn't resist. "We asked other questions," said Yvonne. "Did she scream or anything?" Not a sound, said Harold, who claimed to have been looking at a text message on his phone about Haley's soccer game when Toni disappeared. As he spoke, Harold paced the room. Harold gave different accounts about whether he was looking at his cell phone or Toni's, whether the message came to him about the game or to Toni about a work matter at the eye clinic.

Toni's father was struck as much by what Harold didn't say as by what he did. "I just expected him to say, 'Dad, I shouldn't have taken Toni up there. It was all my fault.' He didn't even mention that, he never mentioned how sorry he was that it happened. It was just like another day at the office." Toni's parents noted how the more he spoke the more animated he became when finally he expressed frustration about the U.S. Park Service. "That was why he was marching up and down," said Yvonne. "He was just so agitated about them accusing him and coming after him. He said, 'I just want to get on with my life and they're bothering me right now.'" Toni's father was aghast. "When he said that to me, I'm thinking: What about my daughter? She's dead. She can't get on with her life."

Stunned, the Bertolets left the basement. Yvonne found her granddaughter sitting alone on the stairs. "She was just staring at me," Yvonne recalled, "and I went over to her, and I was smiling. She said, 'You look like my mama.'" It was a memory that would never fail to bring Yvonne to tears. "I went over and hugged her."

The next day, Tuesday, the medical examiner provided the autopsy findings to Harold and the Bertolet family. "Harold's whole demeanor goes to anger," Todd Bertolet recalled. Incensed that the coroner refused to rule out homicide, Harold railed against authorities. He called Ranger Faherty "Barney Fife." Harold also tangled with the Bertolets over funeral arrangements. Her family wanted her body flown to Mississippi for burial. Harold said he couldn't afford that. When the Bertolets said they'd pay for the arrangements, Harold still balked, saying the cremation had to be done as soon as possible. He said Toni had wanted it that way, though her will said nothing about her wishes. The family then pressed to at least have a viewing of the body. "My secretary called the funeral home, bless her heart, and said, 'Don't do that cremation until Mr. and Mrs. Bertolet get to see their daughter,'" said Toni's father. "That made Harold mad. Yvonne had bought a new dress for Toni to be buried in. Harold would not let Toni wear that dress, even to the cremation."

The viewing took place Wednesday night at the funeral home. "Harold didn't want to go," Todd Bertolet recalled. "He was just almost like he didn't care, just get this whole thing over with kind of deal." During the public viewing, Harold continued to stew. "We're kind of walking around looking at flowers and stuff, and he gets ticked off at us. He's virtually yelling at us," said Todd. The family was looking at something else too. Barry had spoken with the coroner and said the family had suspicions about Toni's death. Barry and Toni's mother gazed into the casket and took a long look at the body. "We did some examination," said Yvonne. "We could tell her neck was broken. The right side of her head was smashed in. On her left hand, where the ring was, there was not even a scratch. Her nails were perfect. I was thinking she was not grasping to hold onto anything when she fell."

A supper afterward brought more mortification Harold wanted Toni's family to see the slide show he'd curated for the memorial the next day. "It was a video thing he'd made with a lady right away," said Todd Bertolet. "My sister's body is not off the mountain yet and he's got photos picked out. Basically, the video is a Harold Henthorn show. There were photographs of just Harold in there. Toni's not even in it at Toni's own funeral." Harold had linked music to the photos. He cranked up the volume so loud the family asked him to turn it down.

On Thursday, Oct. 4, 2012, family, friends, and parents from Halcy's school gathered at Cherry Hills Community Church. In the dramatic confines of the newly built church, faced in tan native Colorado stone with towering stained-glass windows and a hardwood staircase leading to the funeral parlors, the pictures from Tamara Gordon's slide show—what the Bertolet came to call "The Harold Henthorn Show"—played for mourners. There was no casket, Toni's body having been cremated shortly after the viewing. After the service, at the reception, Harold appeared "distraught and under pressure," recalled Mike Whitener, a friend of Harold and Toni's. Still, Mike noted that Harold never cried and his demeanor didn't seem related to the loss of his wife of twelve years. Instead, Harold continued to stew about

the official response to Toni's death. He fixated on park
Ranger Faherty. Harold launched into what Mike called
a "litany" about being embroiled in a legal tangle. He
said the Park Service was being "zealous" in its investigation into Toni's death and that he had to get an attorney. At one point Harold said he felt like he was being
investigated for killing Toni. Mike would later shudder
to realize that Harold never denied it. The thought, Mike
later said, "tormented" him.

On the receiving line meeting mourners, Harold stood
beside Daniel Jarvis, a longtime friend treated as family.
Daniel's parents knew Harold from college at the University of Kentucky and later from church. Every few
years the Jarvis family would visit Harold in Colorado,
through his elementary and high school years. Harold
and Daniel exchanged text messages or an email or two.
"We were very close," Daniel would later say. "I'd say.
He was like an uncle to me."

In April 2012, Daniel was living with the Henthorns
for a month. In the basement Harold had set up a home
office from which he said he told Daniel he worked as a
fundraiser for nonprofit organizations. His job often took
him out of town for a day or two. Once he took a business trip to Grand Junction, Colorado, he told Daniel.
Other times it was just business lunches.

After Daniel moved out, he kept in touch with
Harold, talking or texting once or twice a week. In
mid-September 2012, Harold told him about the anniversary weekend he had planned at the Stanley Hotel in
Estes Park, which Harold said was Toni's favorite place
to go.

Two weeks later, on the evening of September 29,
2012, Daniel got a text from Harold. Daniel said, "It was
something along the lines of: 'Tragic news. Toni fell. She
was severely injured. Flight for Life was requested.

Didn't make it. They couldn't bring it and she passed away.' "

Daniel recalled, "I was completely in shock. I had to read it multiple times just to really understand what the words were saying."

A second text that arrived sometime after midnight generated a different reaction, one of puzzlement. It was from Harold, and it contained attachments.

"He said that he had some pictures that he wanted me to safeguard," said Daniel. "He said it was too difficult for him to keep them on his phone."

The photos showed Harold and Toni on the go—the couple holding hands in front of the Stanley Hotel, Toni in the car sipping from a coffee cup, Toni and Harold on the trail posing in front of the white-barked aspens in full fall yellow, Harold standing on the trail in his U.S. Open hat, Toni on a cliff overlooking the Fall River Valley, Harold standing precariously on rocks on another cliff, clutching a pine tree branch for balance, and Toni high on the mountainside peering through binoculars.

"I started crying," recalled Daniel, "because I knew those were Toni's last moments on Earth."

Now Harold started talking to Daniel in the receiving line. Harold again spoke of the day of the hike and seemed upset.

"They found a map," Harold kept saying. "They found a map."

Daniel didn't know what he was talking about.

Harold's emotions darkened after the reception. Toni's parents were overwhelmed with grief from the funeral when Harold told them something they'd never forget. He complained that his recent frustrations stemmed from Toni's death being investigated by federal authorities instead of local police because she died in a national park. According to the Bertolets, he told them, "If it had occurred fifty yards away, we wouldn't be in this situation."

The Bertolets headed home to Mississippi the next day. "We hated to leave Haley," said Toni's father. "I didn't know how, but we were going to get her and make sure she was all right." As Robert Bertolet sat in the Denver International Airport that Friday morning awaiting the flight, a memory came to him. "When Toni was born, we had a snowstorm in Jackson, Mississippi, of all places. It took me ten minutes to get to the hospital and two hours to get home, "he said. "And sitting there in the airport, I looked out and it was snowing. It was the first snow of the year, according to the newspapers. To us, it was kind of a sign. Toni came during a snowstorm and she left during a snowstorm."

SIX

Not widely known to the millions of people who visit America's National Parks is the fact that the Park Service employs a staff of detectives. They're trained in investigative techniques and evidence gathering and interrogation. They hold the same powers as any big-city police investigator

Elizabeth Shott had been a law-enforcement ranger from 1993 to 2001, completed specialized training in the federal Criminal Investigator Training Program, and since 2001 held the rank of special agent assigned to the Intermountain Region in Denver.

On Oct. 22, she had a speakerphone conversation with Toni's brothers Todd and Barry Bertolet. Shortly thereafter, she also spoke with Toni's parents. The trip to Denver for the memorial service had given the Bertolets a cause. They had become amateur investigators, building a case against Harold. "We were taking notes," said Toni's father. "We had three sets of notes going all the time." Toni's brothers had their notes, the parents kept theirs. "Harold kept talking and then we would compare the stories."

So as Shott queried the family for the first time, four weeks after Toni's death, a wealth of investigative material had already been collected and documented. The Bertolets went over their history with Harold, from that first time they met him, through the wedding, the move to Denver and the birth of Haley. They shared their suspicions about his employment status and his increasingly controlling behavior. Barry Bertolet recounted Harold's statements about Toni's vital signs and how that didn't jibe with what her condition should have been after the fall. And they recounted his behavior before and during the memorial in Denver.

The family had seen him just days before the interview and said his behavior had become even more erratic. Harold had flown into Mississippi with Haley the previous week for a second memorial for Toni for her Southern friends, family, and patients. Visiting Toni's brothers and parents, Harold was oblivious to their grief. To Toni's parents, he provided a graphic account of dragging Toni across the ground and banging her head against rocks to get her to a place to perform CPR. He referred to her as clumsy. "He would constantly downgrade her," said Toni's mother. "She was never clumsy, she was an athlete. She could walk in heels higher than I could. She was very used to doing agile things."

And he obsessed over Ranger Faherty's "vendetta" against him. "He's calling the ranger who's investigating him 'Barney Fife,'" recalled Todd Bertolet. "He's saying, 'He's more a guy telling people to put out campfires and writing parking tickets and busting people for smoking pot.'"

During his court testimony, Faherty would later recall Harold's concerns and contradictions. Harold harped on the fact that Faherty wouldn't leave him alone about the timing of one of the texts that Harold said he received around the time Toni fell: the message from the babysitter about Haley's soccer game. Harold had told the ranger that he was reading the text at the time that Toni went off the cliff. But to Harold's irritation, the ranger suggested the text couldn't have come when Harold said it did. The ranger said the message must have been sent around 6:30 P.M., *after* Toni had fallen and around the time Harold called 911 from the bottom of the cliff. When Toni's brothers asked Harold about it, Harold's story changed. He originally told Barry he had been on his phone reading the text from the babysitter about his daughter's soccer victory when he saw the blur and realized Toni had fallen. Then Harold said he was actually looking for a text message—not at a text message—to see if Haley had already arrived home, the soccer game long over. Finally, Harold said that he was instead looking at text messages from Toni's office. He recalled being perturbed that she was on-call during their special weekend. "He would tell my brother one story and then figure out an issue with the time and then tell me a different story," Todd opined. "He was very proactive. He would try to change the story."

Harold also complained that Faherty kept bugging him about a map in Harold's Jeep with an X written on it. Harold told the Bertolet brothers that it was no big deal: He had scoped out the trail in advance but really had no idea how that map came to get in his Jeep. He thought maybe he had marked the map for a nephew, but he couldn't be sure.

The second memorial service took place on Oct. 19, 2012, at the First Baptist Church in Jackson, the same church where Toni and Harold were married. Harold displayed apparent irritation. "It wasn't a grieving husband that I saw," said Todd Bertolet. "It was a put-out individual. He would just sit there, his legs crossed, shaking his foot like: Hurry up and get this over so he could be someplace else." The more Harold spoke, the more he seemed to have become unglued. He told the Bertolets that he had hired an attorney and a private investigator to figure out what the federal authorities had on him and what other people were telling the feds. "He was telling us that we didn't have to talk to the National Park Service or the feds or whoever was after him," said Todd. Harold told Toni's family he expected to be arrested when he returned home to Denver. "We asked: What are you going to be arrested for?" recalled Toni's mother. "It was something about money. It sounded like bank fraud that he would be arrested for, not murder." He assured them that he'd lined up babysitting for Haley and that he'd be out of jail quickly.

No police awaited Harold Henthorn when he arrived at the airport in Denver from Mississippi in late October 2012. But all of this information had been recorded in the Bertolet family notebooks and reported to Agent Beth Shott.

On October 23, 2012, Shott got a first look at the death scene. Guided by Harold's account of the hike and the photos that had been pulled from the memory card on the camera found next to Toni's body, Shott and Faherty retraced the couple's hike. Starting at the trailhead, they went to where Harold had said they detoured for a picnic spot, but neither Shott nor Faherty could find a trace of the "use trail" that Harold spoke of. Pathways had been carved into the lodge pole pines and other conifers by drainage, but none led to the upper rock "nob" described by Harold. Instead, Shott and Faherty had to wander through the trees over unmarked terrain to reach the overlook.

The next leg of the hike, to the second "nob," brought them one-quarter of a mile down a slope so rocky and steep that Shott had to hold onto tree branches and rocks and in some places, slide down on her backside. One of the last pictures from the camera showed Harold clinging to a pine tree and looking down over the cliff. Shott and Faherty found what they believed to be the same tree. Peering over the edge, they saw directly below them the rocky place where Toni had landed.

They now had what they believed was the "fall spot." The photo of Harold, apparently taken by Toni, was time-stamped 5:00:30—thirty seconds after 5 P.M. If she had gone over the cliff at or around this time, that meant Harold waited nearly an hour to call 911. Harold did say he hiked for another forty-five minutes to get down to his injured wife, which raised two questions. Why didn't he call 911 immediately? And why did it take him so long to get to the bottom of the cliff? Shott and Faherty made it down easily in ten minutes.

Through October, Shott interviewed friends of the Henthorns, each one raising more suspicions about Harold.

Investigators spoke with Cathy Lynch, whose child attended Cherry Hills Christian School with Haley. Cathy described Harold in unflattering terms, calling him controlling and dominating over Toni. He refused to give out Toni's cell number, and anybody wanting to coordinate children's events had to talk to Harold about what Toni would do. Another school parent, Kathy Burr, told Shott that shortly before Toni's death, Kathy heard the Henthorns discuss Haley's baptism. Toni had wanted to get Haley baptized soon, but

Harold cut off Toni, saying he'd already decided on a date.

Myra Whitener, the wife of Mike Whitener, said Harold didn't want Haley spending any time with Toni without Harold around. Since he had no office to go to, this meant Harold hovered constantly. The only respite for Toni was when Harold would take what he called business trips, overnights to places unknown for business he never disclosed.

In September 2011, a year before Toni's death, the Henthorns joined the Whiteners on a vacation. Toni confided to Myra about Harold's controlling behavior with their daughter. Myra quoted Toni as saying, "I just want to be able to read stories to my daughter and sing to her at night, not just when Harold is gone, but when we're home together."

Then, after Toni's death, Harold showed no signs of mourning. In a phone call, Harold complained to Myra, "I miss my best friend. I have to do the laundry and I have to do the grocery shopping."

Allison Talley, a friend of Toni's from Mississippi, recalled a phone conversation with Harold, just days before Toni's death. It was so troubling that Allison had taken notes. On Sept. 24, 2012, Harold talked about a surprise anniversary trip to Estes Park before segueing into a conversation about money. Toni, he said, wasn't making enough of it. Doctors in Colorado could only expect to earn $50,000 a year, he complained. He wanted Toni to quit her job. He next grumbled about Toni's family, griping that they hadn't called her on her fiftieth birthday.

Allison, who was also close to Toni's family, knew this to be untrue and she wondered why he would lie.

Harold's longtime friend Daniel Jarvis, who had been housesitting for Harold during the second memorial, also raised suspicions. He told investigators about the strange statements by Harold in the receiving line at the first memorial service, then recalled how Harold spoke to him further about Toni's death the night Harold returned from Mississippi.

After tucking in Haley for the night, Harold met Daniel in the basement home office. As Daniel would later recall in court testimony, Harold said he received a phone call, not a text, about Haley's soccer game when he looked up and didn't see Toni anymore. Peering over the edge, he saw that she had fallen down an incline that Harold estimated to be thirty feet. After hiking down rough terrain, he found her bleeding but alive, called her cardiologist brother for help with first aid, then dialed 911 to request a Flight for Life helicopter.

"He said that she was alive for about an hour," Daniel later recalled, repeating what he told investigators, "and that he was trying to give her CPR throughout that time."

Volunteer search-and-rescue experience taught Harold the basics in CPR, he told Daniel, but the efforts failed. Daniel recalled that Harold spoke of a long wait for the ranger and that Toni had been dead for three or four hours before they got to her. Her death, he added, left $1 million in life insurance for their daughter. "He couldn't touch it," said Daniel.

Harold then circled back to the map he'd mentioned earlier at the Colorado memorial. "He said that the rangers were making a really big deal about this stupid map," recalled Daniel, "that he had made it for me, meant to give it to me at a lunch, but he had left it in his Jeep and just forgot to give it to me." Harold described the map as "showing some restaurants in Estes Park," said Daniel, "that there was no reason for them to be suspicious of the map."

Harold never mentioned anything to Daniel about an X.

It was more of the same about Harold—self-pity, shifting stories. Toni's family and friends had pictured a marriage in trouble, perhaps on the brink of divorce despite Toni's resistance to that option. Investigators know that a woman is often most at risk of violence from a boyfriend or husband when a breakup looms.

The insurance upped the ante. Harold had said the same thing to Faherty about the insurance: The policy—in this account it was $1.5 million—named Haley as the beneficiary. A check of the insurance records confirmed that Harold and Toni Henthorn had in fact insured her life for $1.5 million through ING Relia-Star, payable to a trust for her daughter.

However, Harold failed to mention important facts. On April 29, 2011, the beneficiary was changed from Haley's trust to Harold. What's more, this wasn't the only insurance policy. In 2001, shortly after the Henthorns got married, a $1.5 million policy with American General Life Insurance was taken out on Toni's life, the beneficiary again listed as Harold with no similar policy taken taken out on him. Then in 2005, yet another policy was taken out on Toni with Genworth Financial for $1.5 million. Once more, the beneficiary listed as the "Harold A. Henthorn and Toni B. Henthorn Trust." The trust was controlled by Harold.

In the end, Toni Henthorn's death meant a $4.5 million payout—all to Harold, according to the evidence later produced at his trial.

Taken together, the evidence—the ever-changing stories, the accounts of controlling behavior, the suspicions of a marital breakup, and the insurance money—all laid waste, in the minds of investigators, to any possibility Toni Henthorn died in a tragic accident. This added up to murder—and worse. Toni's family had mentioned to Shott a couple of times that Harold was a widower at the time he married Toni. Aside from saying his first wife had died in a car accident, Harold said nothing more about her, and the Bertolets never pressed him. Toni had also never said anything about the first wife, if in fact she knew anything. But the information was out there. And now it was in the hands of investigators, convincing them that Harold Henthorn may be more evil than what anybody had ever imagined.

In the days after Toni's death, letters began arriving at the Park Service and the Larimer County Coroner's Office. Over the next three weeks, a total of sixteen emails and phone calls also arrived at the Park Service, the Estes Park Police Department, and the Sheriff's and Coroner's offices of Larimer County—the county where Toni died. All of them said something similar: that Harold Henthorn had been married once before, and that his previous wife had died seventeen years earlier.

"Please thoroughly investigate the death of Dr. Toni Henthorn," one letter read. "Sadly there are many similarities to these two accidents."

SEVEN

Highway 67 is a small, two-lane road that winds down the steep eastern slope of the Rockies from Pike National Forest. It hits a place the locals call Casey's Curve, not far from the remote home of one Van Anthony Hayes. At 10:25 P.M. on the night of May 6, 1995, somebody was at Hayes' front door. He opened it to find a woman in her late thirties or forties who gave her last name as Montoya. There may have been other people with her, he couldn't remember. The woman had driven up to his home in a brown Jeep Wagoneer.

She told him that about a quarter-mile away, in a gravel turnout, somebody was badly hurt and needed help. This was long before the widespread use of cell-phones and the Montoya woman asked Hayes to use his house phone to summon authorities. He dialed 911, relayed the distress call, then left his house for the turnout.

It was a crisp, cool night, but clear and dry—no rain,

snow, or sleet. Temperatures hovered in the mid-thirties. An emergency flare signaled the spot on the roadway to which Hayes pulled up around 10:30 P.M. But for headlamps from Hayes' car, it was pitch black. No street lights lined this stretch of Highway 67.

Getting out of his car, Hayes saw a Jeep Cherokee, whose tailgate was open, parked in the turnout. A man who appeared to be in his thirties crouched beside the Jeep. A woman, who also appeared in her thirties, was on the ground. She lay facedown on the passenger side on the gravel, and wasn't moving. The man had his hand pressed against her neck apparently looking for a pulse. He appeared worried. Hayes told him that help was on the way and to hold on.

A small crowd began to gather. The Montoya woman had returned, and Hayes spotted others with her, including two men and perhaps some children in their car. The men went over to the woman, a "white female," Hayes would say. Somehow she had gotten onto her back and somebody had put blankets on her

Hayes went around to the rear of the Jeep and closed the tailgate. He spotted a flashlight on the ground just under the front part of the Jeep. He picked it up and noticed it wasn't on. Hayes placed the flashlight inside of one of two women's shoes sitting on the hood of the Jeep.

Within minutes, the first sirens of emergency vehicles could be heard approaching. Hayes looked around. The Montoya woman and her group had left.

The emergency dispatcher had relayed Hayes' 911 call to Terry Thompson, the chief of the West Douglas County Fire Protection District, a force of volunteers, alerting him to an accident scene on the highway near the tiny town of Sedalia, about thirty miles south of Denver. Within minutes after getting the 10:27 P.M. call,

Thompson and six of his people arrived at the turnout in their own cars and trucks topped with temporary spinning emergency lights. He saw the Jeep and two of his EMTs attending to what looked like a woman on the ground. Before he got closer, one of his volunteers gave him an urgent request.

"Chief, we need to land a helicopter," he was told. Thompson went back to his vehicle to radio for a Flight for Life helicopter.

Flood lamps mounted atop the volunteers' vehicles illuminated a grim scene. A woman, flat on her back next to a Jeep that appeared to have been jacked up for a tire change. The right-front passenger tire was missing. The woman lay roughly perpendicular to the Jeep, her feet under the wheel well.

Volunteer paramedics Jeffery Schippel and Norm Whipple assessed her. She showed no visible injuries to the head, chest, or throat. But her arms and cheeks exhibited signs of petechiae, red or purple bruising from the explosion of tiny blood vessels caused by the sudden loss of oxygen and blood pressure. Petechiae is seen usually in cases of heart attack or suffocation.

The woman had no pulse and wasn't breathing.

Worried the Jeep could fall on her, Schippel and Whipple moved her "a little further away" and began efforts to revive her. Schippel performed respiration— mouth-to-mouth breathing—and Whippel did chest compressions.

About this time, Jason Kennedy, a patrolman for the Douglas County Sheriff's Office, pulled up in his cruiser at 10:42 P.M., the first law-enforcement officer to get there. With three years at the department after academy training, he was one of several young lawmen responding that night, and his inexperience showed. His handwritten notes marked the location of the incident as

"Kasey Curve," misspelling the landmark, and offered no other details, including mile markers.

By the light of the red sirens and the headlamps, Kennedy spotted between five and seven people. By the early hours of the next morning the number would grow to eighteen. But for the activity at the turnout it was completely quiet. A thick pine forest surrounded them. A car would come by about once every fifteen minutes.

Kennedy spoke with one of the EMTs, who told him that the woman had been crushed by the vehicle. Reports described it as a 1991 Jeep Cherokee, gray with orange and red stripes and "Sport 4×4 written on the side. It happened "during the changing of a passenger side front tire," according to Kennedy's report.

Normally another agency, the Colorado State Patrol, investigates traffic accidents. But since this was a case of a car falling on top of somebody, and not your standard collision or other highway mishap, it was a little more complicated. For now, jurisdiction would remain with the sheriff's office until Kennedy was told otherwise. Unable to get a signal on his portable radio in that remote location, he used his patrol car radio to contact dispatch requesting a detective and probably a supervisor.

Returning to the Jeep, Kennedy began taking notes, jotting down the Jeep's license plate—RDR478—and noting that the front passenger tire had been removed. The "axle drum or brake assembly" was "resting on the ground," his report stated. Beneath what he called the "front passenger side leaf spring" sat an orange colored jack on the ground. A second orange jack was near the front axle but was not actually touching the axle, having apparently been lowered. Two lug nuts were under the car and third was near the "break [sic] drum assembly," he wrote.

A socket wrench with an extension was noted as "laying [sic] underneath," apparently under the Jeep. The tailgate was closed. Through the tailgate window, Kennedy spotted "two full-sized tires" in the rear hatch.

Rescue personnel then directed him to the victim's husband.

"I met with him," wrote Kennedy, "and he identified himself as Harold Arthur Henthorn."

The woman was his wife, Sandra Lynn Henthorn.

"Henthorn appeared visibly shaken," Kennedy recorded in his report. "I asked him if he could please let me know exactly how she was injured, and he told me."

Thus began the narrative described in the yellowed pages of an investigative file long since forgotten. The reports had been stashed away in storage at the headquarters complex of the Douglas County Sheriff's Office, in Castle Rock, Colorado, thirty miles south of Denver, and left unread for the better part of two decades.

The file had been pulled after authorities received the anonymous tips. It now sat before U.S. Park Service Investigator Beth Shott.

Files of long-closed cases have a way of disappearing over time, lost either to fire or cleaning sprees or digitizing efforts that go haywire. This can be true for serious cases, but particularly for ones documenting something like what happened late one night in 1995 on a remote road in the forest, an incident that received relatively little attention at the time.

Deputy Jason Kennedy had been at the scene for fifteen minutes when he spoke with Harold briefly. As they talked next to the Jeep, the EMTs continued to work on Harold's wife while a rescue helicopter landed in the closest open area, a half mile away.

Harold told Kennedy the couple had pulled over to change the tire, which seemed low. "Had maybe a soft tire or something," Harold was quoted as saying in Kennedy's notes. "We have had three flats. Construction on the home."

Harold's wife, held the flashlight while Harold loosened the lug nuts and removed the tire. Harold said that he carried the tire to the back of the Jeep and threw it into the hatch. That's when one of the jacks gave way and Harold heard his wife.

"She began screaming and yelling for him," said Kennedy's report. "He ran up and realized that she was trapped under the car. The car was on her back. She was talking to him. He was trying to get her out from underneath the vehicle. Then she stopped talking to him and stopped breathing."

Harold was somehow able to pull his wife out from under the car and started CPR, he told Kennedy.

Kennedy next radioed the dispatcher from his patrol car to report a "husband-and-wife situation" in which the wife had been pinned under a car and was in serious condition. The dispatcher would relay the information to the sheriff's investigators, who would conduct a more thorough interview with Harold. Because this was now a matter for a detective, Kennedy only wanted to get a brief narrative that he would hand off to the investigator assigned to the case. Kennedy didn't ask probing questions or follow-ups. His report didn't record any observations about Harold's demeanor beyond appearing shaken.

While awaiting the arrival of a detective, Kennedy documented the scene in words and pictures. With a point-and-shoot 35 mm camera, he shot two rolls of film of the Jeep and surrounding area from different sides and angles. The photo log shows thirty-four pictures taken, everything from the trunk to the lug nuts to all sides of the Jeep and the grounds

Kennedy also canvassed the surrounding woods, finding nothing of interest, and started a "crime scene sign-in sign-out sheet" and recorded the names of law-enforcement people, though not firefighters.

At 11:13 P.M., the log noted the arrival of Investigator Robert McMahan. McMahan got the call at about 11 P.M. from his boss, Sgt. Brock McCoy. The area now was swarming with activity and secured. Tape with "Sheriff's Department. Do Not Cross" draped over a sign reading, "Please Do Not Litter, Keep Your Forest Clean." There was also crime-scene tape stretched over the Jeep and attached to a tree.

In May 1995, McMahan was new to investigative work. He had been promoted from patrol about five or six months earlier—he would later say he had been giving no specific training to be an investigator—and his lack of experience also would be evident, starting with his reports. As with the others, he left future investigators with no clear idea of where the incident occurred. His "Investigator's Progress Report" said he responded to "Highway #67 at Casey's Curve on a possible fatal accident . . . near the Giddy-Up-Go," a convenience store, but otherwise didn't narrow down the location.

A briefing with Jason Kennedy established that Harold Henthorn and wife Sandra Lynn—who went by Lynn—had pulled over to change a tire, that the Jeep somehow fell on the wife while she was underneath it for some unknown reason, that she called out his name for help, and that he found her pinned under the vehicle.

By now, Lynn had already been taken by ambulance on a short trip to a Flight for Life helicopter, bound for Swedish Medical Center in Denver. Harold remained on site for the time being.

Fire Chief Terry Thompson told McMahan that the first responders had altered the scene. One of Thompson's crew had lowered the Jeep jack for safety. Otherwise everything was as they found it. Taking notes as he walked around the scene, McMahan recorded the license plate of the Jeep and wrote that the vehicle was facing south on the west side of the highway, "parked in a dirt parking area." Across the road, on what McMahan called the "east side," was another pullout large enough for a fire department vehicle, which was parked there.

The Jeep sat on a turnout covered in tire tracks, a mishmash of no investigative value. The orange jack first noted by Kennedy lay a foot behind what McMahan called "the wheel," presumably the area missing the wheel. Next to it were the ratchet tool and a pair of pliers. McMahan noted the silver jack under the front axle almost exactly in the center of the Jeep. Next to it were pieces of what McMahan described as a "cinderblock," though photos suggest it was a flat concrete paver, broken into three pieces.

Three lug nuts lay below the wheel well, one underneath and behind the well, the other two outside and behind the well, McMahan wrote.

He noted that a plastic bug shield at the front of the Jeep had a corner piece broken off on the passenger side. A blue coat had been draped over the hood and next to it were a pair of women's shoes with a black mini-mag flashlight inside one. Through the passenger side window McMahan spotted a "black standard equipment jack, which apparently belongs to the vehicle" on the floor next to the jack's crank handle and the wheel cover for the spare tire, which normally bolted to the back of the Jeep on the outside of the hatch. This brought the total of jacks to three.

He also made this observation: On the front fender, on the passenger side near where the tire had been removed, "was an apparent partial foot print type mark." The footprint was photographed.

Kennedy explained the findings at the scene, noting the Good Samaritan, Van Hayes had put the flashlight in the shoe.

While awaiting the arrival of a deputy to drive Harold to the hospital, McMahan had a few words with him. Harold said that he and his wife had been returning from a day trip to Deckers, a small mountain town along the Platte River popular with fly fisherman. The couple "were having a great day," said McMahan's report, paraphrasing the interview so that it was unclear whether those were McMahan's words or Harold's. "They were returning to Sedalia to have dinner at a restaurant," McMahan wrote. "They got a flat tire and they stopped to change it."

Harold said he had hoisted the car using two jacks—the silver and orange ones. Harold said he threw the tire into the hatch area, at which point "the vehicle apparently fell off of the jack," said the report. Harold found his wife under the Jeep "with the wheel rotor in her back, somewhere between the middle of her back and her shoulder blades," said the report.

"She was calling for air, stating she needed air," wrote McMahan. "He told her not to talk, and he tried to get the vehicle off of her. She stopped breathing and when he pulled her out she was not breathing."

McMahan examined Harold's hands. The investigator said he "noticed no unusual marks," according to his report. He also photographed the tops and bottoms of Harold's shoes.

Harold was led off to a patrol car and driven to Swedish Medical Center while McMahan stayed behind.

At 11:20 P.M., the Flight for Life helicopter landed at Swedish Hospital in Englewood, just south of Denver. After the four-minute flight, Lynn Henthorn was wheeled into the emergency room. She was unconscious and unresponsive with no pulse, no blood pressure. Her pupils were fixed and dilated.

A quick external appraisal by attending physician Dr. Richard Tillquist revealed no obvious injury or bleeding. That meant the trauma had to be inside, confirmed when she went into the operating room. Stripped of her shirt, Lynn showed a giant purple blotch from neck to waist. Her chest was flattened. Emergency surgery commenced to open her chest and clamp off the bleeding arteries. Fluid had filled her lungs. All medical signs pointed to severe injuries from being crushed.

As his wife was being treated, Harold Henthorn rode to the hospital in the patrol car of Douglas County Sheriff's Deputy Jeffrey Bredehoeft. The deputy had pulled up to the scene at about 10:45 P.M. and picked up Harold at about 11:20 P.M. for the forty-minute drive to Swedish. Bredehoeft drove the speed limit and didn't use the siren or lights.

Along the way, Harold "voluntarily told me the following," Bredehoeft's report said, and contained the following narrative: Harold spoke of driving along Highway 67 and stopping sometime near dark for dinner at the Sedalia Grill. Located at the junction of Highway 67 and Highway 83, the Sedalia Grill was a popular barbecue place for bikers and travelers to the mountain resorts.

After dinner, the Henthorns drove west on Highway 67 when Harold sensed the front passenger tire was low. He repeated his account of removing the tire, putting it in the back, seeing the Jeep go off the jack and, hearing

Lynn scream. He didn't see what happened but had a theory.

"Lynn was on the ground, under the front axle looking for a lug nut," said Bredefhoeft's report, paraphrasing Harold's statement.

Harold told him that after the car slipped off the jack onto Lynn, he placed a second jack in position, lifted the car and got Lynn free. "Lynn was talking to him as he tried to get the second jack in position," said the report. "Lynn lost consciousness and stopped breathing."

A car with four or five people in it stopped to help. "He didn't remember who pulled Lynn out from under the car," wrote Bredehoeft, "and didn't remember who started to give CPR to Lynn."

Shortly before midnight, another Douglas County Sheriff's Office Deputy, this one named Kevin Duffy, arrived at the hospital. His assignment was to collect the victim's clothing and connect with the husband. According to his report, supervisor Sgt. McCoy "advised me that the incident seemed suspicious due to the fact that the victim's husband was with her at the time of the accident and the victim was found trapped under the rim of the car while they were changing a flat tire."

Duffy spoke with the emergency room attending nurse, Suzanne Winders, who handed him a brown paper bag with Lynn's jacket, blue jeans, and sweater. Winders told Duffy that the remaining clothes were still with her in the operating room.

At 12:40 A.M., Lynn was transferred to intensive care, B pod. "Told by staff—survival doubtful," Duffy wrote in his notebook. Duffy asked the staff to hold onto her remaining clothes if she died.

In the next half hour, Deputy Bredehoeft introduced Duffy to Lynn's husband, who'd been in a waiting room.

For the fourth time that night, Harold Henthorn would speak with a sheriff's representative.

Duffy took down Harold's full name and address and the full name of his wife, plus a description that appeared to have come off her driver's license: white female, five-foot-five, 140 pounds, red hair, green eyes. The statement from Harold veered from the incident at hand. For instance, he shared that they had been married for thirteen years and wanted to have children, but Lynn suffered a medical condition that prevented her from getting pregnant.

"About two weeks ago, Lynn had exploratory surgery and was found to have several tumors related to her condition," wrote Duffy in his report, summarizing Harold's comment. "They were going to schedule surgery to remove the tumors in the near future." Lynn was taking Luprin and Endican for her "arthritic condition" and was going to have more surgery in two months.

Harold began again to go through the night's events— he said the couple left their house at 3 P.M. "to drive up to the mountains to the Deckers area," according to Duffy's report. Then the interview was interrupted.

At 1:24 A.M., a hospital staff member pulled Duffy away and, out of earshot of Harold, reported that Lynn had died in surgery.

Duffy returned to Harold, but didn't give him the grim news. Death notification would come later from the doctor. Instead, Duffy continued with the interview, asking Harold about the tire problem.

"The accident occurred on Hwy 67 on a tight curve by a convenience store," wrote Duffy. "They pulled over to change the front tire because it was getting 'mushy' and they thought they were going to have a flat," wrote Duffy—the word "mushy" apparently used by Harold.

Harold said he'd been having trouble with blowouts in his neighborhood because of the nails from construction. "There is one tire with a nail in it in their garage at home," wrote Duffy. In fact, Harold said, he'd stopped two or three times during the day trip to check the tires.

Harold said he had tried to lift the Jeep using the black jack that had come with the vehicle from the factory. "The 'proper' jack was not working properly and was sticking," wrote Duffy. "He tried to get the jack to quit sticking by spraying it with oil but it continued to stick."

That's when Harold used what Duffy called a "silver boat jack" affixed to the front axle of the Jeep. Duffy's report said, "Jack was put on a cinder block. Block broke. Jack was on round axle. Knew that's not where it should be."

Harold said Lynn shined a flashlight as Harold removed the lug nuts and handed them to his wife, who held onto them. At this point, "One guy stopped, asked if he needed help," Duffy wrote. Harold told them they were okay, and the man continued on, his identity unknown.

After Harold got the tire off, he warned his wife to be careful. "He told her not to touch the car or the jack and took the tire off the rim," wrote Duffy. Harold threw the tire into the back—it was now described as a "flat tire." Duffy scribbled, "Vic(tim) stayed by tire."

Duffy quoted Harold as saying, "Lynn called to me" as the Jeep fell. Finding her pinned underneath, Harold couldn't get her out from under the brake rotor assembly. "Lynn was conscious, 'some of the time' but was hurt very badly," wrote Duffy.

Harold again mentioned the next people to arrive, the car that contained "3 males and 2 females" who "stopped and assisted Henthorn," wrote Duffy. Harold told them to call an ambulance. "One stayed—helped get jack into place," Duffy wrote in his notebook. At some point, "the others" returned. "Took their coats off, put on victim, one got a blanket."

Somehow, Lynn got out from under the Jeep. "Henthorn could not remember if he, or the other people, pulled Lynn from underneath the car," wrote Duffy. "Lynn was incoherent and Henthorn checked for a pulse. Her pulse was weak but he did feel a pulse at her carotid artery."

Asked again how he thought this happened, "Henthorn thinks Lynn was reaching for a lug nut that had rolled under the vehicle when the accident occurred."

By 2:40 A.M., the interview was complete. Five minutes later, the attending physician, Dr. Richard Tillquist, came into the waiting room. He notified Harold that his wife had died. If the officer witnessed Harold's reaction, it wasn't mentioned in the report.

A minute later, Duffy got on the phone with Arapahoe County Coroner Jeff Nielsen and "advised him of the situation." Although Lynn died in Arapahoe County, the incident itself occurred in Douglas County. "Nielsen told me he would contact the Douglas County Coroner, Mark Stover, and advise him of the death."

Dr. Tillquist then escorted Duffy into the ICU to see the body of Lynn Henthorn. The officer took note of the "heavy purple/blue discoloring" from the chest to the head with "bulging eyes and swelling to the face." He saw no injuries to the neck, hands, knees, throat, arms, head, or legs. But he did spot two half-inch wide, six-inch long parallel bruises about two inches apart under her right shoulder blade. The high point of the bruising was at the neck running at a 45-degree angle toward her waist.

Duffy took three Polaroid photos of her body and

asked the doctor for his opinion of how she died. "Lynn's injuries," wrote Duffy, "were consistent with a crushing trauma and he believed she died from suffocation due to the trauma."

Duffy met again with Harold and a staff person from the Victim Assistance program at the hospital. Duffy said he "assisted Henthorn," but offered no details of how Harold reacted to the death of his wife.

The officer received a large plastic bag of Lynn's remaining clothes, which he gave to Deputy Bredehoeft along with the paper bag of other clothing to be put into evidence.

At 3 A.M., Duffy left the hospital and returned to the sheriff's office where he put his handwritten notes into the official report.

Back out near Casey's Curve, the investigation continued. Investigator Robert McMahan popped the hatch of the Jeep and found two radial tires—Goodyear Wranglers, size P225/75R15, he wrote in his report—one stacked atop the other. It wasn't clear which tire was the one that had been removed and which was the spare. Both were half flat. Checking the air pressure, the tire on top had 15 psi—half the recommended air pressure— and the bottom tire had 19 psi. The report said nothing of either tire having a nail or other kind of puncture. The other three tires on the Jeep were fully inflated at 30 psi.

The only witness who appears to have given a formal statement at the scene was Van Anthony Hayes. In what appears to be his own shaky hand, he wrote:

> When I got here a flare was burning in the road. The husband was checking her neck for a pulse. The victim was laying on the ground on the passenger side of the jeep. Trunk lid was open. We

put blankets on her. Confirmed a pulse plus breathing. The husband said, The jeep fell on the middle of her back. I said help is on the way just hold on. Three people 2 men 1 lady come to my house. They said please help. I closed trunk lid. I spotted a flashlight under middle of front of the jeep. I picked it up. It was not on. Put it in shoe on hood.

Signed Van Hayes.

At midnight, Sharon Bronner, a crime-scene technician, began the meticulous process of inventorying everything inside and surrounding the Jeep. Her report added details to what the other law-enforcement personnel had mentioned. The jacket on the hood was in fact a blue ski jacket, the shoes black, the mini-mag in the right shoe. That plastic bug guard molding that had been broken away was seven inches by six inches. The shower curtain on the ground was made of vinyl, brown with orange flowers on it.

She noted the four-way lug wrench, the pliers, the gray jack under the axle, the concrete paver broken— she recorded—into three pieces. She mapped on a piece of paper the exact location of the lug nuts that may have doomed Lynn: one next to the gray jack, one behind the wheel base, another a foot away, two more at a spot northeast of the wheel well. That orange jack was hydraulically operated and measured six inches high.

Inspecting the interior of the Jeep, she noted the interior was gray with rug samples for floor mats. Mileage read 54,083; the trip mileage read thirty-six miles. The emergency brake was on. The gear was in either fourth or reverse.

On the floor behind the front passenger seat was that black hydraulic factory jack and its components, a white paper towel, a piece of a shirt, and a pair of gloves. In the hatch area, after removing the two tires low on air, Bronner found a white sheet, garbage bag, umbrella, roll of white paper towels, piece of white plastic, four-way lug wrench, pliers, snow scraper, and several ropes.

At 3 A.M., Bronner sealed the passenger side doors but left the driver side door unlocked for the tow driver, who hooked up the Jeep and hauled it away. Investigator Robert McMahan followed the Westside Towing company driver to the sheriff's impound yard in Castle Rock. The Impound Report, filled in by McMahan, listed the "offense/incident classification" as "suspicious incident/injury." It gave the reason for impounding the Jeep as "Possible evidence of the crime."

Then at 3:19 A.M., on Sunday, May 7, McMahan left the tow yard to write his reports.

Dr. Ben Galloway performed the autopsy on Lynn Henthorn at 12:40 P.M. on Monday, May 8, at Andrews Mortuary in Castle Rock. He was a private doctor who performed the autopsy at the direction of the county's coroner, Mark Stover, who also witnessed the procedure. The coroner's office in Douglas County is an elected position, an administrative post, and Stover was not a medical doctor. Stover's deputy, Wesley Riber, another non-physician who worked as an investigator, also attended the autopsy.

Galloway documented the history of the case from what he'd been told.

"This is the case of a 30-year-old, white female who apparently was underneath the car, looking for a lug nut when the jack gave way and the car fell on top of her. The incident occurred about ten miles west of Sedalia on Highway 67. Apparently the vehicle was a Cherokee and was off the side of the road on a gravel shoulder." The two "apparentlys" reflected the fact that at the time of autopsy Galloway was working with preliminary information.

He noted the woman had been air transported to Swedish Medical Center where "extensive surgical intervention was accomplished" and "the patient subsequently expired."

Using the traditional verbiage of autopsy reports, Galloway described the subject before him as an "unclothed, unembalmed, well-developed, well-nourished body of a white female appearing consistent with the stated age of 30." He measured her at five-foot-six and 150 to 155 pounds. She had red hair, hazel eyes, reddish brown eyebrows, and pierced earlobes. Her teeth were "in a good state of dental repair."

The hospital had delivered her body with some of the hospital apparatus attached. She still had her nose tube and cardiac electrodes on her chest. Tubes still stuck out of her chest. A catheter remained in place. Her right hand was still taped to an IV board. Rigor mortis—the stiffening of joints—was present—as was livor mortis, a bruising-like phenomenon caused by the settling of blood from gravity.

From the external examination, the doctor found that her scalp was "covered by long, thick, blood-stained, red hair," he wrote in his report, though the source of that blood did not come from a wound as he found "no evidence of trauma" to the "external surface of the head." Otherwise there was trauma to the neck. Her fingernails were "intact, short and clean," her hands, arms, and legs, in medical jargon "unremarkable," which is to say free of scrapes or bruises.

Turning the body over, Galloway found a pair of contusions on the back, running parallel at just the place where Harold had said the Jeep had landed on Lynn. Careful measurements were taken of the contusions to compare them with the mechanics of the brake assembly on the Jeep.

All over her body she suffered the blood-vessel breakage called petechiae: inside and outside of her eyelids, the whites of her eyes, her nose, ears, on her scalp, on her forehead, neck, breasts, and chest.

The internal examination found that Lynn's sternum, or breastbone, was cracked, most likely from the vigorous chest compressions from CPR. Fluid filled her lungs, another sign of a body being pressed and squeezed. Otherwise, Lynn's organs suffered no damage—her spleen, liver, kidneys and gallbladder and heart were all fine—and no broken ribs.

The pathologist also found some evidence of fibroids on Lynn's uterus, relating to what Harold said was their issue having children.

Galloway concluded: "The autopsy findings in this case reveal that the cause of death is due to mechanical [positional] asphyxiation secondary to a vehicle slipping off the jack and falling on top of the decedent."

This was the official cause of death. The autopsy offered no clue as to how or why Lynn Henthorn went under the Jeep, the manner of death. The lack of defensive wounds on her hands, however, suggested she didn't put up a struggle. It would be up to Robert McMahan to find more answers.

On the day of the autopsy, McMahan was kept busy on the Henthorn case. At 9:30 A.M., he got a phone call from a woman identifying herself as Paula Devries. She said her husband, Dwight, and their daughter had been driving on Highway 67 the night of May 6 and had stopped to help a man and woman who were changing a tire on their Jeep. She said this occurred around 9:30 P.M.

"She did not know anything further about what had happened but she had heard about the death," wrote McMahan in his report. "She would have Dwight call me as soon as she could reach him."

How she had heard about Lynn's death wasn't stated in the report, though the fatality had earned one small story in the local newspaper, which characterized her death as a road accident.

Later in the day, McMahan called Harold. From McMahan's report, this interview seemed to focus on the subjects of Lynn's health and life insurance. Harold told the investigator that the couple wanted to have children but faced complications. "Sandra had been unable to get pregnant," wrote McMahan. "In December, they found out what the problem was. They anticipated that the problem could be fixed and had planned on Sandra becoming pregnant."

About two weeks earlier, Lynn underwent exploratory surgery. Five benign tumors found on her uterus were to be removed in July. "With the removal of the tumors it was anticipated that she could become pregnant," wrote McMahan. "They got the life insurance in anticipation of the pregnancy in order to provide financial security for future children."

The couple had taken out two policies valued at $300,000 each, one for Harold, the other for Lynn, through CNA in San Francisco. Henthorn provided the policy number and said his agent was one Steve Church. McMahan spoke with Church, who confirmed that the two insurance policies amounted to $300,000 each with no riders. The applications were sent to the couple on December 20, 1994, the company received the policies back on January 3, 1995, and the policies were approved on February 21, 1995. Harold and Lynn were each other's beneficiaries. The policies had nothing to do with their employment and were individual-life insurance policies. McMahan wrote: "To his knowledge, his company has not yet been contacted about Sandra Henthorn's death."

From Harold, McMahan got the name of Lynn's boss, Nancy Hodges, at Denver Options. A call to Hodges revealed that Lynn worked as a Family Services Resource Coordinator—a social worker.

"She knew Lynn quite well. Lynn's marriage appeared to be wonderful," wrote McMahan. "Lynn was very optimistic and happy." As with all the reports, it isn't clear if these were Hodges' words or McMahan's or some combination. "Lynn did not drink alcohol or use anything that would impair her judgment," wrote McMahan. "Lynn was one of the most compulsive detailed safety conscious people she knows."

Nancy Hodges also seemed to know all about Lynn's health issues. "Lynn was unable to become pregnant and underwent some fertility counseling and some exploratory surgery," wrote McMahan. "She and her husband were working this fertility problem out and whatever the next steps were sounded hopeful that she may be able to conceive." As for Harold's health, all she knew was "Harold had a bad back."

Hodges initially described Harold in positive terms, calling him a "very thoughtful man" who would "surprise Lynn with things at work" and even brought Hodges flowers on Valentine's Day. "She was never aware of any domestic fights between Lynn and Harold."

But as the interview progressed, a different picture emerged. "Harold Henthorn is known as a very outgoing man and a 'wheeler dealer' almost overwhelming in a positive sense," wrote McMahan. "This whole incident seems suspicious to her."

By late afternoon, McMahan had reviewed the various reports from deputies Kennedy, Duffy, and Bredehoeft and had some questions. "I noticed that the account of the incident as authored by Deputy Bredehoeft was in conflict with the account authored by Investigator Kevin Duffy in his progress report," wrote McMahan. "I called Deputy Bredehoeft to clarify issues in his report."

McMahan asked Bredehoeft about Harold's demeanor, which wasn't mentioned in the report. "Harold was very excited and almost hyperventilating," wrote McMahan of what Bredehoeft told him. McMahan also wanted to see what Harold had said about his itinerary. Bredehoeft's report had the couple leaving their home at 3 P.M. and taking a day trip to Deckers.

But, after dinner at the Sedalia Grill, they were traveling west when they had the tire problem, which would have taken them in the opposite direction of their home to the north near Denver. Now Bredehoeft remembered that Harold said the couple were in fact going back to the mountains and not home. "Harold did not say why they went back up," said McMahan's report.

McMahan then asked Bredehoeft what Harold had said about which jack he used where, since Harold referenced at least three jacks in various conversations with deputies. Bredehoeft said he recalled Harold saying he'd used only one—the silver boat jack—and didn't recall anything about a second or third jack.

"At this point," McMahan said in his report, "I referred Deputy Bredehoeft to his report, where he mentions Harold using the second jack to try to get the car off of Lynn."

Bredehoeft still was unsure exactly what Harold said, telling McMahan "he would guess the report is more accurate as he wrote it after he dropped Harold off at the hospital, but right now he couldn't remember much about the second jack."

McMahan then spoke to Deputy Duffy, who said that Harold had told him that he used two jacks, the silver one to lift the car and the orange jack to get the car up off of Lynn.

One more angle McMahan would consider was the most unusual. A routine criminal background check on Harold produced a faxed document from somebody named "Sandie" in the records office of neighboring Arapahoe County, where the Henthorns lived.

It was a police report dated March 11, 1994. The box for "Offense Report checked" recorded an investigation at 6901 S. University Ave., Littleton—a J.C. Penney department store. The information came from security guards named James Douglas Bredlinger and James Andrew Butler concerning one Harold Arthur Henthorn who lived on East Costilla Place in Littleton, the Henthorns' current address. Harold's occupation was listed as "self-employed R.D.S Develop" with an address that was a post office box in Trenton, New Jersey.

· According to the report, at 5:26 P.M., Harold, wearing an oxford shirt and blue jeans, was arrested for shoplifting. "Subject apprehended by store security," said the report. Under the list of items stolen, it said "miscellaneous men's underwear." There was no other documentation and from the document it wasn't apparent how the case was resolved.

By the end of the day, McMahan spoke to the crime-scene tech Sharon Bronner, who had gotten a call from Patricia Montoya asking when she could get back her coat that she had placed over Lynn.

"Montoya asked her if we had arrested the husband

yet," wrote McMahan. "Montoya stated that there was no way the woman got under the car like that."

There would be one last conversation with Harold Henthorn. At 8 A.M. on May 9, 1995, McMahan and his boss, Sgt. Brock McCoy, arrived at Harold's home on the 7800 block of E. Costilla Place in Littleton. It was a multistory house, and Harold led them into a downstairs living room. Another man was there: Lynn's brother, Kevin Rishell.

From McMahan's report the meeting appeared to be an effort to get his full account in one sitting and to clarify some points in his four previous statements to deputies. No lawyer was present, and the interview was not tape-recorded

Going over the day one more time, Harold said that he and his wife began their day at midmorning and "did things around the house," McMahan said in his summary report. Between 5:45 P.M. and 6 P.M., Lynn stated that "she wanted to go out," so they took Highway 85, also known as Santa Fe Drive, south to Sedalia, then turned west on Highway 67 toward the mountains. Following the South Platte River, they followed the twisting and turning road for seventy miles as it rose up the Rockies until they got to the Cheesman Reservoir.

"They only stayed a few minutes," McMahan's summary said. "They started getting hungry as they hadn't eaten yet and were headed back towards Sedalia to go to the Sedalia Grill." At about 8:30 P.M., they passed a place called the Sprucewood Inn, another restaurant. Along the way, Harold was concerned about his tires. "He has had some remodeling going on at his house, and there have been many nails in the driveway," wrote McMahan. "He has had numerous flat tires recently."

Heading toward Sedalia, they passed a "little store"—
perhaps the convenience store mentioned in previous
reports—when Harold sensed trouble. "He felt the tire
was soft as he was driving through the curves," wrote
McMahan. "He pulled off on the left side on a wide dirt
flat area to change the tire."

Harold explained that Lynn spread a plastic shower
curtain on the ground as he first tried the black factory
jack—why they traveled with a shower curtain wasn't
mentioned. "This jack did not work," McMahan wrote,
so Harold next retrieved the two "boat jacks"—one silver, one orange—from the Jeep while Lynn put the black
jack away, then returned to help Harold lift the car. The
boat jacks were smaller than the factory Jeep jack and
not designed to lift a vehicle, much less one as heavy as
the Jeep.

"Lynn found a broken piece of flat cinder block,"
wrote McMahan. "He put the silver jack under the axle
on top of the cinder block."

Warning Lynn to stay at least six feet away from the
car, Harold set the orange jack "somewhere behind
the wheel" and removed the lug nuts, starting with the
"special key lug nut." Lynn held the lug nuts in a rag in
her left hand and shined the flashlight that she held in her
right. Around this time, the car came by with two or
three people inside asking if they needed help. "He declined help from any of the people," wrote McMahan.

After removing the "flat tire," Harold carried it to the
back of the Jeep. "The spare was unbolted and was hanging on by the bolt. He threw the flat tire into the back of
the Jeep, which bounced back out," wrote McMahan.
"The spare tire then fell down on the bed of the Jeep
hatch area. He saw the car go down."

McMahan asked: If the tire had bounced out of the
hatch, how had it ended up on top of another tire.

Harold suggested "someone else picked up the spare tire off the ground later and put it in the back of the Jeep."

Harold speculated, "Lynn had dropped a lug nut or a flashlight, but isn't sure." As the car went down, Lynn "called his name" and Harold "came around and saw her pinned."

According to Harold, Lynn said, "I think something's on me."

Somehow, Harold said, he got the silver jack that had been under the axle back in place. He noticed that the cinder block was broken in three pieces. "He got the car lifted, and Lynn was talking in a very strained voice," wrote McMahan. "He knew Lynn was very seriously hurt and thought she had a broken back."

Within a few minutes, a carload of people stopped and asked if he needed help. "He called to this car to get an ambulance," wrote McMahan. "Lynn was lying on the shower curtain face down and stopped talking."

Asked how Lynn got out from under the Jeep, "He doesn't know if he pulled Lynn out from under the car or one of them," the summary said. It became clear that Lynn wasn't breathing and "they"—McMahan's report doesn't say who—"started CPR" and some other unidentified people put coats and blankets on Lynn. "A few other people who had stopped left to make sure help was coming," wrote McMahan.

Harold wasn't sure who they were. He thought one of the men's last names was Tafoya. "This group of people wanted to leave prior to the arrival of fire or police because they had been drinking," wrote McMahan.

Then the rescue workers arrived.

With that, the interview appeared to have ended. There are no references to any more follow-up questions about the insurance, the J.C. Penny arrest, or discrepancies between this account and his previous statements.

There is no record of the house being searched and no hint that Lynn's brother or Sgt. McCoy said anything at all.

That same day, McMahan spoke with Patricia Montoya. Either it was a brief conversation or parts of the report were missing, as the Patricia Montoya statement had little to add. A Denver resident, Patricia said that she and three other adults—Joseph and Manuel Montoya and Maxine Southern—were driving along Highway 67 shortly before 10 P.M. "near Sedalia" when they saw a man on the street "flagging them down," wrote McMahan. "The man said he needed some help and that a car had fallen on his wife and she was underneath the car not breathing. The man was hysterical."

They went back to a store to get help but it was closed. They began looking for a phone. "Someone said they would call the cops," wrote McMahan. "They went back to the man, and the woman was on her stomach, and not breathing." The report said that "CPR was started" and that "she"—apparently, Patricia—"went back to the phone to make sure the cops were coming," wrote McMahan, not saying where this phone was. "When she came back she covered the woman with her jean jacket. They left before police arrived."

If Patricia expressed any more suspicions about Harold, it didn't make it into the report.

This same day, McMahan went to the Evidence Storage Building to examine the Jeep again. His report said he was "assisted by" Evidence Technician Bronner and Douglas County Deputy Coroner Wesley A. Riber. Lifting the Jeep with a floor jack, they looked at the front axle and found "slight scrape marks" on the area where Harold had said the silver jack slipped off, wrote McMahan in his report at the time.

A second report, this one authored by Riber, offered

more details. Riber measured the width of the exposed rotor as 7/8 inch. "This," he wrote, "could be consistent with the space between the two straight marks on the subject's back, including whatever clothing she may have had on." A check of the autopsy report mentioning three injuries confirmed the match. "All three marks are consistent with the possibility of the rotor and the front wheel area of the front axle landing on the subject's back," he wrote.

Looking at the three pieces of what he called a "cinderblock paver," Riber found marks "that were consistent" with the base of the silver jack. "If the jack fell towards the rear of the vehicle there are two marks on the edge of the paver where the jack made contact," he wrote.

"This," he wrote, "is an accidental death."

If any investigation occurred over the next two days, it didn't warrant a report. Instead, the next documentation, on May 11, related to the release of evidence. McMahan wrote a note authorizing the release of the Jeep back to Harold. His friend, identified as a Bruce Haloran, would be given all the rest of the evidence in the case: Lynn's driver's license and registration, purse, as well as the silver and orange jacks, four lug nuts, a lug nut wrench, pieces of plastic, more plastic with brown leaves, a blue coat, black shoes, and a mini-mag flashlight. A report noted that Lynn's blue jeans and sweater were "destroy/dispose of."

The Douglas County Sheriff's Office sent Pat Montoya a note saying, "Please be advised that our department is currently holding property belonging to you. This property is available for release. Property not claimed within thirty days will be disposed of." A later form said that Pat Montoya did, in fact, pick up a jacket.

On May 12, McMahan filed a "Supplement Narrative" concluding: "This case has been investigated and it has been determined that this death was an accident and no criminal charges will be filed."

Sgt. McCoy reviewed the paperwork and signed off on it. The reports were put into storage and not read again for seventeen years.

—

EIGHT

The Lynn Henthorn case got wrapped up within days and forgotten. The Toni Henthorn case was more than a month old and just getting started.

On October 30, John F. Walsh, the U.S. Attorney for Denver, went to a federal judge seeking a search warrant for the cellphone records of Harold Henthorn. This began what would be a detailed and methodical search for every scrap of information they could find on him. The phone records, the government said in an affidavit attached to the search-warrant request, "will show who Harold Henthorn was contacting and where he was traveling to, and if it was for his actual business. It will also give investigators a clearer picture of the events leading up to the death of Toni Henthorn."

It said nothing about how the records would assist in the Lynn Henthorn side of the investigation. But the search-warrant affidavit makes clear that the federal investigators treated her case with considerably more skepticism than the Douglas County sheriff's and coroner's offices did in the mid-1990s. The affidavit pointed to the many parallels between the deaths of the two Mrs. Henthorns: Two wives, two deaths in remote locations under unusual circumstances, with Harold as the only eyewitness. Both times, Harold gave stories that didn't entirely add up. Even the vehicles were the same: Jeeps.

Of all the similarities one stood out: the large insurance policies on both wives, payable to Harold upon their deaths. "He has no business in his name, no partners able to be located by law enforcement to date, and no one interviewed to date knows who his clients are or were," the government wrote in the search warrant, "yet he told investigators he was financially secure, and he was a fundraiser for non-profits like churches and hospitals."

The judge granted the request, freeing up hundreds of pages of records detailing every call Harold had made for months—calls that could be geo-located to a cell-phone tower, establishing where Harold was at the time, plus what number he called and how long he was on the line. The new documents meant more work, and the government expanded the investigative team to include another agent, Mark Caralco from the FBI, working with Beth Shott from the Park Service. Soon, additional federal investigators, including FBI Agent Jonathan Grusing, would be brought in, as would local cops in Colorado.

The scope of their investigation now broadened from one possible murder to two, and Shott and Caralco set out to find family, friends, and documents that would tell them everything they could about the life and premature death of Lynn Henthorn.

Growing up in Potomac, Maryland, in a big close family with a sister and two rambunctious brothers, Sandra Lynn Henthorn went by the pet name "Lynnie-bin." "As a child, she was always on the go, a bundle of redheaded energy," her brother Kevin Rishell would recall. "She organized games, parties, and costumes and plays and was a constant source of entertainment. She loved an audience and stage. As my brother, Eric, and I grew older, we were often the unwilling props in Lynnie's theatrical experiments."

She studied ballet, performing in the *Nutcracker,* and off the stage moved with grace. People would describe her walk as "flowing." With that bright red hair and radiant smile, she made friends easily. "I can't remember her failing at anything," Kevin recalled, "whether it was making something under the stairs in her not-so-secret hideaway or leg-wrestling or playing no-mercy four-square in the driveway or playing neighborhood flashlight tag or studying for tests or practicing her cheerleading drills or field hockey and volleyball smashes or baking in the kitchen or falling in and out of love or helping out with the handicapped children at church."

She was no shrinking violet. "Believe me, that royal redhead had a temper and a sharp tongue when she needed it," said Kevin. "But there was one chink in her armor—she was as jumpy as a cat on a hot tin roof. We grew up scaring her and if it was a national sibling sport me and my older sister, Lisanne, could have earned a gold medal at it."

At James Madison University in Harrisonburg,

Virginia, in the 1970s she majored in social work and psychology and had two life-changing events. The first was spiritual. "As sensitive as she was, she grew sweeter and at more peace spiritually after she made a commitment to follow Jesus back in 1976," said her brother. The other was romantic. She met a husky Virginian with a thick head of brown hair who grew up in Arlington, attending Yorktown High School, and was now studying geology. A couple of years ahead of Lynn, Harold Henthorn became her boyfriend. He seemed to share her Christian way of life, as his next educational and career milestones would be documented in the newsletter of the American Scientific Affiliation, a network of Christian scientists.

After graduating from James Madison, Harold worked on his master's degree in geology at the University of Kentucky in Lexington, spending one summer in New Orleans as an exploratory geologist for Chevron, one newsletter said. The update added that Harold also was active at the university with the InterVarsity Christian Fellowship chapter.

Another newsletter announced that Harold and Lynn were engaged to be married. The newsletter said Harold was "working part-time as a consulting geologist while completing his master's degree." Lynn has been teaching in a total communication class for multiple handicapped children at Christ Church Child Center in Potomac. "After the wedding the Henthorns will move to Denver, Colorado, where Harold will work for Chevron U.S.A., Inc., as a petroleum exploration geologist while Lynn continues part-time study in education," the letter said.

They married in Colorado in September 1982. Lynn wore a gown of white satin with a veil of white lace over her shoulder-length dark red hair and carried a bouquet bursting with white roses. Her family fell in love with Harold. He struck them as strong and protective, smart with money and organization. It was Harold, not Lynn, who handled all the wedding arrangements. "He was in charge of every part of that wedding," recalled her sister-in-law Grace Rishell, who was married to Kevin at the time. "I assure you Lynn only played a small part. It had to be his show. He was just that type of person: over the top."

Lynn's happiness was contagious. She clearly was the favorite in the family. Her brother later also attended James Madison. "As a homesick freshman, I remember how she proudly introduced me to her friends and almost overnight they became my friends, too," he recalled. "She was like a mother hen, very protective of her little brother." Her family would seek her advice about movies and television shows. Lynn was a hugger and a crier—she'd tear up when relatives arrived for a visit and again when they left.

"You wanted to be around her every minute. She was incredibly living and energetic and bubbly," recalled Grace. "She was like a walking cheerleader. Everywhere she went she was about other people, focusing on them, encouraging them, wondering what could she do to make their lives, to lighten their loads. People like that can be annoying. She wasn't that way."

Lynn, according to Grace, "knew how to read people, knew how to connect." It was only logical that she would go into social work. On weekends, she would troll yard sales looking for baby cribs to donate to low-income families. She learned sign language so she could communicate with her deaf and hearing-impaired clients. "She was a strong Christian woman who loved the

Lord," said Grace. "She brought her faith into how she lived. She felt it was God's call how she lived her life."

Her brother Kevin tried to emulate her. "There was a period of time when I would go with her to a small prison in Linden, Virginia, and we would minister to the young inmates there," he recalled. "Her career in social work was a natural extension of her heart, and she would often ache at the plight of the families that she would have to work with. She loved children and she had that rare gift of compassion and commitment. She didn't just talk, she worked; long hours, low pay, and debilitating pain didn't stop her from trying to make a difference in the lives she touched."

Although she suffered painful arthritis in her ankles, she never complained, and she continued to live an active life. She immediately took to Colorado, enjoying the outdoors. She and Harold became part owners of a mountain cabin and they would frequently go boating in nearby reservoirs. One photo shows her standing next to Harold on a gravel turnout in front of a mountain peak with patches of snow. It appears to have been taken in the summer. She's wearing a blue windbreaker and khaki shorts and tennis shoes, Harold in a golf shirt, shorts, and a baseball cap. He's leaning with his left hand against the hood of the gray Jeep Cherokee that would later crush Lynn.

In this otherwise perfect life, Lynn lacked only one thing. "She wanted to have children. She ached," says Grace. "She was a great aunt. Every time we had a family gathering she was scooping up my girls. She had a lot of nieces and nephews and there were birthdays and she always had well-thought-out gifts. I had four babies in six years—bam, bam, bam. I felt so sorry for her. I used to pray: Oh, please grant her this desire."

It was late that Saturday night when Lynn's family got

the news in a phone call. It was so shocking they wouldn't remember who told them, if it was Harold or somebody from the fire department or sheriff's office.

"It was probably around midnight," recalled Grace. "My thought: Oh, my gosh, she's been hurt. We have to pray. We didn't think it was life threatening by any means. We were just waiting by that phone. The second call came from an EMT, or some kind of medical person, saying that she had died."

The family went into shock. "It was unlike anything I had experience in my life at that point, just overwhelming," said Grace. "It was full-on grief, wailing with a pain in the chest and can't stand."

Grace and Kevin stayed at Harold's split-level home in Littleton, Colorado. When the two lawmen from the Douglas County Sheriff's Office arrived, Kevin sat downstairs with Harold while Grace stayed upstairs. She believed that Lynn's other brother, Eric, was there too, somewhere in the house. Nobody wanted to interfere with the work of the police. It never occurred to them to raise questions or interject in any way during the questioning of Harold. They didn't have the strength. When they speak now of her death, they describe that period as surreal and overwhelming.

"When Lynn was killed, I experienced a depth of grief I had never known before," her brother Kevin later said. "I wrote a poem which later led to a book of poetry dedicated to her, and the first poem is called 'Trust His Heart.' It's my way of saying that even when I can't see or understand God's hand in the events that come in our lives, we can still trust his heart."

At Lynn's funeral in Colorado, the family rallied around Harold. They had flown in from around the country to help comfort Harold, whose love for his wife of nearly thirteen years seemed genuine, his grief as palpable as that of her family's. Lynn's father, whom everybody called Papa Rish, sat arm-and-arm with Harold in the church. Friends and families wept and remembered. Most were familiar faces, others not. The family was deeply moved to see that two of the people who had tried to save Lynn's life also attended: Patricia Montoya and her husband. The Montoyas kept a respectful silence about their suspicions of Harold; they were there to support Lynn's family, Patricia later said in court testimony.

A few weeks later, Harold visited Grace's family and spent a week with his in-laws and doted on his nieces. "The first Christmas after we lost Lynn, Harold flew in from Denver and Mama and Papa Rish, Lynn's parents, flew in from Maryland," recalled Grace. "We all gathered together in Scottsdale, Arizona, to comfort each other and to enjoy the children as Lynn would have wanted us to do. Harold presented a framed eight-by-ten photo of Lynn to her parents. I was crying and Papa Rish's face was contorted with tears and deep pain. He was in agony."

Looking back years later, Grace remembers moments, when the fog of grief would lift, that she found aspects of Lynn's death puzzling. Lynn was always the careful, responsible one, never taking chances. Why would she crawl under a Jeep up on a jack? Harold also struck her as safety conscious, never taking any chances when they'd go boating. But any doubts the family would have were squelched by the swift resolution of the investigation. "If the authorities were going to clear Harold, then we were too," Grace says. "The coroner says it's an accidental death. It was actually a relief. I didn't have to entertain any suspicions. I let them all go."

Those close to Lynn were more skeptical than the family. Longtime family friend Mike Walters later told

Inside Edition, "When I heard this story that she had crawled underneath the car on a jack, I just didn't believe it." Lynn's boss Nancy Hodges had already expressed skepticism to authorities about her death being an accident, and continued to wrestle with the subject. She said it long remained a topic of conversation between her and a coworker, Anne McNally. "Lynn believed in this man," Nancy later told *48 Hours.* "Even in her death, we were having trouble maybe second-guessing her. To get from the rhetorical: 'Do you think Harold had something to do with this, Anne?' to 'Harold is a murderer' is a big jump. And I don't think—we just couldn't do it."

But nobody compared notes and none of Harold's friends or relatives said anything to authorities.

About a month after Lynn's death, Harold sent a fax to the records department of the Douglas County Sheriff's Office. "Subject: Police report request." And it said, "This is to please request that you send me a copy of the police report #95-02896 (along with any additional information, accident reports, etc.) relating to my wife, S. Lynn Henthorn; accident of 5-6-95. Please send the information to the above listed address. Thanks!"

It was signed Harold A. Henthorn. Harold needed the police report to collect what he had told investigators was the $300,000 in life insurance on Lynn. He listed as an address the Resource Development Services Inc., which is what he told people was the name of his nonprofit fundraising business, at a post office box on Costilla Place in Englewood, Colorado. That was a different address than shown on the shoplifting report, a detail that went unmentioned by investigators in any reports. When he started using that name for his business isn't known. In the early 1980s, an American Scientific Affiliation newsletter said he worked as a geologist with the Rocky Mountain Division of Chevron (Standard Oil Company of California), exploring for petroleum in southeast Utah.

Over the years, the Rishells continued to treat Harold as one of the family. He stayed particularly close to Kevin and Grace and their daughters. Between visits, they kept in touch by phone and email and, later, Facebook. The girls adored him. He seemed able to talk to them about anything, from school to boys. Harold never forgot a birthday, always bought gifts for Christmas.

In the summer of 1997, two years after Lynn's death, two of Grace's daughters—then ages seven and eight—spent a week with Harold at his cabin in Grand Lake. "He was a father figure," daughter Laura would tell *48 Hours*. "I cared about my uncle very much. Our family had a special bond with him. He helped us all in ways. He was thoughtful. He was there."

It was about four years after Lynn died that Harold did something for himself. He drafted his ChristianMingle profile page, using the screen name "Buzz." One day in 1999 that page caught the attention of a Southern California woman named Sonserae Leese-Calver who was intrigued by the brown-haired widower with perfect vision who dressed rather fashionably, loved telling jokes, drove an SUV, enjoyed long romantic walks on the beach, and had dedicated his life to Christ.

Raised in a very religious household in Orange County, Sonserae admitted to being naïve. "I was brought up in a house where the star football player asked me to a dance at High School and the answer was: 'No,'" she would later tell the *Daily Mail* of the U.K. "There was no dancing, no drinking, so for a long time I didn't really know how to handle myself with men, I wasn't assertive."

After studying fine arts and photography in college,

she put in punishing hours as a visual-effects artist for Sony and Disney. It left little time for a social life, so she turned to the internet, using a Christian-dating site because she felt assured it would attract a better quality of man. And it would be safe.

Sonserae and Buzz flirted online. Buzz professed to be financially independent, heading a charitable foundation, and was charming and well-spoken in their electronic communications. His dating profile exuded confidence, a man comfortable with his station in life, his looks, his faith.

She picked up only a few bad signals. When she asked his real name, he said it was "something grand" like Harold III, as if he were royalty. He said he was a widower whose wife had died in a car accident, but "didn't seem emotional about it," she told the *Daily Mail*. "If he'd told me a car had fallen on her I'd never have agreed to meet him."

Suitably impressed and feeling safe, she set up an in-person date. To Sonserae's surprise, he said he'd be in Southern California visiting his late wife's family—Grace and Kevin—in the Los Angeles suburb of Santa Clarita. He showed up in a salmon-colored shirt and, to her relief, looked like the same in person as his profile picture: a handsome, wholesome man in his early forties.

The date didn't go well. "He seemed kind of arrogant," she later told CBS Denver. "I was turned off by it. It didn't go very far." She said the same thing to 7News in Denver, describing Harold as "more talk than anything." Harold returned to Colorado. They made a half-hearted effort at a long-distance relationship, but it fizzled quickly because of geography and the lack of chemistry between them.

During this time, Lynn's family knew Harold had started dating and were fully supportive. They wanted

the best for him. It was during a visit to the Rishells that
he told them about the woman in Mississippi named
Toni Bertolet. (This was in Christmas 1999 and may
have been the same trip when he met Sonerae.) "Harold
showed us Toni's profile on a Christian dating site and
wanted our approval as he made plans to meet her for
the first time on New Year's Eve in Jackson, Mississippi," Grace recalled.

Toni was a doctor, no less, who had been married
once before. She seemed kind and loving, wanted to start
a family just like he did, and shared his love of Christ.
Their time together in Mississippi went spectacularly,
and the relationship took off. Harold confided to the
Rishells that he wanted to marry Toni. "We said, 'Go
for it,'" recalled Grace Rishell "I just thought he found
the right one."

Harold announced on ChristianMingle.com that he
was officially taking himself off the market:

I'M EXTREMELY HAPPY AND GRATEFUL TO SAY
THAT THANKS TO CCM I'VE MET A REMARKABLE
QUALITY CHRISTIAN WOMAN AND WERE BUILDING
A COMMITTED RELATIONSHIP WITH ONE AN-
OTHER. WE COMPLEMENT EACH OTHER SO WELL
THAT WE'VE ALREADY DECIDED TO BECOME EX-
CLUSIVE. LET ME ENCOURAGE YOU TO KEEP PRAY-
ING HOPING AND WORKING TO PURSUE YOUR
DREAMS LORD BLESS.

After the wedding, Harold brought Toni into the
Rishell family, who adored her. The comparisons to
Lynn couldn't be missed: the red hair, the giving personality, the devout faith, and the strong desire to have
children. In Toni's case, that dream came true when the
couple welcomed their daughter Haley. "He and Toni

were the quintessential aunt and uncle," says Grace in an interview.

It was bittersweet to watch. At the time, Grace Rishell's marriage took a different trajectory. Money problems arose. They lost their house and their ranch. They had to sell their horses, and cars were repossessed. Harold had seen it happening. He listened to Grace and finally offered advice.

"He wanted me to break away," Grace recalls in the interview. "It was actually his statement that woke me up, after ten years trying to keep our marriage together, that gave me the courage. He said, 'You cannot live this way anymore.'"

In 2009, the Rishells separated. Grace, who had spent her life raising horses and homeschooling their children, said, "Now all of a sudden I've got to figure out how to take care of myself and the girls." Vulnerable, scared, she spoke and emailed frequently with Harold. He served as advisor, listener. She considered him like a big brother.

Grace went to work as a music teacher in Texas making $20,000 a year. Harold helped her financially, a few hundred dollars here and there, paying for trips to Colorado to visit him, covering some of her expenses. He encouraged her to move with her daughters to Colorado so they could be closer to him, Toni, and Haley.

All the while, Grace worried about her daughters and how they would fare if something ever happened to her. She had no estate to leave them. Harold always seemed good with money.

Harold hooked her up with a man named Neal Creswell. A longtime friend of Harold's, Neal was an insurance broker who had set up the life insurance policies for Harold and Toni. In late September through the first week of October 2009, Grace and Creswell discussed her options and set a course of action. She signed papers for an insurance policy that, upon her death, would pay $50,000 to each of her four daughters and another $50,000 to her brother. To secure the $250,000 policy, Grace agreed to visit a doctor for a physical examination.

She trusted Harold implicitly and without question and by extension trusted Neal Creswell. She provided him with all of her personal information, her Social Security number, her net worth, her salary, intimate details of her health. Grace would later say that she didn't know everything that she was signing. She left it up to Harold and Neal to guide her to do what was proper. She said she did not know or at least appreciate the implications of signing something called an "accelerated rider benefit."

Grace didn't have the money for the premiums. Harold would carry her over. In October 2009, he wrote a check for $441, what Grace thought was a down payment for the policy, Grace would later say at a court hearing.

On October 15, 2009, Grace saw a doctor in California for the physical. The doctor took her personal and family medical history, her blood pressure, among other things. An appointment was made for a pap smear the following month. She signed more papers, including one saying she was applying for an insurance policy worth as much as $400,000. The pap smear was done on November 5, and she believed that the life insurance policy was on hold, pending results of the test.

These were stressful times for Grace. Her divorce would soon become finalized. Harold continued to help her financially. He sent her $600 for rent one month, $500 to send one of her daughters to Christian camp. Daughter Laura described her relationship with Harold as a "bond with a young girl who is looking for a figure of success and love. Harold seemed to fit this role very well for me. I can still remember being excited to show him a budget project I received an A on because I thought a man of success would be so proud of me."

As much as Grace appreciated, and needed, Harold's help, however, an uneasy feeling took hold. "Harold became more controlling," she recalls. "He just wanted to have a say in my life. He would make me feel so guilty. I had asked him his opinion on whether to do something. If I didn't agree to it, he would say, 'You're ungrateful. You ask my opinion and I give it to you and you turn around and not do it.'"

Harold would threaten to cut off the money. "He was upset that I was not calling him," she said. "I wanted to stop talking on the phone and wanted him to stop emailing me. It wasn't like he was evil or dangerous, but, good grief, he was controlling."

She reached out to others for advice. They told her it was unwise to have Harold involved in her life insurance arrangements. In the spring, she told Neal Creswell that she no longer wanted the policy that Harold had arranged. A second pap smear had been scheduled, and she thought that the policy had not gone into effect yet. She took out her own policy through AAA.

Two years later came the horrific news. History repeated itself. Long-suppressed feelings pushed their way to the forefront. Toni Henthorn had fallen to her death. "It took me about a month. I began to wonder. Oh, my gosh, did he kill Lynn?" she recalled. "My oldest daughter immediately said, 'He pushed her.' I chastised her. I said, 'Don't come to that conclusion.'"

But when she attended Toni's memorial service, she "went with eyes wide open."

She didn't reach out to Toni's family, not yet. "When the Bertolets were ready, I'd help them," she remembered thinking.

Then the two federal agents arrived at her front door.

NINE

The investigative trail led from a cliff in Rocky Mountain National Park to Grace Rishell's apartment in Austin, Texas. Another search warrant had produced Harold's insurance records. In addition to the policies on Toni, they found one for $400,000, taken out in 2009, with ING-ReliaStar, in the name of Grace Rishell. The address listed on the policy was 9457 S. University Blvd., Suite 258, Littleton, CO, 80126, the same address as on the application paperwork and the billing address, which lists him as "Bro-In-Law." A visit to that address showed it to be a UPS Store and "Suite 258" was a mailbox. Shott wrote in the search-warrant affidavit, "I am unable to determine at this time why Henthorn would send mail to 'The UPS Store' as opposed to his home address, which he has owned since 2000." The investigation established that Grace Rishell was Harold's former sister-in-law, married to Lynn's brother.

Beth Shott identified herself as a special agent from

the National Park Service and Chris Calarco as an agent
from the FBI. Grace Rishell was not surprised to see
them. In the six months since Toni's death, Grace had
grown more suspicious of Harold and did everything she
could to distance herself and her daughters from him.
But she knew there was a long paper and electronic trail
connecting him to her and no doubt records of his financial support and involvement in her life insurance.

"I thought it was just for them to see if we had a romantic relationship," she recalled. "We talked on the
phone, he came and visited by himself without Toni.
That doesn't look so good." Grace let the agents in. It
was April 24, 2014.

In a wide-ranging interview with the agents, Grace
denied any romantic relationship with Harold Henthorn.
She said she had thought of Harold as a wise, trusting
older brother—he was, after all, once her brother-in-
law—and a good role model to her children. "You've got
to understand the relationship. A lot of it was because I
needed him for my daughters," Grace recalled, repeating what she told authorities. "I wanted him to be what
I didn't feel my husband could be at the time. I wanted
him to be this strong leader, this Christian man."

She also doubted Harold ever had any romantic interest in her   he always seemed motivated by a heart
felt concern for her, especially for her daughters. She told
them how her view of Harold had changed with his controlling behavior and how since Toni's death she finally
didn't want to have anything to do with him.

There came a time during the interview when Grace's
dogs, her huskies, needed to be taken for a walk. The
tape recorder was turned off and she and Agent Calarco
went out. "I'm the one who brought up the policy," she
recalled, "only in the context of how it showed how controlling Harold was."

Calarco told her that investigators already knew about the insurance policy Harold had taken out on Grace—and a lot more.

As Grace and Agent Calarco walked her dogs, they discussed the life insurance policy. Grace explained to the agent how Harold had helped her obtain it when she was getting divorced and worried about her children's future, how he'd made the down payment on the policy, but how she'd later decided she didn't want Harold so deeply involved in her life. She told him to cancel the policy and took one out on her own through AAA.

That's when Calarco told her the rest of the story. Harold had never canceled the policy. It had remained in effect through December 2012—just four months earlier. What's more, the beneficiaries of the $400,000 were not her daughters and brother.

It was Harold.

Grace was left speechless. Calarco asked why she didn't have more of a reaction. "My reaction was inside my mind. What did I do?" she recalled thinking. "I signed papers, I submitted personal and medical information. What did I miss, what did I allow him to do, why was I so stupid?"

Reviewing her records, Grace found that she had signed things she hadn't read carefully enough. She had misinterpreted a letter about her OB-GYN checkup, thinking it said she still needed another test to get approved for the policy, when in fact it said she had been cleared. But she clearly remembered specifically telling Harold and the insurance broker that she didn't want a policy.

She reflected on the first time she met Harold. She thought of Lynn's wedding and how Harold needed to control every detail—strange then, terrifying now, and yet at the time, it was so easy to overlook. "He could talk forever, and he would overtalk and take over, and he was always right. It didn't matter what the topic was," she said. "But he was friendly and kind and generous and thoughtful and did so many nice things for you. You felt like: Who are you to complain or voice your frustration because he was such a nice guy."

She thought of a time in August 2012, a month before Toni's death, when her daughters visited Harold. Maybe she had him wrong. Maybe he did have a romantic interest in her—and more. "I think he was on a mission. His whole purpose was to systematically detach Haley emotionally from her mother," Grace said. "In August 2012, he was on a mission to get my daughters close to Haley and prepare me for some greater role in Haley's life. I never would have married the guy. But now I wonder what his purpose was."

She recalled one time, after her divorce, that she and her daughters visited him, and they went boating on Lake Travis, near her home in Austin. Grace was wearing a sundress.

"He made some comment like, 'Dang, Kevin sure was a fool,'" Grace recalled. "It was a little bit weird. I was sort of like: Wow. But I just looked at it as he was trying to build my confidence, that I was still attractive. He knew how to do the online dating thing and said he could build an amazing profile for me. I thought that would be cool."

And she thought of the last time she saw Toni. "I took a walk with her. She said, 'Grace, I'm not allowed to talk to anyone about the problems we have in our marriage.' I just felt so sad for her. I didn't think it was a red flag that this guy was going to hurt her. My heart was just burdened. I thought: I hope she stops thinking that way."

It was now, for the first time, that Grace had a terrifying thought—she could have ended up like Lynn and Toni.

TEN

Deputy Myra Buys crouched on all fours and crawled under a Jeep Cherokee that had been hoisted by a floor jack. The right front tire had been removed. Bracing herself with her right hand, she reached out with her left toward a lug nut lying next to a little orange traffic cone. Her fingers could just touch it. She then got on her stomach and shimmied under the Jeep, her back below the tire area, the exposed brake assembly just brushing her yellow fleece sweater between the shoulder blades. She reached out both arms spread eagle. A camera went off.

One day in 2013, in the facility where the Douglas County Sheriff's Office examines vehicles, investigators staged a reenactment of the events that killed Lynn Henthorn. Deputy Muys played guinea pig because she was about the same size as Lynn, who according to the autopsy report stood five-foot-five and weighed 145 pounds.

Since Harold's Jeep had wound up junked at an

Arizona salvage yard, the department found a Jeep of similar weight and wheelbase. "The purpose of that test," sheriff's Detective Dave Weaver later recalled, "was to find out how an individual of the height and weight of Lynn Henthorn could have positioned themselves to have the marks on her back that she had."

A fourteen-year veteran of the Douglas County Sheriff's Department with eight years of detective experience, Weaver was called upon to complete casework prematurely abandoned in 1995, the second prong of the investigation into Harold Henthorn. While the feds worked Toni's death, the sheriff would look into Lynn's. "It was reopened based on information we received from the federal government and from other individuals," he would later say. "They found it suspicious—suspicious that (Harold) had had two wives that had died under questionable circumstances."

Save for a few photos and the reports, nothing was left from the original investigation. The evidence had been returned to Harold, including the Jeep. The jacks, the lug nuts, the wrench, the flashlight, the shower curtain, the broken cinderblock, Lynn's clothes and shoes, and Patricia Montoya's jacket—all of it was long gone. Even the Sedalia Grill was no more; it had changed hands. The most important witness, Harold, had stopped talking to authorities after that interview with Ranger Faherty two days after Toni's death. With the long passage of time, there was the risk other witnesses could have moved or died.

Weaver began with the paperwork, reading the summaries of Harold's various statements and jotting down the discrepancies. These included the different times he provided for leaving the house, different accounts of whether the couple had eaten at the Sedalia Grill, the various versions of what jacks were employed and

how many. Weaver also took note of the places where
Harold seemed vague, not remembering clearly how
Lynn got out from under the Jeep or who performed
CPR on her.

None of these discrepancies was pursued by the original investigators, nor were the concerns expressed by
Patricia Montoya and Lynn's boss Nancy Hodges acted
upon. Montoya got what looked like a very short follow-
up interview. Hodges was never interviewed again.
Dwight Devries was never interviewed. Nobody seems
to have gone back to Hayes or to the Sedalia Grill.
Speaking later about how key witnesses were handled,
Weaver said: "There had been no follow-up."

There was one potential positive: Weaver didn't have
to go far to find those involved in the rescue and investigation. Coroner investigator Wes Riber had gone
on to become the elected coroner and remained active
in local Republican politics, still living in the area.
Jason Kennedy, who as a young deputy was among the
first to speak with Harold Henthorn, was still with
the Douglas County Sheriff's Department, having
steadily risen through the ranks to become commander
of the Investigations Division. Other investigators also
remained. Jeff Bredehoeft had become a sergeant.
Kevin Duffy had risen to captain in charge of the Detentions Division. And Robert McMahan was now a
captain for the department overseeing the Professional
Standards Division.

That meant the most important figures in the case
were literally down the hall from Weaver. This was
not entirely a good thing. While Weaver would have
easy access to the original investigators, he would
essentially have to play the role of internal affairs investigator, dissecting the actions and inactions of the
department's own.

Most of this centered on the work of Robert Mc-
Mahan: what he knew, what he didn't know, and what
he should have known.

Back in 1995, his investigation found that Lynn Henthorn's life was insured for $300,000, payable upon her
death to husband Harold. This he gleaned from interviews with the insurance company, Lynn's boss, and
Harold. While the physical evidence may have been gone,
insurance records live forever. Even after twenty years,
Weaver followed the money trail and discovered that
there were in fact two more policies on Lynn Henthorn
that Harold hadn't mentioned. Both were through USAA.
One was a regular life insurance policy for $150,000.
The other was an auto policy payable in the event of an
accidental death involving an automobile.

The policies amounted to $600,000—double what
Harold had told McMahan—all listing Harold as the
beneficiary.

Working next through the list of witnesses, Weaver
found that Van Hayes, an older man at the time of Lynn's
death, had since died. His only statement would come
from the witness statement written in a shaky hand late
at night on the side of the road. But other people who
were at the scene or who had talked to Harold were very
much alive and most were living nearby.

Terry Thompson, the chief of the volunteer fire department and one of the first on the scene, held the same
position with the department but now as a paid em-
ployee. In the spring of 2013, he sat down with Weaver
along with another first responder, Jeffery Gordon
Schippel, still a volunteer firefighter/EMT with the West
Douglas County Fire Protection District in Sedalia,
Colorado.

Weaver began by asking Schippel if he knew why he

was being interviewed. Officially, the fact that the Sheriff's Office had reopened the case was a secret—the media had not covered Lynn's death since 1995, and Toni's death hadn't warranted a mention in the news since her memorial—but word had obviously gotten out in law-enforcement circles. Schippel said he assumed he was being questioned in relation to the "incident in 1995." According to Weaver's report of his interview, Schippel said he would do the best he could, telling what he saw and remembered all those years ago. Weaver said that's all they wanted him to do.

Schippel's memory turned out to be sharp. He said he was driving his personal car that night when he got the call from the dispatcher around 10:30 P.M. about somebody needing help on Highway 67. He raced to the scene. In the passenger seat was his niece, whom he had just picked up from her job.

She worked at the Sedalia Grill. That meant she would have been at the restaurant the same night that Harold may or may not have dined there with his wife. (The niece was never interviewed by authorities, then or—it appeared—now. There is no indication in the court or investigative files that Weaver ever talked to her, either.)

Within ten minutes, Schippel and his niece got to the scene, which he identified from a photo that Weaver showed him. The official log showed him arriving at 10:37 P.M. The female victim, whose name he'd later find was Sandra Lynn Henthorn, already was out from under the Jeep, lying perpendicular to the vehicle as another EMT worked on her. Lynn was not wearing a jacket. Schippel thought the EMT had exposed her chest so they could perform life-saving actions and would have cut her clothing off to do so. Beyond that he did not recall what she was wearing. He also didn't recall a flashlight on the ground or under the car.

Schippel did remember being told that the victim had no heartbeat or pulse and had been given a powerful medication that would "give a pulse to a stone," as Schippel would later recall in court testimony. Schippel and another volunteer EMT commenced CPR. Schippel performed mouth-to-mouth resuscitation while his partner gave chest compressions with enough force, according to the coroner's report, that it broke Lynn's breastbone.

As they worked on her, Schippel realized that Lynn's feet were still under the Jeep, so they moved her about six feet away for safety. After Lynn showed some faint vital signs, they put her on a gurney and into an AMR ambulance for a short drive to the waiting Flight for Life helicopter.

Schippel related to Weaver how the husband told somebody he thought a lug nut had rolled under the car and his wife was getting it when the Jeep crashed on her, slipping off the jack when he threw the flat into the back. She called out to him and he found her under the Jeep.

"Jeffery said those on scene were shaking their heads regarding the explanation and they thought the explanation smelled bad," Weaver later recalled in court testimony. Weaver asked if Schippel, in his long experience treating car-accident victims, could imagine how a person pinned under a vehicle could be able to talk. "He said unlikely," according to Weaver. "He said the person would most likely have traumatic asphyxiation."

What's more, "Jeffery also said the husband, Harold, was not acting as he, Jeffery, expected, at the scene,"

Weaver recalled. "He, the husband, was pacing back and forth while Jeffery was on the scene."

At one point during the night, somebody told Schippel—he didn't remember who—something unusual. The husband had claimed he did not know how to change a tire and that his wife was the one doing it. This had never been recorded by any of the law-enforcement people that night and contradicted all of Harold's statements that he was the one who had changed the tire.

The experience so unnerved Schippel that he relayed his suspicions to Wesley Riber, the coroner's investigator. But Riber's reports make no reference to this, nor do any of the reports by McMahan.

After the interview, further investigation turned up the first responder who had told Schippel about the conversation with Harold about Lynn changing the tire. In 1995, Roxanne Burns was another volunteer firefighter/ EMT for the West Douglas County Fire Protection District. At the time, she lived in Indian Creek, about three miles away from Sedalia.

Speaking to Weaver, she explained how the volunteer department worked. She said she would respond to accidents and heart attacks and that there were about thirty volunteers in the department at the time. Each carried a pager and would get "toned out" for a call. The page would include the location, the nature of the incident, and they'd respond from home to the firehouse or go directly to the scene.

At 10:27 P.M., she heard the call that a car had fallen on a person; it was not your everyday call for the department, more accustomed to heart attacks and car collisions, and so she remembered it well. The location was eight miles out of Sedalia on the side of Highway 67, in remote, heavily wooded Pike National Forest. As Burns would later recall in court testimony, she told Weaver that she had driven her personal car with her husband, also a volunteer firefighter, directly to the scene while others went to the firehouse to get the trucks. When they arrived, the fire truck was already there and soon a rescue truck and ambulance would also pull up. Floodlights mounted on the trucks lit the scene where two EMTs already were performing CPR—"pumping and blowing," she said, using the lingo of EMTs, on the victim, who lay on the ground next to the Jeep.

Burns noticed that one of the EMTs' feet was under the Jeep, which was missing a wheel and seemed to be teetering on a jack. For their safety, she told them to move, which they did. The woman also was moved about six feet farther away.

Burns asked the EMTs if they needed help on the victim.

"We've got this covered," one of them told her. "Go talk to the guy."

Burns was led to a man who stood at the front of the Jeep watching the EMTs work on his wife. Somebody said they thought he was the husband. She asked his name, and he told her Harold Henthorn.

"He wasn't very upset," Burns later recalled in the court testimony, repeating what she told Detective Weaver. "I've seen a lot of people where they've had an accident and they're like screaming and jumping up and down and just very upset. And he didn't seem that upset to me."

He stood by the hood, then would pace back and forth in front of the Jeep. She asked him what happened. He said that a car had fallen on his wife while she was changing the tire. Burns did a double take.

"She was changing the tire?" she asked Harold.

"Yeah," said Harold, "she was changing the tire because I don't know how to change a tire."

Burns was surprised because she assumed that all men knew how to change a tire.

As Burns asked Harold if his wife had any health issues or was allergic to any medications, she silently wondered how this woman managed to get under the Jeep while she was changing a tire.

She asked that of Harold, who speculated she crawled under the Jeep to get the lug nuts as he tossed the spare into the back, dislodging the Jeep from the jack. This made even less sense to Burns and seemed to contradict what she saw at the scene. The spare tire was not in the back of the Jeep where Harold said he tossed it. Instead, it was propped up against the side of the vehicle.

Burns asked Harold why he and his wife were driving so late on the desolate road. He told her they were going on a drive to clear their heads.

"He really didn't look at me all that much," Burns recalled later in court. "I mean, he kind of kept his head down and he would walk away from me while he was talking to me. And then I would go back over, and I'd say, 'Can you give me a little bit more information?' And so I would be like walking with him. He didn't seem like he was that upset. He wasn't always looking over to see what was going on with Lynn."

Burns said that after the Flight for Life helicopter landed, and the EMTs wheeled Lynn into the ambulance to take her to the landing spot, Harold asked her what was going on and if Lynn would be okay. Burns told him that his wife had regained a pulse and that the ambulance likely was taking his wife to Swedish Medical Center. What she didn't tell him was how dire Lynn's condition was. One of the EMTs had delivered a shot of Epinephrine directly into Lynn's heart. It didn't get much of a beat from Lynn's heart, more like a flutter, but Lynn Henthorn was technically still alive.

That ended Burns' interaction with Harold. Later, the volunteer EMTs gathered to reflect on the night's events. A fatal incident was rare for them, so a mental-health expert came to help them deal with any stress. But all they could talk about were the circumstances of the call. Burns couldn't decide what was more strange—that a car landed on top of a woman or that a grown man would admit to not knowing how to change a tire.

Finding Dwight Devries, the would-be Good Samaritan whose wife had called the sheriff's department, proved the easiest task of all. He had the same address and phone number listed in the original reports. Devries' memory also proved clear. He told Weaver it was between 8 P.M. and 9 P.M., well after dark, when his headlights caught a man and woman on the side of the highway next to a Jeep. Pulling up to them, Devries asked if there was a problem. The man told him that the Jeep had a flat tire. Devries offered to help change the tire or even shine his headlamps on them, but the man declined and Devries went on his way, reluctantly.

Something didn't feel right, Devries said to Weaver. "He told me that it appeared the woman appeared scared or frightened," said Weaver.

Patricia Montoya, too, still lived in Colorado, but at a different address and with a different marital status. In an afternoon interview with Weaver that was recorded on video, Patricia had the most vivid memory of all.

It was, she recalled, a cool and dry night, no mud on the side of the road. She was in a car carrying her then-husband Joseph Theodore Montoya and his brother Carlos Manuel Montoya. There was a woman in the car named Maxine Southern, but she didn't know what became of her or how to find her. The others in the car were her sons, Bentura, Manuel, and Franki Montoya, all too young at the time to remember anything, she said.

Although Patricia had not kept a diary or journal, she had a clear-enough memory to be able to draw a diagram of where she came upon the couple next to the Jeep and the position of the vehicle. Shown a picture of the area as it looked today, she said that was the right location. Weaver would later use this diagram to help position the test Jeep in his re-creation.

Patricia, who was a passenger in the car, spotted a man on the side of the highway flagging them down by waving a triangle-shaped warning sign. Patricia initially feared the man wanted them to stop so he could rob them or steal their car. Another car ahead of them passed the man by without stopping, she said.

But feeling secure that they would outnumber any would-be robber, the Montoya group pulled over. That's when they saw the woman on the ground under the car on her stomach with both of her arms stretched out in front of her head. She wore blue jeans and a short-sleeved blouse or T-shirt but no coat despite the cold. Patricia couldn't remember if the woman had shoes on.

Patricia watched as one of her group, either her husband or brother-in-law—or both—pulled the woman from under the Jeep, which Patricia thought had already been jacked up off of her. The woman's face was pale and her lips were blue. She wasn't breathing. Patricia and the others put their jackets on top of her. Gently, the woman was turned onto her back.

While this was going on, the woman's husband "only stood watching," said Weaver's report of his interview with Patricia, "and eventually found some plastic, rolled it up and put it under his wife's head." Patricia thought the plastic was trash from the side of the roadway. It was dirty, and so Patricia's husband and brother-in-law removed it and put a coat under her head.

As Patricia's husband and brother-in-law searched for a pulse and then began CPR, the husband grabbed them and told them not to touch his wife, Patricia recalled.

Patricia then drove off looking for a telephone to call 911. They found a nearby house—that of Van Hayes. Returning to the scene, Hayes joined them with blankets, which they put over the woman. The husband, Patricia said, again stood watching and didn't take off his own coat for his wife. CPR was resumed, this time without interference from the husband, and the woman started to breathe again.

During the course of these events, the man identified himself as Harold Henthorn and said his wife's name was Lynn. He told the Montoya group that he was putting the tire in the back of the car, closed the car's tail gate and the car fell off the jack onto his wife. He said Lynn was under the car getting a lug nut that had gotten under the car when he was putting the tire in the car.

At no point did Patricia recall seeing Harold getting anything out of the car. Nor did she see any tires on the ground—Harold would later say one of the tires bounced out of the back hatch. Patricia also never saw anybody put the tire into the car.

When the sound of a siren could be heard approaching, Harold flashed a look of what Patricia called "fear."

He wasn't the only one concerned. The Montoyas had been drinking earlier that day; they didn't want to get into trouble, Patricia said. They drove off before the first rescuer arrived.

The next day, Patricia called Van Hayes to find out what became of the woman. He told them that she had died. That's when Patricia called the sheriff's office, reaching the evidence technician Sharon Bronner, asking first about getting their coats back but also to express her concerns.

Weaver asked Patricia when she first suspected foul play. She said it was from the very start, as soon as she got there and heard Harold's story, and then how he was acting, physically trying to stop the men from giving Lynn aid. Patricia had changed a tire herself before, and this certainly was no way to do it. As she reflected on Harold's behavior, she had the impression that he had flagged them down, not to help his wife, but to provide a witness to prove that she was already under the Jeep.

When Patricia and the others went to Lynn's funeral, keeping a respectful distance from Harold and the family, her lingering impression of Harold's demeanor was that he looked happy.

The interview with Carlos Montoya, brother of Patricia Montoya's ex-husband Ted, was conducted by FBI Agent Jonathan Grusing. Carlos provided much the same account as Patricia had, filling in additional details. He confirmed they had been returning from a day in the mountains when they pulled over to help a man flagging them down.

Carlos recalled the man said something like: "My wife is dead."

Walking around to the passenger side of the man's Jeep, they found the woman lying on her back, her eyes open and unblinking, as if she were staring at the sky. As Carlos and his bother Ted put their coats on her, they asked the man what happened. The Jeep fell on her, he said, but couldn't exactly explain how—something about lug nuts rolling under the car.

Touching the woman's throat, Ted detected a pulse,

but she wasn't breathing. He and his brother performed CPR—Carlos doing the chest compressions, Ted breathing into her mouth—while Patricia and the other woman, Maxine Southern, went searching for a phone to call 911. Eventually, the woman started breathing again. When he heard the sirens, they left because they'd been drinking.

A few days later, Carlos, Ted, and Patricia attended the woman's memorial service. "The family of the woman thanked them," wrote the FBI agent in his report on his interview.

Saying he thought his brother might remember things better, he provided the contact information for Ted, who next was interviewed by phone by Grusing. Theodore Montoya recalled driving that night, and acknowledged his group had been drinking that day. When they pulled over and first saw the woman, her lips were blue and she wasn't breathing. The man seemed odd.

"The man was just standing there," the FBI agent said in his report on the interview, "and Ted asked him for his coat so they could prop her head and open her airway. The man refused to give Ted his coat, so Ted and Carlos used their coats to cover her and they propped her head up."

Ted began to "massage the woman's heart" and asked Carlos to breathe into her mouth, but Carlos didn't want to. So Ted did the mouth-to-mouth while Carolos handled the chest compressions, getting the woman to breathe again.

"Ted looked and saw that the two passenger tires were on the vehicle and he told the man that he did not understand why he would ask her to get a single lug nut while the car was on a jack," wrote the agent. "Ted added that the four other lug nuts would easily hold the tire in place and they could pull forward to get the other lug nut."

Asking the man how all this happened, he told them the account of his wife retrieving the lug nut under the Jeep when it fell on her. Ted didn't believe him.

The re-creation of Lynn's death sought to answer three questions. The first was whether she could have physically done what Harold said she did. From the original investigation reports, on the night of the tire blowout, she had somehow gotten under the Jeep on her stomach. The autopsy found those parallel marks on her back that matched the shape and measurements of the brake assembly. Weaver wanted to see if that was physically possible.

Based on the measurements and photos taken at the scene, the Jeep used for the re-creation was positioned as close to the same position and lifted to the same height as it was in 1995. The orange mini traffic cone was placed where one of the lug nuts had been found. Deputy Buys then walked around the front of the Jeep and got down onto her stomach. Her body thickness measured 8 inches, which enabled her to fit under the Jeep and the brake assembly. "She essentially had to contort herself to get in the position that we believe Lynn would have been in for the Jeep to fall on her and leave the marks as they were described in the autopsy report," Weaver said.

The reenactment concluded that it was in fact possible for Lynn to have gotten into that position, but it would have taken some exertion.

A second test examined whether the lug nuts could have ended up in the positions that they did, particularly the one that Harold speculated Lynn was reaching for. According to Harold, Lynn had been holding the flashlight in one hand and the lug nuts in the other.

It wasn't known exactly where she was positioned at

the time—the only potential witness, Dwight Devries, who had stopped to help, was sent away by Harold. But it would be logical that Lynn had to have been standing somewhere close to the right front tire where Harold was working the wrench.

For this test, Weaver brought the reenactment Jeep out to Highway 67 near Sedalia. The vague and inconsistent descriptions from the reports of the location of the Jeep made it impossible to find the spot. The best he could do was make an educated guess. The road had changed little over the last twenty years, with no major construction or re-grading. He picked a day with similar weather—no rain or snow—and a site with the same dry, gravely surface and positioned the Jeep.

A Crime Scene Investigator stood next to the right-front passenger tire and dropped a handful of nuts the way Lynn may have done while Harold was throwing the soft tire into the hatch. This was done several times: One lug nut dropped, three dropped at a time, all four at time. They were dropped from different heights and different places around the wheel.

The lug nut that Lynn would have been reaching for when the Jeep went down was, according to the reports, located twenty-two inches inside the wheel drum. But in Weaver's test, not a single lug nut landed anywhere near that. The nuts wouldn't, on their own, roll that far under the Jeep. Somebody would have had to toss them.

The last test centered on the most important question: How could the Jeep have come off the jack or jacks. Weaver hoisted the test Jeep using a similar kind of jack that Harold used, placing the jack under the front axle as Harold had said he did. All the tires were filled with the same air pressure as measured by Investigator Robert McMahan. With the Jeep now up on the jack and the right-front tire removed, Weaver re-created what Harold said he did next.

"We tried various ways of placing the tire in the back of the Jeep, placing it gently, a little force, and actually to the point that we threw the tire in the back of the Jeep," Weaver later recalled in court testimony.

Nothing could dislodge the Jeep from the jack. "The Jeep never teetered," Weaver said in the testimony.

They kept trying, tossing the tire every which way into the back of the Jeep, from different angles and using different force, and still the Jeep would not budge.

"The only way I could get the Jeep to go off the jack," he said, "was when I went to the passenger side and pushed it."

Pushed it from the same place where McMahan had found that footprint.

ELEVEN

"It's important to emphasize right from the start, this man that we're talking about has not been charged with anything and says he did nothing wrong."

Brian Maass, the investigative reporter for KCNC-TV, better known as CBS Denver or just Channel 4, spoke in measured tones. "We've been looking into this case for the better part of a year," he continued, "and it turns out that three law-enforcement agencies are doing the same thing."

A well-known figure in the Mile High City, Maass also is a local boy, a product of the University of Boulder. He has spent more than thirty years at the station in Denver and has broken one story after another about official corruption and crime. In addition to filing reports for the station, he writes for the Channel 4 website, his email address a click away from his byline.

Days after Toni went off a cliff, an anonymous email arrived. It referenced an earlier article Maass had not au-

thored. Headlined, "Victim Identified in Fatal Fall in
Rocky Mountain National Park," it was a rewrite of a
Park Service press release about Toni Henthorn.

"Your story above is very interesting," wrote the
emailer. "This man's first wife died in a tragic and freak
accident as well."

Maass considered the message. "It was just a cryptic
email," he recalled, "those one or two lines. It certainly
got me curious. I started to work on it."

In a business known for ratings-grab flash, KCNC
gives Maass time, resources, and space to do his job.
He can spend months on an investigation. At the time,
Maass was juggling several stories. He added this one
to the list and was in no hurry. "You have to look at this
in a light most favorable to Mr. Henthorn," he said. "He's
a guy who's a victim of nothing more than really bad
luck."

Beyond those early press release pickups, there was
virtually nothing written about Toni Henthorn and even
less about Lynn Henthorn. He found one local newspaper account that characterized her death as a tragic accident. But through his sources, Maass got his first big
break: He obtained Toni's autopsy report, which was
filed under seal and strictly off-limits to the public and
even Toni's family. This was in keeping with the federal
government's silent-running strategy. Every document
was under wraps, including the investigative file into
Lynn's death. Family and friends who had been contacted by agents, meanwhile, had said nothing to the
media, though they openly spoke among themselves.

When Maass read the part of the autopsy report with
the coroner's conclusion—"The manner of death is
undetermined. The circumstances of death are under
investigation at the time of this report. Homicide cannot be excluded."—he knew he had a major story. The

only question was how much more material would he need to go to air. "Honestly, we had a lot of internal discussions here, a lot of discussions with my editor," recalled Maass. "When I got the autopsy report on Toni where it said homicide could not be excluded, that she died as a result of a fall or push, that's not language you see every day."

Maass and the station sat on it. They wanted more details, and they wanted to hear from Harold. "I very gingerly went about trying to talk to Mr. Henthorn, leaving phone message, emailing, leaving notes on his door. He never would contact me, which I found to be curious," said Maass. "So I went down some different avenues, a lot of it behind the scenes talking to sources in law enforcement."

He also reached out to the families of Lynn and Toni. He told them what he was working on and kept them up-to-date on when his story may air. He gave them the opportunity to comment, but they declined. "It was a hard story to do. It took a ton of work. It took a ton of time," he said. "For a lot of the media these days it's easier to do the easier story, the fast hitter, the story you can do pretty quickly and move on. This one took months and months of work and footwork, going into Mr. Henthorn's neighborhood, talking to the Rishell family, talking to the Bertolet family, reaching out to the FBI, the various federal investigators."

Exposing people who are under investigation but not formally charged with a crime poses legal risks. If it was handled improperly, Harold could sue for libel. Since Harold was not a public official, the station would have to show that it possessed no malice toward him and that it didn't recklessly disregard the truth. Working with his editors and the station's attorneys, Maass began pounding out a rough script.

Finally, with all legal and ethical bases covered, Maass went to air. The story appeared in a telecast on October 31, 2013, after more than a year of research.

Maass began by laying out the timeline. He noted that the deaths of both of Harold Henthorn's wives had initially been reported as freak tragic accidents, but now they had attracted the attention of a number of law-enforcement agencies, including the FBI, the National Park Service, and the Douglas County Sheriff's Department. The parallel investigations into the two deaths, he said, began right after Toni's fall.

From the start, Maass displayed the depth of his sourcing in law enforcement. He reported for the first time that Harold had told investigators he was preparing to take a photo when Toni fell and that he hadn't witnessed the plunge because he was looking at his cell phone. Maass quoted from Toni's autopsy report, saying that she "fell or was pushed" and that homicide could not be excluded.

Then he got an official on-the-record statement. It was a comment from FBI spokesman Dave Joly confirming that Harold was under federal criminal investigation, a journalistic coup as federal authorities almost never confirm the existence of an investigation.

"It's ongoing," Joly said. "We're hoping to bring it to a conclusion sooner rather than later. It's something we're taking a look at very seriously."

The story also offered the first on-the-record confirmation from the Douglas County Sheriff's Office that it too was looking into the death of Harold's first wife, which Maass noted came with a $300,000 insurance payout. (He didn't yet know about the additional $300,000.)

Next came the public's first glimpse of Harold Henthorn. It was through the windows of a silver BMW in his driveway. Maass was seen handing a business card through the passenger side window while saying, "I'm Brian Maas from Channel Four. I've been trying to reach you, trying to talk to you about the investigations that are going on."

The driver through the tinted windows said, "I've really got to run."

"Is there a time we can get together with you?" asked Maass, but the man backed out of the driveway, waving.

The online version of the story had an additional quote from Harold. "I want to cooperate with you," he said. "But I know you spoke with my attorney and ask you to speak to him." The lawyer, Craig Truman, told the station, "I'm sure when all the facts are known in this difficult and complicated case that justice will be done."

It was left to a friend named Steve Reynolds to come to Harold's defense, calling him a loving husband and father and decrying the investigation as a "witch hunt," with the FBI not having "one shred of evidence." Harold had no criminal background, Maass noted, and in recent years was a stay-at-home father raising money for nonprofits, while in line not only for Toni's life insurance money but a chunk of her inheritance from the oil business.

After the story aired, Toni's family cautiously broke their silence. They did so to help investigators find more witnesses. "We had been getting messages from investigators and from others out there that it's possible that there were people who would come forward, but since we were supposedly supporting Harold, they didn't want to offend us," said Toni's brother Todd. "So that was kind of weighing heavily on us. We finally decided we would come out." The question came down to how much they would say. "Brian Maass was doing a second story and asked us if we wanted to participate, and we said we would," said Todd. "That's when we exposed our feelings. We didn't come out and accuse him of being a killer. We had tried to be political about it."

Five days later, their hometown paper, the *Natchez Democrat* in Mississippi, quoted Toni's father Bob Bertolet—"formerly of Natchez," the paper noted—confirming that the investigation into his daughter's death was "very intense" and "ongoing." He declined to say more. Her brother Todd Bertolet said authorities had revealed little to the family but that he did believe an indictment would come "sooner rather than later." But he didn't know exactly when and he didn't say who would be indicted.

"Obviously, we will all be witnesses if any future trial comes about," Todd said, explaining his reluctance to say more. "They don't really tell us anything or talk about anything outside of what we know, if it's any procedure, any scheduling or anything like that, they don't share that information with us."

Two weeks later, the Bertolets opened up more. In another scoop for Brian Maass, the family went on the record and all but accused Harold of killing Toni. "Nobody has that much bad luck," Todd said, contending that Harold's account of her death didn't add up. "I just felt immediately he was responsible."

They also spoke out about the characterization, in Maass' previous story, of Harold as a work-at-home fundraiser. The Bertolets scoffed at years of letters they received from Harold claiming his many work successes, only to hear him admit that he hadn't been employed in years, a contention Maass was able to confirm by checking records. "The trophy of the family was tarnished by a loser who doesn't pull his weight, has no job, is not a good person and is a liar," said Todd. "That's not what my parents had envisioned for their daughter."

Their suspicions deepened, he said, when the family got more details of how Harold's first wife had died—he had told them it was in a car accident, a "lie of omission," claimed Todd, who found it "ridiculous" the Douglas County Sheriff's Department dispensed with the investigation in a week. Worse, Todd said, Toni didn't know how Lynn had died. "I feel like if she knew the real story about the first wife there would have been a lot more scrutiny of Harold Henthorn as a fiancée and husband," Todd told Maass. "I think she was deceived a lot about a lot of things. I think the deception started from day one and it never ended. To have two wives die in freak accidents, the odds are better you will win the Powerball lottery."

The Bertolets also voiced their suspicions about Harold over Toni's injury at the cabin. "I told her, 'Toni, I don't think I would be with him alone in a secluded place. I just don't have a good feeling about it,'" her mother Yvonne Bertolet said.

The floodgates now open, more people went public. Mike Walters, a friend of Lynn's, told *Inside Edition:* "When I heard through friends that Harold's wife had died through similar circumstances, hours and hours away from anyone else, very mysterious circumstances and so forth, candidly I immediately called the authorities." He simply refused to believe it could happen twice. "Two wives die under those kind of circumstances with large insurance policies. I think there is enough smoke there to indicate to me there is fire," Walters said.

Behind the scenes, investigators had come to the same conclusion. As witnesses in Lynn Henthorn's death gave statements, federal authorities continued to proceed on a second track with the probe into Toni's death. The $4.5 million in life insurance provided plenty of motive, particularly when Harold's financial picture came into view. Park Service Agent Beth Shott obtained from one of Harold's friends a photo of his business card. It read: "Development Services Inc. Not for profit fund Raising" and listed as an address their home address. Next to Harold's name were stamped the letters "CFRE," which Shott discovered stands for Certified Fund Raising Executives.

But a call to the CFRE organization revealed that Harold had never received nor applied for certification. And a check of Harold's 2011 federal tax returns found he reported no income from any source, according to a search-warrant affidavit filed by investigators. There was no claim for income or loss from "Development Services Inc.," in fact no references to Development Services Inc. or affiliated businesses at all, the affidavit said. There was no record of incorporation for Development Services, and Harold was not listed as the registered agent for that or any other business. All wages on the tax returns reflected Toni's sources of income.

The financial evidence did more than add hard evidence to support the impression by Toni's family that she was the family breadwinner. It helped authorities prove that Harold was a liar. All his big talk about clients and fundraising campaigns turned out to be bunk. Interviews with the workers at a local Panera store found that Harold spent most of his days sitting at a table surfing the Internet.

Linking Harold's phone calls to cellular towers, Shott also could trace Harold's movements. In the summer and fall before Toni's death Harold made nine trips to Rocky Mountain National Park—not the two or three visits he said he'd made to Ranger Faherty. One of those visits came on September 16, 2012—that same Sunday that Harold had told longtime family friend Daniel Jarvis he was out of town for business and couldn't be at church with Toni and Haley.

Reviewing his calls for the day of Toni's death, Harold had turned off his phone at 2:18 P.M., about an hour into their hike. The phone went back on later, and at 5:54 P.M. he received a text message from the babysitter. One minute after that he called 911. This conflicted with Harold's initial statement that he received the text at the same time Toni fell and then called 911 from the bottom of the cliff about forty-five minutes later.

An interview with the Henthorn family babysitter, Katy Carvill, spelled more trouble for Harold. Katy watched Haley and occasionally went out to Friday night dinners with the family. Katy said that Harold dominated the conversation and would interrupt Toni any time she tried to voice an opinion. He acted, she said, as if he were superior to her. Haley, meanwhile, consumed Harold's attentions. He seemed to Carvill more interested in Haley than in Toni, making all the decisions for their daughter. For all of Harold's romantic gestures at Toni's office, the marriage appeared loveless. They slept in separate bedrooms, she said.

Asked what Harold did for a living, the babysitter didn't have any more clue than anyone else. Most Thursdays Harold left for what he called business trips while Katy watched Haley. Harold would return the next day saying he was traveling to Grand Junction and other locations. But Katy noticed that he never took any luggage. Sometimes Harold told the babysitter he had a flight to catch at a certain time, then would leave the house after the supposed flight time. Katy came to wonder whether he was having an affair.

Investigators thought they had another explanation:

Harold was out scouting Rocky Mountain National Park for a place to kill Toni.

On the day of Toni's death, Katy got a call from Harold from Estes Park, where the couple were spending their anniversary weekend. It was unusual for Harold to call; he normally texted her. Harold then passed the phone to Toni so she could speak with Haley. This, too, was out of character for Harold, who never let Toni speak with Haley on his phone.

Katy had in fact sent that text to Harold's phone as reflected in the records. The soccer game had just ended and she sent him a picture of Haley with a note saying they had won the game. But Harold never replied, she said.

As for Harold's other version of the fall, in which he said he was looking at Toni's phone at the time because he was annoyed she was on duty, investigators found that would have been impossible. A friend had retrieved Toni's cell phone that she had left at the office in her haste to leave with Harold. A check was made for calls from Toni's answering service, Contact One Call Center. None went to either her phone or Harold's.

A new review of recordings of Harold's 911 communications and his text messages from the side of the mountain brought more damaging information. The Estes Park law-enforcement officer who tried to guide Harold through CPR would tell federal investigators that it didn't seem like he was doing any such thing—that he didn't seem to be listening to her or following her instructions. On the 911 tape, Harold did not in fact seem to be counting along with her on the chest compressions and very quickly abandons the whole thing.

So what was he doing up there?

At 7:31 P.M., according to records, he called his friend Jack Barker. The call lasted only two seconds. Harold then dialed Jack on another number for a call lasting twenty-seven seconds. He immediately called that number back for a call lasting thirty-five seconds.

Then he texted Jack: "Urgent . . . Toni is injured . . . in estes park . . . Fall from rock."

A second text followed: "Can you get Steve t and drive to estes pk. ASAP.

"What do you need?" Jack texted back

"Do not call others/Haley not told," texted Harold, followed by: "you," "prayer," "doing cpr," "Call 911 when you arrive."

"911?" texted Barker at 7:36 P.M. "Oh crap."

"Tell me your eta," responded Harold. "Flight for life requested."

But as he sent this, Harold knew that no rescue helicopter was coming. He had been told repeatedly that rescuers would reach him by foot. It was around this same time that he texted his brother-in-law Barry Bertolet, again saying he was doing CPR while giving vital signs that made no sense to Barry.

To authorities, all signs pointed to Harold lying about trying to resuscitate Toni and lying about her condition to her brother. The reason, they believed, is that he had no reason to do CPR or check her vital signs. By the time he started contacting people, she may well have been dead.

Harold's apparent lies, before, during, and after the day of the hike, emerged as what authorities saw as the cornerstone of their case against him. If he lied about all those things, then it wouldn't be a big leap to suggest to a jury that he also lied about his innocence, authorities felt. Documenting each apparent lie consumed the better part of the investigation, a slow and tedious task.

From the official standpoint, time was on their side. The more lies they believed they could find, the more

Sandra Lynn Rishell and Harold Henthorn
met as students at James Madison University
in Harrisonburg, Virginia, in the 1970s.
He seemed to share her deep Christian beliefs.
Courtesy: Grace Rishell.

Lynn and Harold married in 1982
in Colorado. Her family was surprised
that Harold insisted on handling all
of the wedding arrangements.
Courtesy, Grace Rishell.

Harold and Lynn shared a love of the outdoors and traveling;
here they stand in front of the Jeep Cherokee that would
later crush Lynn to death. *Courtesy: Grace Rishell.*

On the night of May 6, 1995, the Henthorns' Jeep Cherokee slipped off jacks and landed on Lynn, crushing her to death. Harold said the accident happened while he was changing a tire that appeared "soft" or "spongy." *Court file, courtesy US Attorney's Office.*

Harold told investigators the Jeep fell off the jacks when he tossed the tire into the back hatch. *Court file, courtesy US Attorney's Office.*

Harold told investigators he used this silver "boat jack" placed on a concrete paver and another, orange "boat jack" because the factory tire jack wasn't working. Investigators never tested the factory jack to confirm his story. *Court file, courtesy US Attorney's Office.*

Investigator Robert McMahan photographed and made note in his report of this "partial foot print type mark" on the fender right over where the Jeep fell on Lynn. But McMahan never revisited the finding nor did he apparently ever ask Harold about it. *Court file, courtesy US Attorney's Office.*

On the right front passenger fender of the vehicle, towards the rear of the fender right behind the wheel well of the missing wheel, was an apparent partial foot print type mark.

From my initial observations, there were three lug nuts visible on the ground below the wheel well of the vehicle; one underneath and behind the wheel well and two outside and behind the wheel well.

The initial official reports referred to the Lynn Henthorn case as "suspicious" and "possible evidence of crime." But those suspicions would quickly, and mysteriously, disappear. *Court file.*

Toni Bertolet had met Harold Henthorn on a Christian dating site in 1999; they were married within months in September 2000. Her family was happy for her but worried that she was rushing into the marriage. On the couple's 12th anniversary weekend, they spent the night at the historic Stanley Hotel in Estes Park, CO..
Court file, courtesy US Attorney's Office.

On May 28, 2011, a large piece of wood fell on Toni from atop a deck where Harold was doing work at their cabin. Her family believed that Harold had tried to kill her.
Court file, courtesy US Attorney's Office.

The morning of Sept. 29, 2012, the Henthorns drove in
their Jeep Cherokee—the same make and model, but newer version,
of the vehicle that killed Lynn—from the hotel to the Deer Mountain
trailhead for a day hike and picnic. Harold likely took this photo.
Court file, courtesy US Attorney's Office.

The Deer Mountain trail is
considered "moderate," a
six-mile trek that covers
rocky soil and goes up
steep switchbacks, but
offers spectacular views of
the valley below. Toni's
family were puzzled why,
with two bad knees both
subject to surgery, she
would try such a hike.
*Court file, courtesy US
Attorney's Office.*

Harold snapped this
selfie at or near the
end of their hike. He
had given the photos
to a longtime family
friend to hold onto.
*Court file, courtesy
US Attorney's Office.*

LEFT: Toni on an outcropping overlooking the valley.
Court file, courtesy US Attorney's Office.

RIGHT: Toni looking through binoculars; she plunged off the cliff within moments after these photos were taken.
Court file, courtesy US Attorney's Office.

The cliff from which Toni plunged to her death. *Court file, courtesy US Attorney's Office.*

The site at the bottom of the cliff where Harold had called 911 and set a small fire, leaving the black mark. He had dragged Toni from where she had landed to this spot, bumping her head on rocks along the way. An officer tried to lead Harold through CPR via the phone but she doubted he actually did the procedure. *Court file, courtesy US Attorney's Office.*

The conclusion on Toni's autopsy report in which the pathologist said homicide "cannot be excluded." Harold was said to have been outraged when he found out the coroner wouldn't flatly determine Toni's death an accident. *Court file.*

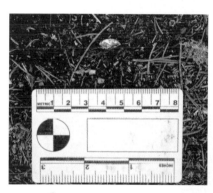

The diamond from Toni's engagement band was later found at her death scene; officials suspected that Harold had placed it there after originally taking it with him the night she died. *Court file, courtesy US Attorney's Office.*

Sheriff's investigators recreated the circumstances of Lynn's death; they were unable to get the Jeep to fall off the jacks in the way that Harold said it did. *Court file, courtesy US Attorney's Office.*

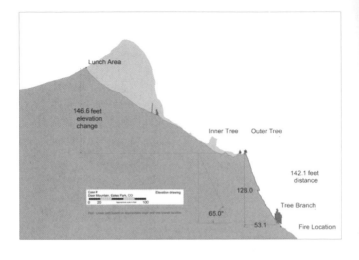

Chart and photo that prosecutors showed to the jury to illustrate the circumstances of Toni's death. *Court file, courtesy US Attorney's Office.*

guilty Harold would look. They had little concern that he would flee. They kept him under occasional surveillance, both with plainclothes spotters and through an electronic tracker affixed to his car, and he didn't appear to have any designs on going anywhere.

Toni's family understood and accepted the pace of the investigation. "We knew what they were doing, we knew that there was a timeline they had to investigate," said Toni's brother Todd. "They were all over the place, investigating every story that this man had told. We knew that this was going to take a long time. They told us from the start that this is not a two-to three-month investigation, that they're looking at a minimum of a year." Through most of the investigation, the Bertolets remained active participants. "We stayed in the mode that we're in, listening and not arguing with Harold," said Todd. "We went an entire year that was for gathering information about what Harold was telling us. That was a pretty good year for us. If we had talked to Harold we would write it all down and submit it to the FBI. Harold being Harold, he talked a lot."

Part of the ruse depended on Harold thinking the Bertolets supported him. With investigators interviewing Harold's friends and the parents at Haley's school, it was no secret to those close to him that he was a target of the federal inquiry into Toni's death, and people at the school began complaining about allowing Harold on the property. "We knew that the second Harold suspected we didn't support him he would cut us off from Haley," said Todd. "My parents would go out to Denver strictly to visit their granddaughter. They would go with Harold to Haley's school and get introduced as Toni's parents. Harold's whole argument was: If I did this, why would the Bertolets support me? Harold kept speaking for the family and telling these stories that were not true.

We certainly didn't support Harold, and it got to the point where it was more damaging acting like we did."

The decision came with a steep cost. Once the Bertolets went public with their suspicions of Harold's guilt in October 2013, everything changed.

TWELVE

The morning of Thursday, November 6, 2014, unfolded like any other for Harold Henthorn. He dropped his daughter off at school then drove to his home in Highlands Ranch. It had been nearly a year since news broke of the investigation, and Harold had become a pariah at the school. Grumbling about his presence had built to a vocal protest by parents fearful that a killer lurked in their midst. Harold refused to stay away, and the school had little recourse since he had not been formally accused of a crime. Harold also now openly clashed with Toni's parents. After going public against him, he cut off all contact with them and refused to let them see or talk to Haley. Letters they sent her went unanswered. Gifts they mailed went unacknowledged. The Bertolets could only imagine what Harold was saying about them to Haley.

Toni's parents responded by hiring a lawyer and going to family court in Denver, seeking grandparent visitation

rights. Harold got his own lawyer and fought back.
Since the proceedings are confidential, no records are
available, and the Bertolets shared only a few details.
Very quickly, they found that going public against Harold
would cost them. "Harold said [to the judge] that
because we came out and accused him that turned the
parents against him at the school and the children were
criticizing little Haley," said Toni's father, Robert Bertolet.
"That caused all sorts of problems. The judge seemed to
take that into account." Also at issue was the fact that
Harold had yet to be formally charged with a crime.
"There was too much of a potential conflict between
this and Harold's Fifth Amendment right," said Robert.
"If we asked if he murdered his wife, he didn't have to
answer." The judge put off a decision on visitation until
authorities decided whether to charge Harold in the
deaths of Toni or Lynn.

The court inaction meant that Harold retained custody of Haley and could continue to keep her from seeing her grandparents. All the while, tensions increased
between Harold and the Bertolets and between Harold
and the other parents at the school.

To protect her interests, the court assigned Haley her
own lawyer. In March 2014, Barbara Cashman began
serving as Haley's *guardian ad litem*. The phrase "ad
litem" is Latin for "for the suit" and in the legal world
it's usually attached to a lawyer who acts on behalf of
somebody else, normally an incapacitated adult or, in
this case, a child, providing a voice for those who can't
express themselves.

Cashman met Haley for the first time on a Saturday
in April 2014, having secured a court order approving
of the session. "Haley was punctual and polite," Cashman later recalled in court testimony. "She was understandably a bit wary of me. I know this was partly

because of what Harold said to her in advance about our meeting." What Harold had said would become apparent as the meeting went on.

The meeting was critical for Cashman in developing an understanding of Haley's personality in a setting away from her father. "That afternoon, Haley was all put together and carried with her a little backpack, the contents of which were carefully designed to support the conclusion that everything is just fine," Cashman said. "But there were cracks in that veneer, evident not just by the effort Harold put into creating the package, which was the report card; the scrapbook, with her mommy's picture in it; a picture from a soccer game where she was the goalie and, she added somewhat boastfully, ended in a shutout, and the book she was reading, which she reported was above her grade level; her need to convince me of something, her boastfulness, which didn't fit her demeanor, these all concerned me."

On the surface, Haley appeared to have "the trappings of a well-adjusted eight-year-old," said Cashman. "But as we walked around the gardens, talking about school and skiing and other things, I saw how she carried herself, how she spoke about herself at times, as if in the third person. These were some of the red flags I noted from that first meeting."

From that point on, Cashman worried about Haley's well-being with her father. Cashman talked to the staff at the child's school, who recounted her problems in the classroom. She didn't get along with other children. She would hide a lot. Another problem was Harold's behavior, at home and at the school. Because of him, school doors were locked during the day and he was banned from attending field trips and other school activities.

The pressures took their toll on Haley. "She was a germaphobe who washed her hands just a few too many times," Cashman recalled. "When I asked her if she had any pets, she told me, without any elaboration at all, that she was allergic to pets. Not any particular kind, just pets. I didn't want to ask her how she arrived at that conclusion. Because I suspected that she hadn't made that determination."

It was, Cashman concluded, "just one of a countless number of lies Harold told her." Cashman gave an extensive analysis of Harold's and Haley's relationship as part of the court proceedings against Harold. The more time Cashman spent with Haley, she later said in court, the more times she heard words coming from the child's mouth that clearly had been planted there by Harold. "Things about her mother that as a young girl she would not have come up with on her own, like my mother was very clumsy," Cashman said. "Or another reference that her mother was not really very smart about certain things."

"I sensed that Haley was subject to Harold's ongoing need to dominate and control her. He was trying to alienate those happy memories she held for her mother, to somehow erase the love that Haley felt for her," said Cashman. "Harold's efforts to alienate Haley from her mother's family are well documented. Haley was being trained to be emotionally dependent on her father."

Infantilizing the child, Harold had trained Haley "to doubt her own capacities, doing her homework, continuing to cut her food for her, and strictly minimizing contacts with the outside world, so it would remain foreign and scary to her without Harold's assistance," said Cashman. "Harold's exertion of control over so many of the small details of her life was an attempt to shrink her down to a puppet that he hoped to manage so as to have her completely emotionally dependent on him."

In this, there were strong echoes of what Toni's family

and friends had seen in the ways that Harold treated his wife. "I understood that Harold viewed people and particularly women only as property, as a means for his self-gratification," said Cashman. "I sought more help for Haley in her very difficult emotional state. I knew that Haley as a child was at risk of serious psychological and physical harm."

Then, on that morning in November 2014, as Harold returned from the school, agents from the FBI and National Park Service were waiting at his house.

After more than two years of investigation, Harold Henthorn was arrested without incident on charges contained in a federal grand jury indictment handed up the day before. The indictment read: "On or about September 29, 2012, in the State and District of Colorado, and within the special maritime and territorial jurisdiction of the United States, namely Rocky Mountain National Park, the Defendant, HAROLD HENTHORN, willfully, deliberately, maliciously, and with premeditation and malice aforethought did unlawfully kill Toni Henthorn."

It charged him with one count of murder in the first degree with a maximum penalty of life in prison and a fine of up to $250,000.

Harold was still being processed into federal custody—photographed, fingerprinted, and booked—when the U.S. Attorney's Office issued a press release trumpeting the success of the more than two-year investigation, with each agency getting a quote.

"The indictment charges Henthorn with the first-degree murder of his wife in Rocky Mountain National Park," said U.S. Attorney John Walsh. "The United States Attorney's Office will work tirelessly with the National Park Service and the FBI to ensure that justice is done for the victim and her family."

"The National Park Service is always concerned for the protection of our visitors," said Mark Magnuson, Rocky Mountain National Park Chief Ranger. "When a violent crime such as this occurs in a national park, one of our nation's most treasured places, we work hard to ensure that those responsible are held accountable and the victim and the victim's family are afforded justice. In this case, we will continue to work closely with the FBI and the U.S. Attorney's Office toward a just resolution."

"Working with our partners from Douglas County and the National Park Service, FBI agents took Henthorn into custody this morning," added FBI Denver Division Special Agent in Charge Thomas Ravenelle. "As with all defendants, Henthorn will now be afforded his day in court after an extensive investigation." This case was investigated by the National Park Service and the Federal Bureau of Investigation with "assistance" from the Douglas County Sheriff's Department.

Toni's family got word of the arrest in a phone call from investigators. "It was our fifty-fifth wedding anniversary," said her mother, Yvonne. Her father said, "We feel like it was the best anniversary present we ever got."

Toni's family, too, issued a statement from Mississippi. "Today's arrest of Harold Henthorn is a culmination and validation of the efforts of some exceptional people with the National Park Service and the FBI. This judicial process is not only warranted, but is deserved by a wonderful lady that was my sister, Toni Bertolet Henthorn. We obviously did not choose to be placed in the position that we find ourselves, but we fully support this process in effort to seek justice for my sister."

Todd Bertolet added in an interview with CNN: "It was a day we were looking forward to." Harold Henthorn said he was a businessman who owned a company, but Bertolet said no one in the family really knows what he did. Todd said Harold controlled the couple's finances, and he questioned his sister's relationship with Harold. "He was so dominant over my sister and the child. It was almost like whatever he said, went," Bertolet said to CNN.

By afternoon, Harold made his first appearance at the Alfred A. Arraj U.S. Courthouse on 19th Street in downtown Denver. He wore a University of Kentucky pullover sweatshirt as he stood before Magistrate Judge Kathleen M. Tafoya. Harold didn't enter a plea, and the matter was held over for another week.

His attorney, Craig Truman, didn't want to talk about the cases outside the courtroom, but issued a statement: "I'm sure when all the facts are known in this difficult and complex case, that justice will be done." It would be the only public statement he'd make.

The indictment and government press release said Harold was charged only in Toni's death and said nothing of the Lynn Henthorn case. It was left to the Douglas County Sheriff's Office to issue a brief statement. "We can only say that there is an open, active investigation into the death of his first wife," said sheriff's spokeswoman Deborah Sherman. "We can't release anything else because of the investigation."

Haley was placed into temporary custody of Henthorn family friends. "They were good friends of my sister and Harold," said Todd Bertolet. "Harold agreed to allow them to be guardian. They were really good people that worked out for the best." It was then left to Cashman to explain to Haley what had happened and why in ways a child would understand.

"When I told Haley about it, I was aware of Harold's preparation of her for such an event, by telling her about the bully men who might come to get him," Cashman later said. "I carefully explained to her that a federal grand jury does not return an indictment based on hurtful things that might have been said by uncles or grandparents. I told her that an indictment was based on evidence from a law-enforcement investigation." But an understanding of the legal system was the least of Haley's problems. "She was a hurting and emotionally needy child, in need of nurturing."

After Harold's arrest, the family court allowed Toni's parents to visit Haley. They were not allowed to take her out of the state, and all visits were conducted under the supervision of the guardian ad litem. Yvonne and Robert Bertolet saw their granddaughter for the first time in a year at a Denver area teahouse. "She had been told something about us by Harold and we still don't know what it was," said Toni's mother. "So at first, she just kind of eyed us like: I'm not sure about you." Soon, though, the ice began to melt and Haley jumped into their laps, clung to them, and laughed.

Each visit got easier. Yvonne recalled one at the Henthorn house, where Haley frequently stayed with the temporary guardians to avoid too much disruption. "After Haley warmed up, she said, 'Grammy, would you come up in my room with me?" recalled Yvonne Bertolet. "We went upstairs and I sat on end of the bed with her and she said, 'Grammy, I never stopped loving you.' And I said, 'I never stopped loving you, either.' From then on, she knew that nothing had changed between us."

THIRTEEN

"All right," said U.S. Magistrate Judge Kathleen M. Tafoya. "We'll call case Number 14-CR-448, United States of America versus Harold Henthorn. May I have appearances, please?"

"Good afternoon, Your honor, Suneeta Hazra and Valeria Spencer appearing on behalf of the United States," said Assistant U.S. Attorney Hazra, who then introduced the two federal agents in the courtroom, Jonathan Grusing and Beth Shott.

The judge then turned to the defense table.

"Judge, my name is Craig Truman, and I represent Harold Henthorn, who's present at my side."

On November 12, 2014, Harold returned to court. He wore a prison-issued tan jumpsuit.

"We are here in his matter for an arraignment, a discovery conference and a detention hearing," the judge said. "Are you prepared to go forward with the arraignment at this time?"

"We are, your honor," said Truman. "The court should know that Mr. Henthorn has received a copy of the indictment, he has read it, he has been advised by the court as well as counsel. We waive formal reading or further advisement. We would ask the court to receive our plea of not guilty."

With that the legal wheels began turning, the first act in a courtroom saga that could end in Harold being set free or locked up for the rest of his life in a federal penitentiary. As he formally denied the murder charge against him, Harold—widely described to investigators as a big mouth—wisely let his lawyer do all the talking this time. Harold would not say a word.

"The not guilty plea will be entered to this one-county indictment," said the judge.

The plea now entered, the prosecution formally informed the defense of when it would turn over all the evidence it had collected against Harold over the last two years—all the paperwork of alleged murder: the police reports, the records of phone calls, the autopsy reports, the reports on witness interviews and the final photos taken on the ridge before Toni fell to her death. Truman acknowledged that he expected the evidence would be "voluminous."

Dates and deadline set, it was time to address whether Harold would be released on bail until trial and, if so, how much that bail would be. The government objected to any bail and called its only witness: Dana Chamberlin, an auditor in the Economic Crime Section of the U.S. Attorney's Office who investigates economic crimes.

"I have reviewed bank accounts, investment accounts, insurance documents, tax returns, as well as the Quicken file that Mr. Henthorn had at his home," she said under questioning by Hazra.

The result of her inquiry showed that Harold was that rare murder defendant who actually had money: a bank account with $12,000, investment accounts totaling more than $800,000, IRAs worth $219,000, for a total of more than $1 million in ready cash.

And that wasn't all.

"Are you aware of an additional $500,000 that Harold Henthorn transferred to his brother in early 2014?"

"I am."

According to the auditor, Harold made two transfers, one for $200,000 at the end of January 2014 and the second for $300,000 around the middle of February, both to a Bank of America account in the name of Robert Henthorn's business, something called Ameritrade Holding. After this, more money was moved around to another holding account under a different name. This occurred just as federal investigators had obtained a search warrant for his computer and insurance records and were completing the last of the interviews.

"Based on what you know about this, what was Mr. Henthorn's explanation for why he transferred $500,000 to his brother?"

"He wanted to invest in his brother's business, who was doing quite well according to Mr. Henthorn, and he was looking to get a guaranteed rate of return anywhere from 5 to 7 percent on this investment."

She didn't say how she knew that was Harold's intention—whether she talked to the brother or somebody else. But she did find out that before he transferred that money, these accounts for this supposedly promising business opportunity had less than $10,000 in them.

"So just to sum up the sort of total financial picture of the amount of money Mr. Henthorn currently has access to, what is the total amount of money, roughly?"

"Roughly $1.5 million."

Turning to the insurance records, Chamberlain confirmed that three life insurance policies were active at the time of Toni's death worth a total of $4.5 million, plus interest, to Harold. He had not yet received any of the money, however.

That wasn't the case with his first wife's death. The death of Lynn Henthorn paid Harold $496,000 in life insurance benefits, which apparently sustained Harold for five years until he married Toni, according to an examination of his financial records.

"What is the nature of his employment as he's held it out to be?"

"As a fundraiser for nonprofit organizations."

"And based upon your review of the records, has Mr. Henthorn received any income from this position?"

"Not to my knowledge, no."

His tax records showed no evidence of any money from a W-2 filing, no income recorded on his Social Security records and no paycheck deposits on any of his bank statements.

The judge turned to Truman. "Cross-examination?"

Truman stood. "Ms. Chamberlin, I don't have a lot of questions," he began, "but I do have several."

In the first preview of how the defense would challenge the evidence against Harold, the attorney asked about Harold's insurance agent, Neal Creswell, who was told by Harold about wanting to invest in his brother's business. This was according to Chamberlin, who added that Robert Henthorn had spoken to federal agents.

"And Robert Henthorn was frank, forthcoming and open with them?"

"I know that the brother was interviewed," said Chamberlin, "but I don't know what the results of the interview are."

"Nothing illegal about investing money with your brother's company?"

"No."

As for Toni's insurance policies, Chamberlin said that one claim was made quickly—on the Monday after Toni died. She said it was an "associate" of the insurance agent Creswell who started the claim process.

"It wasn't Mr. Henthorn?" asked Truman.

"Not to my knowledge, no," said Chamberlin.

"You have no information from your investigation that Harold Henthorn ever asked that a claim be made on the Monday after Dr. Toni Henthorn's death?"

"I don't know."

As for the other policies, "You and I both know that none of those insurance policies have paid the claim?"

"That's my understanding at this point in time."

"And do you know why that is?"

"I would assume of because of what's going on here today."

"Let's talk about another hearsay incident. You say that Mr. Henthorn had told people he was employed as a fundraiser for nonprofits?"

"Correct."

"Who'd he tell?"

"Several people."

"Do you remember who they were?"

"Friends and associates. Neal Creswell."

As for collecting on Lynn Henthorn's death, he asked, "They were paid after an investigation by the Douglas County, Colorado, Sheriff?"

"I don't know how long after, but it was after I believe they had done their investigation, yes."

Truman consulted his notes. "Ms. Chamberlin, I'm sure we'll talk again. Thank you. I have no further questions right now."

Hazra had only one line of inquiry on redirect questioning.

"Having reviewed Mr. Henthorn's financial records, was this $500,000 investment typical of money he gave to his brother?"

"No, it was not typical."

"Had he ever done anything like it at all previously? $500,000?"

"Not that large dollar amount, no."

With testimony over, Hazra urged the judge to deny bail. The fact that Harold transferred the half-million dollars to his brother when he did, the money finding its way into different accounts, "is particularly suspicious," she said. Plus, Hazra insisted Harold "pushed" his insurance agent to collect on Toni's death. This is combined with the fact that he has very little tying him down to Denver.

"Mr. Henthorn has no employment. Despite his repeated statements to everyone that he was employed, he has none. He has no family here in Colorado except for a very portable 9-year-old child, all his family's back East. He essentially doesn't really have many ties to the community, and his ties to the community have been frayed by the nature of this charge."

Frayed was putting it mildly. "Law enforcement have talked extensively over the last two years to a number of potential witnesses and acquaintances and friends and family of Mr. Henthorn," said Hazra. "Many of them are very concerned for their own safety, but more importantly they're very concerned about the safety of his daughter."

Saying that the prosecution "shares that concern" about Haley, Hazra revealed that the girl's school had sought a "no trespass request" barring Harold from the grounds. "He's committed first-degree murder," she said. "He's told multiple conflicting stories about what's happened since then, all of which make him both a danger and a flight risk." Everybody at the school, she said, is "frankly terrified of him."

In the defense portion of the arguments, Harold's attorney began by complaining that "we're caught up short here" because he had not had any of the police reports or other evidence on which the prosecution made its claims of a terrified school. Nor had he seen any of the evidence purporting to support one, much less two, murders.

"We'd like to see those, of course, and in due time we will, and then we'll answer those allegations." Without that evidence, he said, he was also unable to address one of the factors in denying bail: the strengths or weaknesses in the prosecution's case.

What he could say was, "It is not correct to say Mr. Henthorn has no ties to this community. Of course, he's a longtime resident, owns property in Colorado, has a family tie"—presumably Haley—"and many family and friends, certainly friends in the community, a longtime church relationship.

"Irrespective of that, Your Honor, we're mindful of the nature of these charges, and have said this small piece without benefit of knowing what the government's evidence looks like, we'll submit this case on the record as it presently stands," he said.

Ruling from the bench, the judge acknowledged that a person can't be detained without bail merely because of the severity of the charge of murder. If anything, the law presumes bail if appropriate. Still, the fact that a grand jury had considered the evidence and voted to indict spoke somewhat to the strength of the prosecution's case.

Although Harold had no criminal history, the judge

noted the large amount of money available to him. "To have really pretty ready access to $1.5 million in cash is very troubling in a case of this kind because it means that the defendant has the means to flee," she said. "Most people do not have that kind of money readily available."

She added, "I don't know where the money came from, and I'm not making any particular findings about why there's so much money, just noting that there is a lot of money and it is not explained by any kind of employment of this defendant."

Mostly, she said, "What's really troubling, though, is the movement of money, the half-million dollars that has been more or less hidden." Recapping the testimony of Chamberlin about the different accounts, the judge said, "There's many different reasons why people hide money, but one of them could very well be to have a nest egg if you flee, especially to a country with no extradition."

Concluding, the judge said, "I am going to find that the defendant is a substantial flight risk and I will find for that reason that he's not entitled to bond." Further, she found that "there is a risk and danger to the community."

Harold was led back to jail to await his next day in court. On the docket was a pretrial hearing to determine what evidence would be allowed to go before the jury. This would prove to be one of the most important hearings of the case, perhaps more important than the trial itself. For the prosecution intended to admit more than just evidence that Harold killed Toni, Hazra told the judge.

"The government also will plan to try to introduce evidence of the first wife's death," she said. "We don't believe this is his first murder. He actually committed a previous murder of his first wife in remarkably similar circumstances."

Even though Harold would not be formally charged in Lynn Henthorn's death, the prosecution had a legal theory that would allow the jury to consider that evidence all the same. It meant that Lynn's family could have its day in court. It also meant that the competency of the Douglas County Sheriff's Office so many years ago would also be put on trial.

FOURTEEN

Douglas County Coroner Lora Thomas lived in Highlands Ranch, not far from where Harold and Toni Henthorn and their daughter attended church. Their social paths never crossed, but they had common neighbors. A day or two after Toni plunged to her death, a neighbor came to Thomas's door. The news had called it an accident, but the word rippling through this part of Douglas County was something else.

"He was telling me a lady at the church just around the corner from us had died and my neighbors knew of her and my neighbor said, 'God, Lora, that was not an accident. Her husband killed her,'" Thomas recalled.

The neighbor wasn't the only one to suggest that.

"Right after Toni died, a teacher at the school where Haley went had said something to somebody, and my friend knew this teacher and that's how it came to me," Thomas says. "This person said, 'I think her husband killed her.' He went on to say, 'Lora, that's not all. The husband's first wife died in Douglas County and I think he killed her too. You've got to do something."

Thomas went to her office in Castle Rock and pulled the 1995 file for Lynn Henthorn. It contained medical records from Swedish Hospital documenting her arrival by helicopter and the futile efforts to save her. It also had the autopsy report. And there was a report from Wesley Riber saying that the manner of death was "accident."

There were no supporting investigative reports, nothing reflecting the work of the sheriff's department. The gap between the injuries described by the autopsy report and the finding of an accidental death seemed vast and unsupportable, at least by the scant documentation in the file.

Thomas walked next door to the Douglas County Sheriff's Office in search of the investigative file. The clerk looked up the reference number on the computer and found the case file in storage. Thomas brought the file home and went through it with a yellow highlighter. Like other elected coroners, Thomas was not a doctor. But as a 26-year veteran of the Colorado State Patrol, working her way up from dispatcher to the department's first woman captain, Thomas knew how to analyze reports.

"As I'm going through this report, I'm appalled at what I am reading," she says. "When I was done reading the report, I remember sitting back and thinking: I cannot believe it. This was a classic case of a Keystone Kops. They're all running around doing something and accomplishing nothing."

The official death certificate said Lynn died in an accident. If it was wrong, Thomas wanted to change it.

Through her contacts in law enforcement Thomas discovered that Lynn's death was being investigated by the FBI as part of the probe into Toni's death, which at the time had not been publicly revealed. She saw no reason to implicate herself and so, "After that I just patiently waited," she said. Over the next two years, she'd bring the case up to a friend privy to the investigation, and she'd hear that the National Park Service was on it and that something may break soon.

After the arrest of Harold Henthorn, Thomas waited no more. In a November 10, 2014, email to Park Service Special Agent Beth Shott, Thomas introduced herself.

In reviewing this report which I've attached, I see that it does not list a manner of death. However, the death certificate was signed out as an accident."

She said she'd read the sheriff's investigative file and was "wondering if it would be appropriate to have a discussion about changing the manner of death on the 1995 death certificate for Sandra Henthorn to "undetermined."

Thomas said Shott called her back but referred her to investigators with the Douglas County Sheriff's Office. On December 3, 2014, Thomas sent an email from her smartphone to sheriff's Detective David E. Weaver.

Hi Dave,
I understand that you are the detective assigned to the re-opened Henthorn case. Is that correct?
I'd like to meet with you on Friday. Will that work?

Thank you
Lora.

"Of course, I heard nothing," Thomas recalled. This didn't surprise her. As so often happens in Douglas County, politics intruded.

Of the county's 219,223 registered voters, nearly half—102,660—are Republicans, only 43,597 are Democrats. A larger group of 72,966 are listed as "other." That sets the stage for intra-party skirmishes, GOP vs. GOP, for a variety of races. It can be especially fierce between the coroner and sheriff, both elected positions. Candidates can score points during the primary, the only election that matters, by trashing the other. Afterward, hurt feelings linger, sometimes for decades.

In her 2010 bid for coroner, Thomas faced Carter Lord, a deputy to Coroner Wesley Riber, the same Wesley Riber from the Lynn Henthorn case who was leaving office because of term limits.

"It was an ugly race," Thomas said. She had accused the coroner's office, under Riber and his predecessors, of wasteful spending and other forms of inefficiencies and sloppiness. She got enough votes at the Republican General Assembly to a win a spot on the GOP primary ballot, and went on to beat Lord.

But the fallout from the campaign put Thomas at odds with the sheriff's office. In the heat of the election, Thomas had accused the sheriff at the time, David A. Weaver (no relation to the sheriff's detective on the Lynn case) of backing her opponent Lord. Weaver denied this and Thomas countered by saying she had photos of the sheriff embracing Lord at a campaign event.

After the election, Thomas said Sheriff Weaver retaliated by locking her and her staff out of the justice center's gym and vending machine areas, which were controlled by the sheriff's office.

Weaver then claimed that a spiteful Thomas responded

by releasing to the public sensitive information about a double-homicide that the sheriff didn't want out.

Thomas later admitted that her actions were a "terrible mistake on my part"—but that didn't stop her from making enemies.

Inventorying her office after the election, she found that a gun seized in a case was missing from evidence storage. She turned the matter over to the Colorado Bureau of Investigations, and in 2012, the missing gun was linked to her predecessor, Carter Lord. He was charged with the theft of two firearms—one of which he sold for $500—embezzlement of public property and forgery. In 2014, he was sentenced to three years' probation.

Having stirred things up in both the coroner's and sheriff's offices, Thomas went one step further. In October 2013, she announced she was running for Douglas County Sheriff to fill a suddenly open position when Weaver left the department to become a Douglas County Commissioner. Weaver's temporary replacement was Undersheriff Tony Spurlock, a thirty-year veteran of county law enforcement. Thomas went up against Spurlock and Castle Rock Police Department Commander John Anderson at the GOP caucus, but this time failed to get enough votes to make the primary ballot.

Spurlock was nominated and would face no Democratic challenger in the general election. (In yet another twist, his only general election opponent was Brock McCoy, formerly the sergeant from the Lynn Henthorn case, now retired and running on the Libertarian ticket).

Spurlock easily won, and Thomas became a lame duck with few friends at the sheriff's office.

Thus, the fact that nobody responded to her email to Detective Weaver asking about the Lynn Henthorn investigation came as no surprise, the county's top law-enforcement leaders were no longer on speaking terms. So Thomas, now insistent on finding out what the sheriff was up to with Lynn Henthorn, filed a public records request, which produced several internal emails. It turned out that Detective Weaver had not in fact ignored her; he had forwarded her email to his supervisors with the message: "Comments? Suggestions? Guidance?"

A few names on his forward list stood out. One was Jason A. Anderson, a sergeant, who also happened to be the son of Thomas's opponent in the sheriff race, John Anderson. Another was Capt. Jason Kennedy, the same Jason Kennedy from the Lynn Henthorn case, now a top supervisor.

As lines blurred all over the place between politics and official duties, the past and the present, Thomas pressed on. "I know that I will get zero cooperation with the sheriff's department," she recalls. "I'm thinking: What should I do in the meantime? I do not want to change the death certificate on my own. That's when I hired Mr. McCormick."

From her years in law enforcement, Thomas knew a lot of retired detectives with homicide investigation experience. Charlie McCormick wasn't among them. A former homicide detective with the Denver Police Department, McCormick had done presentation on another case at a law-enforcement seminar that Thomas attended, and she was impressed. She inquired with her friends in police work and heard of his reputation for integrity and meticulousness. McCormick now worked as a private consultant to lawyers with trial preparation. He lent an experienced eye on reports, reconstructing investigations, looking for those overlooked details, documenting the mistakes. His clients came from both the defense and the prosecution side.

In late 2014, Thomas hired him to examine the work of the Douglas County Sheriff's Office and then generate a report with his findings. "For political reasons, I thought it was best to hire him to review the case," she said. "He's not a buddy. This would be very clean."

Although he was working independently from the Douglas County Sheriff's Office, McCormick began his work the same way Detective Weaver had, by reading the investigative file. He immediately knew things were missing, particularly photos referenced in the log but nowhere to be found in the file. McCormick, however, ascribed no evil motive to this. From his experience, he knew this wasn't unusual for a file now twenty years old—things had a way of getting lost. He'd do the best he could with what he had.

Going through the reports line-by-line, McCormick spotted references to the Sedalia Grill and was intrigued. Harold said they'd been on the way there when the tire problem happened, but at another point said they'd already eaten there.

"I'd never been out that way. I just went up there to see what it was like. It was kind of interesting. It was the hell out of the way," he said.

For years, the Sedalia Grill was a popular eatery at the intersection of two little country roads out in the middle of nowhere. It featured hand-carved wood booths, and in the front, you could see the cool motorcycles through mostly clean windows; "cheap beer & grub," said one Yelp review. There were tacos and burgers, friendly waitresses, a smoking patio out back. Bathrooms were clean enough. You never left hungry.

As he drove by the restaurant site, McCormick saw that the Grill was gone. It had been sold, redecorated, upgraded, and replaced by an establishment the new owners called the Buckskins Saloon. There was still cheap beer—$3 Coors Lite pints during Broncos games, $18 prime rib dinner specials on Tuesdays—but now added were country line-dancing classes and a general store that sold handmade soaps.

But while the restaurant had changed, the setting spoke volumes. This little isolated road made for the perfect place for a murder, particularly at night. The restaurant served as a symbol of everything wrong with the investigation.

McCormick's findings would be compiled into an eleven-page report that spelled out a number of deficiencies in the sheriff's department's work.

His first note was that nobody had ever conducted a formal, recorded interview with Harold. The file contained only his various—and variously conflicting—statements to different deputies. The closest thing to a formal interview, at Harold's house, also wasn't recorded and appeared far from probing.

McCormick was particularly surprised McMahan didn't confront Harold about the apparent shoeprint right over the area where Lynn was crushed. It was, after all, McMahan who had ordered the shoeprint photographed.

"I found no further mention of this important observation in any of the reports in the file, nor is it included in the photo log compiled by Technician Sharon Bronner," said McCormick.

Harold also wasn't pressed on his ever-changing account of their itinerary. "Unfortunately, the autopsy report makes no mention of the stomach contents, or lack thereof, in Lynn's body," wrote McCormick. "There is no indication in the file that the employees of the Sedalia Grill were interviewed to confirm whether the Henthorns ate dinner there on this evening."

Harold alternately said he'd left his house at 3 P.M. and

6 P.M. for a trip to Deckers and the Cheeseman Reservoir, a drive on the winding roads that would have taken about one and a half to two hours. Harold said he passed the Sprucewood Inn at 8:30 P.M. and then a "little store," which from his road trip McCormick knew was now called the Ridge Trail Store, and that he stopped within a mile to fix the tire. Had he changed the time of departure, knowing that he couldn't have left home at 6 P.M. and gone up to the mountains and back by 8:30 P.M.?

If he had in fact passed the store at 8:30 P.M., why did the 911 call for help come at 10:27 P.M.? What was Harold doing for those two hours on the side of the road? Somehow this time gap didn't get noticed—or made no impression—on the original investigators.

It was one of the similarities between the circumstances of the deaths of the two Mrs. Henthorns. The long time-gap would be repeated seventeen years later when Harold waited some forty-five minutes between Toni's fall and calling 911.

From the reports, McCormick also couldn't tell which direction Harold said he was driving or even where the tire problem occurred. The reports variously describe it as "8 1/2 miles west of Sedalia on Highway 67," "on Highway 67 at Casey's Curve,"—which is only 7.6 miles west of Sedalia—"west of Rampart Range Road on Highway 67," "north side of road, facing south on west side of highway," "left side of the road pointed in a north-westerly direction," "and 10 miles west of Sedalia at Casey's Curve."

Even if the investigators accepted what Harold ultimately told them about his itinerary and the blowout, the story, taken as a whole, didn't pass the smell test.

"It seems ironic that a vehicle that contains three car jacks being driven by a man who admittedly had some recent experience with changing flat tires (caused by construction debris around his house) would have such difficulty changing a tire on this occasion," wrote Mc-Mahan.

The jack, however, was never tested. Nor was the oil-can found—or if it was, it was never logged by the otherwise meticulous crime scene analyst Sharon Bronner.

The more McCormick read, the more questions he had. McMahan had carefully checked the tires for air pressure but made no note about whether the tire that caused all the problems had a puncture in it. Was there a nail in it as Harold had suspected? The passenger side doors were locked—who had locked them and why? How did the tire that Harold said had bounced out of the Jeep get back in the jeep with the hatch locked? If they had traveled all the way up to Deckers—120 miles round trip—why did the trip odometer read only thirty-six miles? The investigation turned up no sign he'd stopped for gas along the way—no receipt was found in his car, and he apparently was never asked about this.

The only part of Harold's story that did seem to measure up was the position of Lynn when she was crushed. One of the lug nuts was found just behind the front axle. "If, in fact, Lynn was crawling under the rotor when the car fell on her, this lug nut could very well be what she was trying to reach," he said.

In the report, McCormick didn't venture to speculate why the investigation was dropped as quickly as it was or why the investigators concluded against all this evidence and contradictions that it was an accident. The report that he submitted to Coroner Lora Thomas on December 3, 2014, stuck only to the facts as he found them—or didn't find them.

But McCormick couldn't help but wonder. Why would Deputy Coroner Wesley Riber conclude the death was accidental while the investigation still seemed to be chugging along? Nothing in the report seemed to support that, even though it seemed to have a major impact on the course of the investigation. For everything stopped.

McCormick later guessed the investigation's end had something to do with the power dynamics between the coroner's office and the sheriff's office, echoes of political forces Lora Thomas would encounter twenty years later. The coroner made a finding of accident and the sheriff didn't—or wouldn't—contradict it. McCormick had been around long enough to know the score.

"That would pour cold water on any investigation right away," said McComick later of Riber and the coroner's office's finding. "But why he reached that conclusion at that particular point in time is a mystery to me."

Lora Thomas read McCormick's report and, on December 19, 2014, sent a letter to Lynn Henthorn's brother Eric:

Dear Mr. Rishell,
Enclosed are the three certified copies of the corrected death certificate for your sister, Sandra Lynn Henthorn, that we discussed by phone yesterday.

As I explained to you, I reached out to the Douglas County Sheriff's Office to discuss the case and received no reply. I then hired a consultant to review the files to determine if changing your sister's death certificate was warranted. After reading Mr. Charlie McCormick's report and discussing the case with him, I believe that changing the manner of death from ACCIDENT to UNDETERMINED is the correct decision.

At your request, I also forwarded you via e-mail

a copy of the autopsy report for your sister. I can only imagine how difficult this must be, but if we can be of assistance, please feel free to contact our office.

Thomas's decision on manner of death would come with the backing of another consultant she'd hired. A report by Accident Reconstruction Services Inc. of Wheat Ridge, Colorado, which came in after McCormick's report, not only raised the same questions as he had but added a bunch of its own. Reviewing the police file, the consultants amassed more than two dozen questions that apparently were never asked and never answered. They wondered, for instance, why Lynn—if she had shimmied under the Jeep—didn't have any dirt on her hands. Or why she wasn't covered in oil and grime from the Jeep landing on her. Or why Harold's hands were also apparently clean if he'd been removing a tire, throwing it into the hatch. They wondered whatever became of the rag that Lynn was said to have been using to hold the lug nuts. And on it went.

"Based upon our initial examination and analysis of the materials, reports and information, provided and developed, it was determined that there were substantial issues related to the investigation and results of the investigation in this death case." Those questions and issues were of sufficient magnitude that they would support the change of the case of death from "accidental" to "undetermined," concluded the consultants, Arnold G. Wheat and David W. Lohf.

After receiving the revised death certificates, the Rishell family spoke out for the first time in twenty years, issuing this statement:

"Our family has known Harold Henthorn for nearly forty years—first as a college friend, then as our sister

Sandra Lynn's husband. After Lynn's death, he remained part of the extended Rishell family. Over the years, we spent time with Harold, Toni, and their daughter on vacations and visits to the East Coast and to Denver. When we learned of Toni's death two years ago, we were shocked and saddened. At the same time, however, the baffling circumstances surrounding Toni's death gave us a strong sense of déjà vu. As the investigation into Toni's death progressed, it became clear that Harold Henthorn was not the man we thought we knew, and that he had in fact been lying to us for many years."

Eric Rishell elaborated in an interview with Brian Maass, calling the change in the death certificate "symbolic of the direction we think everyone is working toward in these proceedings. We appreciate everyone's continued due diligence in this case and are hoping and praying for the right outcome."

Less than two weeks remained in Lora Thomas' term. In December 2014, in her parting act as coroner, she released McCormick's report to the public. The fallout was immediate.

In late January 2015, Tony Spurlock had been sheriff of Douglas County for all of a month, his swearing-in occurring in December, and he immediately faced a maelstrom. The Harold Henthorn "black widower" story had become huge international news, the London tabs finding the story particularly fascinating. The network shows *48 Hours* and *Dateline* were amping up coverage. *People* magazine slapped the case on its cover with a photo of Toni and Harold on their wedding day and the headline, "Did He Kill Wives?"

That prompted Harold's former online date, Sonserae Leese-Calver to alert her Facebook friends of her role in the *People* article. She posted a photo of Henthorn smiling and hugging Toni Henthorn during a hike and wrote: "At least this is one tragedy that was dodged! I may not have any jewelry but at least I'm not at the bottom of a cliff. I'm very sad for the women who lost their lives to this EVIL MAN. Not many people can say they dated someone who's featured in PEOPLE MAGAZINE but THIS IS NOT what I had in mind."

Thanks to the candidate Spurlock had defeated for sheriff, nearly every step and misstep in the Lynn Henthorn investigation became public knowledge. Colorado's alternative weekly, *Westword,* published an in-depth cover story (by this author) drawn liberally from McCormick's review and from leaked reports from the original investigative file.

Soon, the whole file would go public when it was attached to a court filing by Harold's attorney. The judge in Harold's case also unsealed twenty-one search warrants and affidavits reflecting much of the work by the Park Service and FBI investigators, from details of Harold's actions up on the mountain—including a transcript of his cell phone text messages—to the interviews with Toni's family and friends, to details about Grace Rishell and the insurance policy.

Even Patricia Montoya surfaced. Brian Maass at Channel 4 tracked her down. "We all thought the same thing. It didn't seem like that was an accident," she said. "We were all very surprised. We all felt they would come and find us. And they never did."

On January 29, 2015, Spurlock went public, speaking out about the renewed investigation into Lynn Henthorn's death.

"Over the past 27 months of the investigation, approximately 40 interviews have been conducted and additional information has been uncovered that was unknown and or unavailable at the time," began a statement released to the media by his office. "DCSO

detectives continue to work diligently on this case, meticulously going over the case file, evidence and new information related to this death investigation."

There would not be full disclosure, the statement said.
"Because the overall investigation is ongoing, there are
details that Douglas County Sheriff's Office (DCSO) is
not at liberty to discuss," said the statement. "Rather, the
purpose of this release is to disseminate what can be released at this time and to ensure the public that this
case continues to develop and that we are working in co-
ordination with federal agencies on this case."

The department confirmed that that on May 6, 1995,
the sheriff responded to a "report of an injury accident" on Highway 67 west of Sedalia," that the initial
responders learned that "Harold Arthur Henthorn reported that they had been driving and pulled to the side
of the road to tend to a flat tire and at some point, according to Harold, the vehicle jack gives way and the car
crushes his wife, Sandra 'Lynn' Henthorn." The response
included "patrol, investigations and lab" and that Lynn
was taken to the hospital, where she died. The department then "opened a suspicious death investigation at
that time," said the statement.

As for why that investigation ended, the sheriff point-
edly shifted responsibility. "After a ruling that the
death was an accident by the Douglas County Coroner,
the case was closed and listed as an accidental death,"
the statement said with no elaboration.

Everything changed, Spurlock said, when the second
Mrs. Henthorn died. "While the original investigation
took place almost 20 years ago, this new information
merited additional investigation," said the statement,
which then included a couple of direct comments from
Sheriff Spurlock.

"It is hoped that this new information and a second

look at this case will provide a clearer picture of what might have happened," he said. "We owe it to the family and friends of Sandra "Lynn" Henthorn." He added: "This case is extremely complex and over the past 27 months our dedicated detectives have tirelessly re-examined this case and will continue until we have ex-hausted every aspect. In the past 20 years, investigations and investigative techniques, as well as technology have not only changed drastically, but have allowed many cases to be reopened."

Much of this last part was bluster. There were no technological changes at issue in the new investigation—there was no DNA or trace evidence or any other scientific evidence in the Lynn Henthorn case. In fact, there was no physical evidence at all to examine—the original investigators either destroyed it or gave it all back to Harold. And the department statement all but admitted how little headway the reopened probe had made. It noted that "no arrests have been made at this time" and said, "It is very possible there may be additional witnesses related to this case and we would encourage anyone with additional information to contact the Douglas County Sheriff's Office."

Walking a fine line between keeping the peace at headquarters and maintaining credibility with the public that voted him into office, Spurlock gave his one, and only, interview about Lynn's death to Brian Maass. "Based upon the information I've been briefed on up to this date . . . I do not think it's an accident," Spurlock told him. "I don't think it was an accident and I think it's very suspicious. That information leads my detectives to determine this is probably not an accident."

Still, he stopped short of second-guessing the original investigators who now dominated his command staff. "It's very easy to point fingers. It's more difficult to take the evidence that you have today and move forward, and that's what we're going to do. I think that if we had a chance to do it over again we would do things differently," said Spurlock. "Things are always different when you look back. Hindsight is 20-20. It serves me no good to look back 20 years or 30 or 15 years and make a judgment on what was done at that point, because I can't change that."

While Spurlock didn't want to look back, the U.S. Attorney's Office was more than eager to do so. The timing of the sheriff department statement was no accident. That same day, the U.S. Attorney for Denver, John Walsh, filed a motion formally asking a judge to allow the jury in the trial to determine whether Harold murdered Toni Henthorn to also hear evidence about Lynn Henthorn's death.

FIFTEEN

"Good morning, sir, can you state your name for the court reporter."

"Yes, it's Jason Kennedy."

"Thank you, sir, what do you do for a living?"

"I'm a deputy sheriff for the Douglas County Sheriff's Office."

"What is your official title there?"

"My title is captain."

"Let me direct your attention to May 6, 1995. Captain Kennedy, did you receive a dispatch call that you responded to?"

"I did."

At 8:47 A.M. on Monday, May 11, 2015, almost exactly twenty years to the day after the Lynn Henthorn case was officially closed as an accidental death, a hearing was held in courtroom A902, before Judge R. Brooke Jackson, who had taken over the case from the magistrate and who would preside over the trial. Jackson would hear testimony related to the prosecution's request to introduce evidence in three areas not directly related to Toni's death. In addition to details of Lynn Henthorn's death in 1995, the prosecution also wanted the jury to hear about Toni's injury from falling wood at the cabin and the life insurance policy Harold had taken out on Grace Rishell.

"The government plans to introduce other evidence that it anticipates will take no more than one trial day," the motion said. "Given the nature of this case, that evidence is critical to proving Henthorn's intent, motive, and plan. It will also establish that the death of his wife Toni was no accident."

It was just as critical for Harold that the evidence not be admitted. The murder case in Toni's death was solid but by no means a slam-dunk for the prosecution. Years of investigation had still failed to turn up an eyewitness to Toni's death, besides Harold. Nor had Harold confessed to anybody that he'd killed her. On the contrary, he vigorously proclaimed his innocence. The prosecution had built a case on circumstantial evidence and would ask a jury to infer that Harold's behavior, contradictory statements, movements shown by the cell phone records and the motivation of money should be seen as incriminating.

Allowing the introduction of details from Lynn's death and the life insurance policy on Grace Rishell would strengthen the prosecution's hand. Therefore the defense vigorously objected to that evidence. Harold's attorneys called the evidence irrelevant to Toni's death and said it was intended only to smear his character and inflame the jury's emotions.

Although each case turns on its own merits, prosecutors could take some comfort—and Harold some trepidation—over Jackson's earlier ruling in another high-profile case. He also presided over the civil lawsuit against the owner of the Aurora, Colorado, movie theater where James Holmes opened fire in 2012, killing twelve people and wounding seventy. In a pretrial hearing the previous summer in that case, Jackson ruled Cinemark could have reasonably enough anticipated the danger of such an attack to be held legally liable. "Although theaters had theretofore been spared a mass shooting incident," he wrote, "the patrons of a movie theater are, perhaps even more than students in a school or shoppers in a mall, 'sitting ducks.'" Jackson appeared in this case at least to favor inclusion over exclusion.

As Harold watched quietly and impassively next to his attorneys Craig Truman and Josh Maximon, prosecutor Hazra delivered her opening statement. At the prosecution table with her was co-counsel Valeria Spencer. Assisting them in court were Park Service Agent Beth Shott and FBI Agent Jonathan Grusing. A dress rehearsal for the opening remarks to a jury, Hazra's remarks would offer the first look at how the prosecution would attempt to put Harold Henthorn away for life.

Using photos that Harold and Toni Henthorn had taken to illustrate the presentation, Hazra recounted the couple's anniversary weekend, from the overnight at the Stanley, to hitting the trailhead at 1:15 P.M., to veering off into a rugged area to stop for lunch at about 3:30 or 3:45—even though they had dinner reservations at 7 P.M. The prosecutor described how they hiked down a steep, rocky incline to a knob—the "fall location."

Despite the late hour and despite fifty-year-old Toni's bum knees, they ended up at the fall location and "you can see the body-recovery location is where Toni falls over 140 feet." She showed the judge a close-up of the rocky knob, a natural rock ledge, a ledge of about two feet high and two feet across. "The rocky knob is treacherous, there's a sheer 140-foot drop-off over the ledge and the footing is uneven."

A photo showed Harold standing on the rocky ledge holding onto a tree and below him the sheer drop. Another photo showed Toni on the knob, a little bit away from the picture of Harold, "seated in a cautious position, looking out."

As for events the prosecution wanted admitted, the prosecutor deferred to the arguments contained in her previously filed court papers, which boiled down to this: Grace's life insurance policy, Toni's cabin injuries and, most of all, Lynn's death all served as the build-up to Toni's ultimate death. The similarities were haunting—connected by Harold's inability to tell the truth, said prosecutors.

"In the coming years, Henthorn offered more bizarre stories about Lynn's death: She was bending over in the trunk when the hatchback fell on her neck and killed her," prosecutors wrote. "A lug nut shot out and pierced her lung. A rod from one of the jacks shot into his wife's chest and killed her. The cabin on the flight-for-life helicopter or plane depressurized and collapsed her lungs. She died in a head-on car collision from which he escaped uninjured. He even told a Sunday School class that she had died from cancer and lost a baby she was carrying to chemotherapy."

Seeking to prove that the death of the first Mrs. Henthorn was practice for the more lucrative death of the second, the prosecution called Jason Kennedy to the stand. If Kennedy felt any pressure at all, he didn't let it show. His testimony would be clear and non-defensive, his recall crisp.

Asked about that late-night call so many years ago,

he could still remember the trees and the dirt and the darkness. He remembered the Jackson Fire vehicles—civilian cars tricked out with spinning sirens since the responders were volunteers—and getting the word that a vehicle had fallen on somebody, and how that changed this from a regular accident to something that would require an investigator and maybe a supervisor, so he radioed it in.

He didn't remember seeing Lynn on the ground, only the EMTs working on somebody, but did recall his brief conversation with Harold, though he couldn't say exactly where they were standing, only that it was close to her. And he remembered Harold's eyes.

"He appeared visibly shaken, and looking around, darting his eyes around," Kennedy told Valeria Spencer.

"Can you describe that a little bit more, what you mean by that?" she asked.

"Just that his eyes were wider than, you know, a normal, you know, individual that had not been in an incident like this. And he was—his eyes were darting back and forth as he was kind of surveying the scene as I was speaking with him."

He remembered getting the basics from Harold: how they'd been driving on the road, then stopped to change a tire, got out of the car, how Lynn was helping change the tire, how he threw the tire into the rear, how the jack gave way and he heard his wife "yell for him." He remembered it was a narrative, not a Q&A, that he didn't press, that he didn't ask clarifying questions, since he knew investigators were on their way and they would handle that. Kennedy took notes and wrote a report and documented the scene. If Harold said anything more, he didn't remember.

Kennedy recalled how Deputy Bredehoeft arrived, at which point Kennedy handed off Harold while Kennedy took some pictures with a point-and-shoot camera. He recalled calling dispatch again to inform them that this was a "husband-and-wife situation" and that the wife had been pinned under the car in serious condition. He remembered the jack under the vehicle, the wrench with the extension, the two lug nuts under the brake assembly and just outside of it, the rear hatch shut and two full-sized tires inside.

He recalled speaking to "Mr. Hayes," whom he called the "RP"—the reporting person who had called 911—who told him about the two Hispanic males and a Hispanic female whose last name may have been Montoya who came to his home a quarter mile away saying they needed help and to call 911, and how he went to the scene to see Harold checking Lynn for a pulse.

"And did Miss Henthorn have a pulse at that time, according to Mr. Hayes?"

"Yes, and was breathing."

Hayes told him about covering Lynn with blankets to try to comfort her and then picking up the flashlight from under the Jeep and placing it in one of her shoes on the hood, going around to close the hatch.

And he remembered that a helicopter arrived to take the victim to Swedish Hospital. Prosecutors showed him the photos taken that night, the Jeep, the license plate, the broken concrete, the jacks, the jacket put on Lynn, what appeared to be a shoe impression in the dust on the front fender, and the underside of Harold's shoes.

And that, he said, was all he remembered.

When it came time for Harold's attorney, Craig Truman, to cross-examine Kennedy, the questioning was gentle. It was, after all, the Douglas County Sheriff's Department which concluded Harold did nothing criminal.

"When you talked to Mr. Henthorn," asked Truman, "among other things that he told you was that they had had a lot of flat tires in their neighborhood due to construction?"

"I don't remember hearing that directly from him," said Kennedy. "But I did write that in my notes."

As for Harold's demeanor that night, the lawyer asked, "Mr. Henthorn appeared visibly shaken?"

"That is true."

"His eyes were wide?"

"That is true."

"You've seen that before with people who suffered traumatic events?"

"I've seen that with people who have gone through traumatic events."

The defense brought Kennedy through the rest of his work that night—how he protected the scene, how he took photos, how he worked with other officers and the crime-scene tech—but asked no more questions about Harold. Kennedy was excused from the stand and another detective called to bring a fresher perspective on the case.

Detective Dave Weaver, overseeing the reopened investigation into Lynn's death, explained that his department took a new look at Lynn's death "based on information we received from the federal government and from other individuals."

Prosecutor Spencer asked, "Well, specifically, what was it that made you open the file and talk to your supervisors that the case needed to be relooked at?"

"We learned that Mr. Henthorn's second wife, Toni, had died in September or October 2012. And as a result of her death, Larimer County Sheriff's Office, different law-enforcement agencies, received information, some sourced and some anonymous, that Lynn Henthorn's death in Douglas County should be relooked at because they found it suspicious."

"Suspicious that the second wife had died or suspicious on its own?"

"Suspicious that he had had two wives that had died under questionable circumstances."

Weaver explained how he went through the file, made notes, and noticed the discrepancies. He spoke of interviewing Patricia Montoya and Dwight Devries, and of speaking with the original investigators and first responders. And he spoke of the new lead in the case, the statement from paramedic Roxanne Burns about how Harold said it was his wife, not him, changing the tires.

Spencer next asked whether Weaver found one part of Harold's story credible: that Lynn could have called out to him when the Jeep went down. (In her question, Spencer used the phrase "Lynn is squished by the axle.")

"I found that unusual based on the fact that her cause of death was listed as what I think was traumatic asphyxiation, which would usually indicate there was no air in her lungs; and with the weight on her, it's unlikely she would be [able] to reinflate her lungs and speak."

"Have you spoken with any medical personnel about that opinion?" asked the prosecutor.

"They're hesitant to say absolutely it's impossible, but they will say it's highly unlikely."

"In your review of McMahan's interview of Mr. Henthorn at his house on May 9, is there anything to indicate to you that Detective McMahan confronted Mr. Henthorn with any of these discrepancies or asked for explanation?"

"I don't believe Mr. Henthorn was confronted with any of his apparent contradictions."

It was the closest anybody in the department would

come during the hearing to directly criticizing the work in 1995, and the prosecutor let the matter drop, directing Weaver back to his own efforts. The defense, so forgiving of the original investigation, took aim at the new investigation.

In the cross-examination, Truman pressed Weaver, suggesting that witness recollections, including that of Devries, who said Lynn appeared frightened, could be clouded by the passage of time.

"He wasn't even aware of what month in the year this incident occurred in, is that right?" asked the defense attorney.

"He said he could not recall exactly when it occurred, that's right," said Weaver.

"All he could tell you what he wasn't sure what month it was and he thought it was dark?"

"He remembered it was dark, correct."

"And he thought that the tailgate was open, but he wasn't even sure of that?"

"Correct. I believe—I have to pull up some memory cells here—he was driving by and saw the vehicle on the left-hand side. He believed the tailgate was open. He made a U-turn and then saw the back two tires and the front passenger tire, that's what I recall him telling me."

"Well, he wasn't even sure that the tailgate was open, was he?"

"I don't think he said with any confidence it was open or closed."

Truman also took aim at the reliability of the more recent statements by the original investigators.

"When you talked to those people, did you interview them on tape or make a report?"

"Not at this juncture. The case was still open."

"So no reports were made. You were just visiting?"

"I don't know if I would use the word 'visiting.' But, again, I gave them an opportunity to tell me if they recall or recollect anything, you know, here's your report, can you remember something that may not have been in the report? Gave them an opportunity. But, again, my case is still open."

"But you've made notes about those interviews, of course?"

"I have all kinds of notes."

Truman took particular issue with the recent statement of Patricia Montoya.

"She also told you that they were drinking that day?" asked the attorney.

"Yes."

"They had been drinking all afternoon?"

"Well, (Montoya) just said they had been drinking."

"Did you ask her about how much they had been drinking?"

"I think voluntarily she—and when I subsequently interviewed her ex-husband, or ex-brother-in-law, they had been drinking beer pretty much all day, playing horseshoes."

"They told you, all of them told you, the reason they left the scene was so that they wouldn't be arrested, because they were too drunk?"

"They said they were afraid they would get in trouble."

"In fact, one of them, Theodore, told you last month [that he] thought he was too drunk to drive and if they had stuck around, he thought he would be leaving in handcuffs, right?"

"I think words to that effect."

"Let's talk a little bit about your tests," said Truman,

turning to the Jeep re-creations. "And the purpose of that test?"

"The purpose of that test was to find out how an individual of the height and weight of Lynn Henthorn could have positioned themselves to have the marks on her back that she had, that Lynn had."

"And you found that it was possible for that contortion to have occurred?"

"Correct."

As for the second test, to see if the Jeep could get knocked off the jacks by tossing the tire into the hatch, Weaver said, "We were not able to recreate the jacks failing."

"And of course, those jacks were not on a cinder block?"

"No."

"And you found that that would have made no difference irrespective?"

"We believed it would make no difference."

"So you can't tell Judge Jackson what would happen if one of those boat jacks was sitting on a cinderblock and the cinderblock broke?"

"Well, we call it more of a paving stone than cinderblock."

"So you can't tell Judge Jackson what would happen if one of those jacks was on a paving block and that paving block broke?"

"I could not."

With the third test, dropping the lug nuts to see how far they'd roll, Weaver acknowledged that he couldn't say for certain whether they had brought the test Jeep to the exact location of the original incident.

"We could not determine the exact location," he said, "because there was at that time no GPS available."

"And of course, it was done on the shoulder of the curve?"

"It was done in the area, according to the photographs taken in 1995, it was done in the area that we believe it occurred, based on everything we have, as far as descriptions of location."

"Any changes to the area in the last 20 years?"

"The only way I can answer that is most likely."

"Yeah, you didn't check with bridge and roads to see if they had repaved or regarded that area?'"

"Well, I can tell you that the area that it took place is not a paved area. . . . I know that they did change the signs there, that I can tell you."

"So you know at least they've changed the signs. You can't tell us anything about the—"

"I can't tell you, I'm sorry, Mr. Truman."

"You can't tell us anything about the grade of the road?"

"I can't tell you the grade of the road in 1995 and I can't tell you the grade of the road—how do I say it?— the slope. I can tell you that generally speaking it appears to be similar to how it was in 1995."

"Just the same as it was 20 years ago?"

"I said similar, not identical."

"And so when you were doing the lug nut test, you had no idea the position that Lynn Henthorn was in when she dropped the lug nuts?"

"We don't know her posture at the time."

"And so you don't know how the lug nuts came to be under the vehicle?"

"We don't."

"And so you were trying to replicate that which you didn't know?"

"We were trying to find out the probability of lug nuts, a lug nut, lug nuts, if they're dropped from various heights, in that convenient area, how they would roll, if they would roll, how they would interact with each other."

Truman wrapped up the cross-examination by trying to suggest that Investigator McMahan didn't do that terrible a job.

"You knew from reading the reports that those inconsistencies were not lost on Investigator Robert McMahan? He was aware of them?" asked Truman.

Weaver wouldn't bite: "I can only speculate that he was aware of them."

Asking about the interview with Harold at his house, "It was there that Investigator McMahan and Sgt. McCoy questioned him about the inconsistencies?" asked Truman.

"They did question him, correct."

"And that interview wasn't recorded, was it?"

"I found no documentation any interview with Mr. Henthorn was recorded. Nor did I find any documentation that Mr. Henthorn actually wrote a statement."

"But in the McMahan report, his discussion with Henthorn is meticulously documented?"

"Your description, sir," said Weaver.

"You certainly know that the inconsistencies were called to Mr. Henthorn's attention?"

"I believe they were raised."

"And Mr. Henthorn was asked to explain them?"

"I believe he was asked. Or given an opportunity."

On redirect examination, Spencer made it clear the prosecution was not impressed with McMahan's work.

"What did you see in the report from Detective McMahan that indicated that he looped back and asked any questions whatsoever to have Mr. Henthorn explain the discrepancies?"

"I don't recall any indication that Mr. Henthorn was actually ever subjected to any kind of adversarial type of conversation or interview."

Following Weaver to the stand was his federal counterpart on the investigation, FBI Agent Jonathan Grusing. Grusing was called to bolster the prosecution's request to introduce evidence about Toni's cabin injury. The agent recounted how his inquiry into Toni's injury at the cabin found shifting stories by Harold in the official reports.

"In all those reports, is Harold Henthorn on the deck flinging the wood?" asked Suneeta Hazra.

"Not all the reports, just in the very first report to EMS is he flinging wood."

"In all of the reports, is your understanding that Harold Henthorn is not on the ground with Toni?"

"Yes, that is correct."

"Did Harold speak to family and friends about this incident?"

"Yes, numerous."

"Did he tell consistent stories about what happened?"

"No, he did not."

He told his neighbor Dennis Dahl, for instance, that Toni was injured when Harold was up on a ladder repairing fascia on the roof when both Harold and a small piece of wood fell off the ladder and the new piece of fascia hit Toni on the back of the neck. At the time, she had three life insurance policies on her, down from four earlier in the year.

"And these were all Toni Henthorn is the person, entity insured?"

"That's correct."

"And who is the beneficiary of those policies?"

"Harold Henthorn."

"So if Toni Henthorn had died in May 2011, how much would Harold Henthorn have received, approximately?"

"$4.7 million."

Similarly, Harold was listed as the beneficiary of his former sister-in-law's life insurance policy—the third piece of evidence the prosecution wanted introduced at trial.

"Who did Grace think would be the beneficiaries of this $250,000 policy?"

"Her daughters," he said, clarifying that after going through the application process and getting a physical exam, Grace changed her mind.

"She told Mr. Henthorn that she was going to get her own life insurance and she had indeed gotten it?" asked Hazar.

"Yes."

"And Grace Rishell had no idea prior to that point that Henthorn had gone ahead and gotten the policy?"

"That's correct."

"Did Harold Henthorn, after learning Grace Rishell did not want the policy, tell Neal Creswell to go ahead and get it?"

"Yes, he told Neal Creswell: Let's go ahead and proceed on the QT and let's keep this to ourselves, basically that he knew what was right for Grace Rishell, even though Grace had told both Mr. Creswell and Mr. Henthorn that she did not want the policy."

"Were there any life insurance policies on Lynn Henthorn in May of 1995?"

"Yes, there were."

"How many?"

"There were three primary life insurance policies."

"Was anything required in order to get that amount?"

the prosecutor asked in reference to the accidental death benefit.

"Yes, it's an accidental death benefit. So it had to involve an automobile accident."

Then there was the third policy for $300,000, for a total of $600,000.

"Who was the beneficiary of all of these life insurance policies?"

"Harold Henthorn."

"Did Harold Henthorn disclose all three of these to law enforcement back in 1995 when asked?"

"He only disclosed the CNA to law enforcement."

"After both Lynn Henthorn and Toni Henthorn died, what did Harold Henthorn choose to do with the bodies?"

"Both bodies were cremated shortly after their death."

He recalled interviewing Chuck Bowman, director of the Horan and McConaty funeral home in Littleton, Colorado, that handled Toni's remains and service.

"Mr. Bowman told me that he has done over 3,000 cremations, and Toni's death reminded him of one other cremation he handled approximately 20 years ago."

"And what was that one other cremation?"

"Mr. Bowman explained that when he was working at Chapel Hill Mortuary, a man came in, and his wife had been crushed by a vehicle in Douglas County, on a remote mountainous road, and the man was insistent that she be cremated immediately because he could not rest until her remains were cremated."

The cross-examination by co-defense attorney Josh Maximon stayed far away from this chilling revelation, focusing instead on Toni's and Harold's demeanor after the cabin injury.

"There was no indication of any fighting?"

"There was not," said Grusing.

"And was there any kind of police report or police activity in relation to this?"

"No."

"And was there any indication from the EMTs that Toni thought that her injury was the result of intentional conduct?"

"No."

"Is there any information in the medical file from Granby that Toni thought that her injury was from intentional conduct?"

"No."

"Was there any indication from the Swedish Hospital, in their medical reports, that her injury was from intentional conduct?"

"No, there was not."

Harold's lawyer also tried to establish that the life insurance policy on Grace Rishell, taken out through Harold's agent Neal Creswell, was appropriate.

"And she signed it?"

"She signed it, yes," said Gruswell, acknowledging that the paper trail told one story and Grace another.

"There's no question, in all the paperwork we've gone through, that there was an insurance policy related to Miss Rishell that went into effect on December 15, 2009?"

"That's correct."

"So when you said earlier that she changed her mind about the policy in February or March of 2010, the policy was already in place."

"It was, but she tells me that she was not aware of that."

Agent Grusing's testimony wrapped up the prosecution's case to convince the judge to allow the jury to hear about Lynn's death, the cabin injury, and Grace's insurance policy.

SIXTEEN

Jeff Bredehoeft, a deputy sheriff working patrol in May 1995, had gone on to work as a detention sergeant, a training sergeant, and an investigator. He was now a sheriff's sergeant working with the Rocky Mountain High Intensity Drug Trafficking Area program. Out of the twenty-three-year career, the events from 1995 fit into a two-and-a-half-page report about a fifteen-minute conversation between Bredehoeft and Harold Henthorn in the patrol car on the way to the hospital after Lynn was crushed by the Jeep.

"What was his demeanor?" Craig Truman asked the first defense witness about Harold.

"Sad, reserved, not anything, I guess the usual attitude when somebody's been hurt in an accident, I don't know how to describe it," said Bredehoeft.

Bredehoeft only "vaguely" remembered what was said in the patrol car—Harold talking about going to dinner at the Sedalia Bar and Grill, traveling west on 67, pulling over to change the tire, the car falling on his wife.

"I don't recall who, if he said who took the tire off," he said, "but he returned the tire to the back of the car and at that time Lynn had crawled underneath the car to grab a lug nut that had come off or that they didn't have control of, and when he put the tire in the back of the car, that the car fell off the jack and fell on top of Lynn. And he heard a sound, which I wrote down. I believe it was a scream."

The next defense witness, Kevin Duffy, also professed memory lapses.

"What was Mr. Henthorn's demeanor?" the defense attorney asked.

"Oh, I can't recall," said Duffy, noting that what he knew of that night came from his long-forgotten report. "I didn't document it in there. I just know we had a conversation."

Now a division commander for the detention facility, Duffy had been with the Sheriff's Office for twenty-six years. His long resume included stints on criminal intelligence on street-gang detail, investigations, a sergeant in patrol and on a drug task force, a lieutenant in detentions, an investigator in the major-crimes division, and a lieutenant for special investigations. He had just been promoted to captain.

What he did remember all these years later, he told Spencer under cross-examination, was that the conversation with Harold was not an interrogation.

"It was definitely casual," he said. "I was trying to get as much detail for the investigators who I knew were going to be the leads on this. To get from the only person who was there who could tell us what was going on in his words what had happened."

This set the stage for the testimony of the man who

did have a more detailed talk with Harold—and the most important figure in the investigation.

Robert McMahan was now a captain in the professional standards division, having worked twenty-seven years as peace officer—twenty-five of them with the Douglas County Sheriff's Office. His career followed a similar path, working patrol before being promoted to investigations, where he was assigned in 1995. He'd later move up to sergeant, then to lieutenant and captain.

Under gentle questioning by Truman, McMahan too had to constantly refer to his reports to refresh his memory, his answers terse. Even his recollection of arguably his most important observation of the night was fuzzy.

"Looked like there was a partial footprint-type mark," McMahan said of the impression on the fender over the Jeep tire.

"What did you do when you saw that?" asked Craig Truman.

"I don't recall."

"Did you have it photographed?"

"I don't recall, sir."

He did remember looking at Harold's hands.

"Why did you do that?"

"I was looking for signs of injury or a fight."

"Part of your standard investigative circumstances?"

"Yes, sir."

"What did you find?"

"I find no unusual marks or anything on his hands."

"How would you describe his hands?"

"Unremarkable, nothing to note."

He also recalled going to the vehicle evidence yard with crime scene tech Sharon Bronner and coroner investigator Wesley Riber, looking at scrape marks on the Jeep's axle.

Truman asked: "What did those marks mean to you?"

"They were consistent with the story that Mr. Henthorn portrayed about how the accident occurred."

"Later did you make a decision as to how to sign this case out?"

"Yes, I did."

"How did you sign it out?"

"As an accident."

"When you sign out a case, does it have to be reviewed by a superior?"

"Yes."

"Who reviewed this one?"

"Sgt. McCoy."

"And how did he sign it? Accident?"

"Yes."

The questioning took a sharper tone during cross-examination. Prosecutor Valeria Spencer briefly exchanged "good afternoons" with McMahan before launching into him.

"Back in May of 1995, how long had you been an investigator?" she asked.

"I believe about five, six months."

"And what sort of training did you have to become an investigator?"

"I don't believe I had any at that point."

"When you look back on this now and the things that you did or did not do, do you see things that you should have done differently or would have done differently if you had had better training?"

"Yes."

"What sort of things would you have done different if you had better training?"

"Well, there were some witnesses that could have been further examined. For instance, Miss Henthorn's supervisor said that she had heard some accounts of how this accident had occurred, and I would have liked to, at this point, go back and examine some of those accounts and compare how those things occurred."

"How about Mr. Devries, who had stopped to offer help and been shooed away by Mr. Henthorn, would you have spoken with him?"

"Yes, ma'am."

"Would you have spoken more thoroughly with Ms. Montoya or anyone else in her car?"

"Yes, ma'am."

"You didn't interrogate him [Harold Henthorn] about the discrepancies that he offered in the various stories?"

"No," acknowledged McMahan.

"You didn't push him on that in that interview at his house about which version he was going to go with on that day?"

"Correct."

Noting that he had checked Harold's hands at the scene and found nothing to report, she asked, "Do your hands get dirty or greasy after you change the tire?"

"They can, yes."

"Did you notice anything like that on Mr. Henthorn?"

"Not that I noted, no."

About the scrape marks on the axle under the Jeep, she asked, "I think you actually said it was consistent with Mr. Henthorn's story. What it's consistent with is the jack slipping, not HOW the jack slipped? Would that be a more accurate way to put that?"

"Yes, ma'am."

As for whether Harold had told another first responder a different story about the tire, that Lynn was actually the one who changed it, McMahan said, "I'm sorry, I don't recall that."

He did, however, check on the insurance and said he believed that the only policies in effect were the ones that Harold and Lynn's boss had mentioned.

"But you were not aware of an additional $150,000 policy with USAA, were you?"

"No."

"Or a rider for another $50,000 in case of death by automobile accident?"

"No."

"Do you recall what Mr. Henthorn's demeanor was like when you spoke to him on May 9?"

"I would say it was unremarkable. Appropriate for the time. I don't recall specifically anything else."

"You note nothing in your report," she said. "If he had been hysterical, sobbing, that sort of thing, would you have noted that in your report?"

"Yes."

"Captain McMahan, as you went through this investigation period, you had the mindset that this was an accident, correct?"

"I did."

"And so when you closed it out on May 12 as an accident, that was consistent with what you had predetermined before you went through the whole investigation?"

"I don't know that 'predetermined through the whole investigation' would be accurate. But I did believe it was an accident, and that's how I closed it out."

"Within six days of the accident occurring?"

"Yes."

"Thank you, captain."

Truman tried to rehabilitate McMahan under redirect questioning, eliciting that Sgt. Brock McCoy, who did have a number years of investigative experience, had supervised at every step of the way.

"Did you ask for any additional help in this investigation?"

"No."

"Think you needed any?"

"No."

Claiming to have the worst memory of all was the next witness, former coroner investigator Wesley Riber. The man whose signature seemed to do more than anything to abruptly end the Lynn Henthorn death investigation said he had only the haziest recollection of his work.

"From my memory is a car that had fallen on her," he said in testimony marked by fractured syntax. "Up in the Ranch Park Range area, and the autopsy was from the pathologist that was used by the coroner. She died from the car being on top of her."

Truman asked: "Did you have any opinions to the cause of death?"

"Through my—from what—I asked him for more information."

"Him being?"

"The coroner," said Riber, referring to Dr. Mark Stover, " 'cause I work through him, he's the boss. And that information wasn't supplied, and he ruled it as accidental, and that's what closed the case in the office in those days."

"The report of May the 9th is over whose signature?"

"That's my signature."

"And when you signed that, what did that mean to you, sir?"

"That means that that's the information I had gathered for the case. And then the last part was the coroner's ruling on what that case was."

"What was your determination and the signature line of your signed report of the cause of death in this case?"

"Without looking at it exactly I can't tell you. But it was from the car being on—on her."

"Let me show you, sir," said Truman, placing the document in front of him. "A two-page report. Do you recognize that?"

"Yes."

"How is it titled?"

"Final investigative report."

"How is it signed?"

"By me as deputy coroner."

"And the last line of the report?"

"It says this is an accidental death."

"That was your opinion on May the 9th, 1995?"

"That was the ruling the coroner said was on the case."

"Why did you sign it?"

"Again, I say it's a synopsis of my whole work that I did on that case," said Riber. "What I did, what the coroner said the end of it was, and that's what it was. I was—in this office, the coroner had the ultimate responsibility to rule on each and every death. And that's what his ruling was on that information that I gave him and from the pathologist."

"Tell us how you based the accidental-death decision over your signature."

"I think I just did."

"Just 'cause the coroner told you to?"

"Pretty much."

Truman tried to pin him down more, but any effort by the defense to establish the rationale for the accident failed.

"This has been 20 years ago," said Riber, "and I had the opportunity to look at that piece of paper for a few minutes a couple weeks ago."

"But if it's in the report, it was something you found at the time?"

"Yes, sir."

"So if it's a factual predicate, that's not something the coroner just told you to write in there?"

"No, sir, those are my findings."

Asked, again, how he came to those findings, he said, "You're quite lengthy ahead of me on. It's only been 20 years."

He said he only "vaguely" remembered inspecting the Jeep and thought McMahan was there with him and a crime-scene tech whose name he didn't remember. Again, Truman showed him the report. Reading it, Riber acknowledged finding that the scratches on the axle confirmed that the Jeep had been lifted by the silver jack and that the broken paver's cracks were consistent with having been broken under the weight of the jack and Jeep and that the marks on Lynn's back matched those of the brake rotor.

"And then your next statement was this is an accidental death?" asked Truman.

"That's what the report reads, yes, sir," said Riber.

Under cross-examination by Spencer, Riber claimed that at the time he "did want more information" about the incident but that he was "never awarded that opportunity from the coroner."

"And how would you have been awarded that opportunity? Explain what you mean by that."

"I told him what I'd like to see, and it wasn't, he didn't request it. He didn't want it. I don't know. It was just never brought forward for me to know of, anyway."

"I think you've been pretty clear on this," said Spencer, losing patience, "but Mr. Stover was the coroner. You're aware that he signed the death certificate on May 8?"

"Yeah, if that's when it's signed, then that's correct."

"And then on May 9, you finished your report according to the date on the final investigation report," she said. "As you've indicated, the coroner's conclusion was this was an accidental death and that's what you signed off on?"

"Yes, ma'am."

Thus ended the first courtroom examination of the death of Lynn Henthorn, the officials involved unapologetic, the missing pieces from the reports to remain forever missing, lost in a haze of bad memories and petty inter-office politics. If the judge were to allow the evidence at trial, the prosecution would gain nothing from the original investigators and would have to rely instead on the new work by Weaver and others and the information contained in the reports, however incomplete.

Only one witness remained at the hearing. The defense called Neal Creswell, the insurance agent and financial planner who worked with Harold. Under direct examination, Creswell described his relationship over the years as a friendship as much as it was professional.

"I met Harold and his first wife at our church," explained Creswell. "When my wife and I met with a group of younger couples. I guess they determined that we had such a good marriage that we would be a worthwhile couple to counsel these young people. That's when I first met him. That's probably 20 years ago."

"And would you say that you're friends?" asked defense co-counsel Josh Maximon.

"Oh, yeah, we were friends. Not close friends. We knew each other. And we would see each other occasionally at church."

"You also helped him buy a policy related to his sister-in-law, Grace Rishell?"

"Yes, uh-huh, he asked me to help him get Grace insurance."

Creswell's understanding was that Grace was in financial straits, recently divorced.

"During that time leading up to that divorce, Harold told me that he had helped Grace financially," said Neal. "Because she was now a single mom without any help from her ex-husband with four teenage daughters. And the extent of her income, as I recall, was, she was teaching piano."

Harold hooked him up with Grace, and in a phone call he asked her how much insurance she could afford.

"She could afford $20 to $30 a month, and I told her that wouldn't buy much life insurance, at her age," recalled Neal. "And at that point Harold said, 'Well, Neal, let's get her insurance but I'll pick up the premium.'"

That's when they talked about $400,000 with a payout of $100,000 for each of the daughters. "Harold told me that if anything happens to Grace, I will see to it that each of these girls has a hundred thousand to go to college," Neal recalled. "He also counseled against making the girls the beneficiaries because they were teenagers and they had some irresponsibility in their history at that point. So he named himself the beneficiary. And I took that as, since he had helped Grace in other ways, that he was acting out of the goodness of his heart as an un-appointed trustee for the family."

Neal sent the application to Grace, who provided her private and financial information. "She was happily cooperating with me in answering the questions so that I could complete the insurance application. She was appreciative."

The beneficiary, Neal insisted, was clearly listed as Harold.

"And you're aware that Miss Rishell claims that you

and Mr. Henthorn forged her signature seven times on the documents that we just discussed?"

"I've heard that."

"Did you forge any signature?"

"No," he said. "I think that's Grace's signature. I don't know why there would be any forgeries after I had a pleasant hour-long conversation with her, and her very kind response to Harold's—her gratitude, her response of gratitude to Harold's kindness in buying this policy for her."

He noted that she did inform him in the summer of 2013 that she wanted out of the policy having gotten her own policy.

"Then it was terminated, is that correct?" asked Maximon

"Well," he said, "ultimately, yes. But Harold was not comfortable terminating it without a letter with a signature guarantee or a notarized letter from Grace asking him to terminate it."

"Ultimately, it was terminated?"

"Ultimately, it was terminated, yes."

Only that's not exactly what Neal Creswell had told investigators, prosecutor Suneeta Hazra suggested in cross-examination.

"Do you recall telling them that Rishell didn't want this life insurance policy and she didn't want Henthorn to be involved in her finances?"

"Yes," he acknowledged.

This was the first time this contradiction came to light. Until now, Harold's camp had portrayed Grace Rishell as a willing participant in the life insurance, from beginning to end. Creswell now was corroborating what Grace had been saying all along: that she had changed her mind about the policy and was stunned to learn, from the FBI, that it had remained in place, causing her to fear that she had been targeted as another of Harold's potential victims.

"Do you recall," Hazra continued, "that Henthorn told you to do it on the QT and quietly paid the premium?"

"He might have told me that. But he wanted the premium paid so that the insurance would be in force."

"And he said, 'I'll pay the premium, let's keep it to ourselves'?"

"Uh-huh."

Hazra asked: "Do you recall telling Grace Rishell in the spring of 2010 that she had cooked her own goose because she didn't want this policy?"

"I said that to her?"

"Yes."

"Not that I'm aware of."

But after more prodding, Neal said, "Well, if the difference is between Grace not accepting Harold's generosity . . . then I might have told her she's cooking her own goose."

As the attorneys delivered their arguments, for and against introducing the other incidents, a curious thing happened. The events of twenty years earlier began to yield to those of a century before. Prosecutors had one last unusual card to play: Harold was confronted with a ghost.

SEVENTEEN

George Joseph Smith was a London man of early middle age, neither handsome nor ugly, with a receding hairline, a bushy mustache, and eyes as black as death. He went to a reformatory school at age nine for petty theft and graduated with an advanced education in crime. In 1898, in the waning years of the Victorian Era, he assumed the alias of Oliver George Love and married a housemaid named Caroline Beatrice Thornhill, who—either voluntarily or under pressure from her new husband—stole from her employers and gave the money to him. This ended when she turned him into police and he went to prison for two years, having learned exactly the opposite lesson authorities intended.

"After the experience with his wife Smith subsequently preyed on more vulnerable women who seemed to be unaware of how he was manipulating them and unable to escape from his cruel conduct," wrote Brian P. Block and John Hostettler in *Famous Cases: Nine Trials*

That Changed the Law, which explores the Smith case in detail.

Fearing her husband upon his release from prison, Caroline fled to Canada while George married another woman while still legally wed to Caroline. He cleaned out the new wife's savings and ran away, in what would become a criminal pattern—two more aliases, two more illegal polygamous marriages, to an Edith Pegler and to a Sarah Freeman, two more cleaning out of their finances. Sarah offered the most lucrative return—400 pounds in cash and war bonds, a lot of money in the year 1909, when working-class men could expect to make about 150 pounds annually.

George juggled his various wives by spending little time at home; he told them he had to travel for work, which he claimed was selling antiques.

In 1910, he took on the name Henry Williams and married Beatrice "Bessie" Munday. One morning in July 1912, she was found dead in the bathtub, her head submerged, her feet sticking out. With no sign of a struggle, a doctor testified at an inquest she had suffered an epileptic fit and drowned. The inquest issued a verdict of death by misadventure. Her will, drafted five days before her death, left her husband 2,579 pounds.

A year later, now assuming the surname Burnham, George met a woman named Alice Smith, who was so enamored with him that they wed, in November 1913, despite the objections of her father. The father would later speak of George's "very evil appearance, so much so that I could not sleep whilst he was in the house as I feared he was a bad man and that something serious would happen."

One night shortly after the wedding Alice took a bath in their rented apartment. She was later found with her head under water at the foot of the bath. An inquest determined she died of heart failure. It was later found that, at her husband's insistence, she had taken out a life insurance policy of 500 pounds payable to him.

The following year, going under the name of John Lloyd, George married a woman named Margaret Elizabeth Lofty, who insured herself for 700 pounds. One day in December, she visited her lawyer to draft a will leaving her estate to her new husband.

That night she took a bath while her husband went out, he'd said, to buy tomatoes. When he returned, he found her dead in the tub, he said. Another inquest followed, this one also returning a verdict of accidental death. The husband had told the undertaker to get the funeral done as quickly as possible.

The marriages and deaths all stopped in 1915 when one of George Joseph Smith's landlords, who owned the house where Alice Burnham died, sent a letter to police with newspaper clippings about the inquests into Alice's death and that of Margaret Lofty. The letter pointed to the obvious similarities.

The resulting investigation and arrest of George Joseph Smith, first on bigamy charges and then for murder, caught the attention of the press, which dubbed it the "Brides in the Bath" case, a name that would stick for one hundred years. The resulting publicity brought to police attention the first bathtub death, that of Bessie Munday, for which Smith ultimately went on trial.

It was the most sensational trial in decades in England, and the prosecution mounted a vigorous effort, calling 112 witnesses and entering 264 exhibits. But the prosecution could produce not a single person who had witnessed Bessie's murder. In fact, aside from Smith's use of various alias, the wills and insurance money and Smith's obvious bigamy, the prosecution had no direct evidence of murder at all. Instead, the Crown relied on the tactic of introducing evidence of the subsequent two dead brides to show that Bessie's death was no accident.

To bolster their theory, attorneys for the Crown called a coroner to conduct reenactments. The baths were those of the era—made of tin, five feet long, portable, and not hooked up to plumbing. They were filled by buckets of water.

The reenactments were intended to show how the women, all over five feet tall, could drown in such small tubs without any sign of struggle. Early experiments using women divers of the same size as the brides proved fruitless; the subjects could all easily resist being pushed underwater. Then the coroner surprised one of the divers by suddenly yanking up her feet, causing her head to slide into the water. Before she could react, water rushed into her nose and mouth. It took doctors ninety minutes to revive her. When she came to, she said she remembered nothing other than feeling her legs tugged.

The defense vigorously objected to admitting into evidence details of the other two brides' deaths, but to no avail. The jury deliberated for twenty minutes before finding Smith guilty of murdering Bessie Munday and condemning him to death by hanging.

On May 12, 2015, attorneys argued over whether to allow the introduction of evidence of Lynn Henthorn's death, the cabin accident involving Toni and the life insurance policy on Grace Rishell. The prosecution said the events were all linked, part of Harold's ongoing plan to murder Toni. The odds were simply too long that all of this would have happened otherwise by pure chance.

Harold's attorney Craig Truman begged to differ, and now conjured the hundred-year-old specter of George Joseph Smith.

"The reason it's not admissible is because I think the doctrine of chances, while it might have been good in England in 1915 in the Brides in the Bath case, is not the present mathematical learning concerning what chances and things happen in this type of thing," he said.

"We all learn about the Brides in the Bath case, we learned that in law school," said the judge. "Why isn't that this case?"

"Your Honor, it isn't this case because I think that the learning concerning the probabilities, chances, and things randomly occurring in terms of a pure mathematical circumstances has radically changed since 1915."

"But neither side presented any evidence on that," said the judge.

"That is correct, Your Honor," said Truman.

"Neither side presented any expert testimony, for example, on the law of chances."

"That is true, Your Honor," Truman conceded again.

"So what do I do?" asked the judge.

Try as he could, Truman couldn't vanquish the spirit of George Joseph Smith once he had summoned it and the legal principles that survived generations.

"The court in that case, and if I remember, it involves a succession of brides who drowned in the bathtub," said the judge.

"Three, Your Honor," acknowledged Truman.

"And the first one was just a tragic accident, the second one raised eyebrows, and the third one convinced people that foul play was involved."

A little over two weeks later, on May 29, 2015, Judge Jackson issued his ruling. It took him eighteen pages to explain his reasoning. The decision was heavy on references to the various legal statutes and theories guiding him. Though the judge never mentioned the Brides in

the Bath case, its imprint was all over the ruling. The
judge did cite a previous ruling that put a modern twist
on the Brides case: "The man who wins the lottery once
is envied; the one who wins it twice is investigated."

Harold was investigated. Now, as with all defendants,
he benefited from a longstanding legal tenet that a person's character can't be put on trial. Just because he
looked like a wife killer, based on what happened to
Lynn, to Toni at the cabin, and regarding Grace's insurance, didn't mean he in fact killed his second wife. Evidence of a propensity to commit crimes generally is
barred from trial as irrelevant and inflammatory.

The exception derives from crimes in which the previous acts could help show planning and intent for the
act charged. Was Lynn's death a dress rehearsal for
Toni's? Prosecutors argued that it was, while the defense
argued that prosecutors were just trying to slime him.

In the ruling, Judge Jackson expressed reservations
about the Rishell insurance issue. The prosecution had
argued that it showed Harold's "common plan" of developing relationships with women, taking out life insurance on them, luring them to remote locations and
then killing them in ways to make their deaths look like
accidents.

"The court is at a loss to see how this could be," wrote
Jackson. "First, no allegation has been made that Ms.
Rishell was lured to a remote area where she was manipulated into a risky situation that soon became deadly
followed by an attempt by Mr. Henthorn to collect the
insurance proceeds from her policy. And it is disconcert-
ing to consider that the foretelling of unperformed acts
could be used to portend an individual's intent with re-
gard to a past, completed act. This evidence might be
relevant to a charge of attempting to defraud Ms.

Rishell's insurance company, but that is not the issue before me."

He ruled that this evidence would be barred from Harold's trial.

Lynn's death, by contrast, had many parallels with Toni's. "The similarities between these two otherwise disconnected acts is significant and may aid the government in establishing the requisite elements of its case without improperly relying on the jury to find that Mr. Henthorn has a propensity towards the commission of the crime charged."

The more difficult decision concerned the cabin injury. "Being hit by a board dropped from ten feet may well cause a serious injury, depending upon the size of the board and where the victim is hit, but it seems to me to be markedly less likely than the other incidents to result in death," the judge wrote. "If Mr. Henthorn was determined to kill his wife, dropping a board on her strikes me [as] an odd way to attempt it."

Still, the judge said, it wasn't up to him to make that final call—only whether there was sufficient cause for a jury to be allowed to make that decision. He found that there was. "Here we have three accidents where Mr. Henthorn's wives were the victims," he wrote. "Each of them occurred in unusual if not bizarre circumstances. The only witnesses in each instance were Mr. Henthorn and his wife. In each incident, the wife was either killed or seriously injured. Each time, at least in retrospect, Mr. Henthorn is said to have told inconsistent stories about what happened. . . . Viewed in isolation each incident reasonably could be viewed as an unfortunate accident. Viewed collectively, however, the 'doctrine of chances,' discussed above, argues against the conclusion that all three were accidents."

The final score was two-to-one for the prosecution, but the overall impact was much more severe for Harold. The trial was set to start within days of the judge's decision, and it was yet to be seen whether the defense could recover.

EIGHTEEN

The Alfred A. Arraj U.S. Courthouse is the pride of America's federal court system. Newly built with all the environmental bells and whistles, the ten-story highrise houses ten district courtrooms, four magistrate judge courtrooms, and one special proceedings courtroom. The General Services Administration boasts of the courthouse's silver rating for Leadership in Energy and Environmental Design, a number of green features for emergency efficiency and to keep utility costs in check. Natural daylight streams through massive floor-to-ceiling windows while a state-of-the-art "underfloor air distribution system" with air ducts at floor level provides an advanced filtration system. More ominously, the courthouse is designed, a GSA description reads, "to fulfill expansion needs for the district of Colorado." Crime and litigation appeared to be a growth industry in the expanding Denver region.

On September 2, 2015, the first prospective jurors to

sit in judgment of Harold Henthorn filed into Judge R. Brooke Jackson's courtroom on the ninth floor. Reporters swarmed the halls and TV news satellite trucks were parked outside. Prosecutors promised a long witness list and more than 300 exhibits; the defense had a leaner case. Judge Jackson minced no words: the upcoming trial, he told the jury prospects, "will be a doozy."

Each prospective juror filled out a questionnaire with several dozen questions to determine their exposure to publicity and their ability to remain fair and unbiased. What news programs do you watch or listen to? What TV or radio shows? How do you keep up with the news? What Internet sites do you regularly visit? What newspapers and magazines do you regularly read? Do you watch police reality shows?

About half the first batch of prospects said they'd heard at least something of the Henthorn case in the news. "You can't necessarily believe everything you read in the paper or see on TV," the judge warned. Some said they had an opinion they could set aside, others not. A few were excused when they said they had already made up their minds or couldn't be fair to Harold, who sat at the defense table. He wore a dark gray suit and scribbled notes. He'd look up at the jurors and smile now and then, betraying no sign of the stakes facing him.

It had taken twenty years for Lynn Henthorn's death to be considered by a jury, nearly three years for Toni's. This jury was selected within two days—neither side finding cause to bounce too many jury candidates.

On the morning of September 8, 2015, less than four months after the judge's ruling on the prior acts, friends and family of the two Mrs. Henthorns took their seats next to reporters and friends of Toni's, chatting amiably, the traumatic circumstances creating the usual temporary intimacies.

Harold, who once said in his online dating profile "friends would also probably add that I'm active, adventurous, trustworthy," sat still, a pariah among his in-laws, neighbors, and fellow school parents. If any friends came to support him, they couldn't be identified and they certainly didn't call attention to themselves.

Shortly after 9 A.M., Assistant U.S. Attorney Suneeta Hazra stood before the jury, said good morning, and began a story.

"On the weekend of September 28, 2012, Harold and Toni Henthorn headed up to Estes Park, Colorado," she began. "Toni Henthorn thought she was going to celebrate her 12th wedding anniversary with this surprise trip to the Stanley Hotel. The defendant, Harold Henthorn, knew he was going there to murder his wife. He intended to kill her so that he could collect $4.5 million of life insurance that she did not know about. And on the next day, he took her to a remote area in Rocky Mountain National Park, and he shoved her off a cliff."

Toni Henthorn fell 128 feet, the prosecutor said, landing in the trees and the rocks below. "The fall broke her neck and all the ribs on her right-hand side," said Hazra. "The fall also essentially scalped her. She bled out so much that there was not enough blood left in her for the coroner later to test. The defendant claimed that this— that her death—was an accident. But this was not the first time that the defendant claimed that a wife of his died in an accident."

Hazra then proceeded to tell jurors what Harold never wanted them to hear. "The defendant's first wife, Sandra Lynn Henthorn, also died in a remote location, far from help, where the defendant was the only witness and the sole beneficiary of her life insurance," she said. "And evidence will show you, ladies and gentlemen, that these deaths were not accidents."

And so, due to the century-old precedent of the Brides in the Bath case, Suneeta Hazra would bring before the jury the events of 1995 near Sedalia and of 2011 by Grand Lake. She spoke of the car landing on Lynn Henthorn and the wood crashing onto Toni Henthorn, of the various stories Harold allegedly told, of the massive insurance payouts.

Hazara showed photos of the death scene and of Toni's body and video clips of a ranger struggling to negotiate the steep, rocky descent to the cliff where Toni fell. Another video shot by a drone took jurors on a dizzying plunge from the fall spot. She played sections of Harold's 911 call. And she told the jury a little something about Toni and Harold's relationship, the fast courtship, the marriage, the daughter, the accusations of manipulation and control.

And she told the jury about Harold's alleged lies— about his job, about how his wife died—lies exposed by friends, family, and even a photo: Harold had said he performed mouth-to-mouth resuscitation on his dying wife. Showing a picture to the jury of Toni's face in death, Hazra noted, "Toni Henthorn's lipstick is still intact and on her lips."

Concluding her opening statement, Hazra said, "As you just heard from Judge Jackson, the defendant is charged with the first-degree murder of Toni Henthorn. The elements of first-degree murder are up there on the screen in front of you. It's first, that the defendant caused the death of Toni as named in the indictment. Second, that the defendant killed Toni Henthorn with malice aforethought.

"Third, that the killing was premeditated. And last,

that the killing took place within Rocky Mountain National Park. Malice aforethought means to kill a person deliberately and intentionally. A premeditated killing is one that is the result of planning and deliberation. In determining whether the Government has proved the intent, you may consider the evidence of the death of the defendant's first wife, Sandra Lynn Henthorn.

"And at the conclusion of all this evidence, ladies and gentlemen, Miss Spencer and I will return and ask that you find this defendant, Harold Henthorn, guilty of first-degree murder."

From the audience, Todd Bertolet listened intently and occasionally glanced at Harold at the defense table, unable to see how Harold reacted. "His back was to us the whole time. He never turned around," says Todd. "The only time we could see his face was when they brought him in in handcuffs. In a way, it was kind of sad. He was looking kind of haggard. I'm not feeling sorry for Harold. It's just not the way you want to view anybody." As the prosecutor spoke, Harold sometimes shook his head or took notes on a legal pad. He would whisper something to his attorney, and the attorney would whisper something back. "I think his attorney told him: You sit and be still," says Todd.

Defense attorney Craig Truman began his opening statement in similar fashion to the prosecution, with a narrative, albeit alternate version of what happened on Deer Mountain. "It was over in an instant," Truman told the jury. "Harold Henthorn saw his wife Toni Henthorn sitting on the ledge getting ready to stand up, and as he looked down to his texts coming in from the nanny, she was gone."

This will be proved, he said, by the text messages retrieved from Harold's phone late in the afternoon "on this dreadful day." Truman said Harold's 911 call "came in less than a minute after that"—one of many facts the prosecution would dispute at trial. "He then scrambled down the mountain to get to his wife, and when he found her, she was in a dangerous position," said Truman. "And so he moved her the best he could. She was bleeding and she was in an extreme physical state. He moved her the best he could to get her to a place where he thought she was the safest."

This will be borne out by the audiotapes of the 911 call, he said. "You'll hear how that goes. Here's Mr. Henthorn in extremis, he's hysterical, worried about the death of his wife. She's dying in front of his eyes," he said. "You'll hear Mr. Henthorn asking, please, where's Flight for Life. I don't care what it takes, let's get Flight for Life here, my wife is dying in front of me."

But, said Truman, "There was no helicopter. You'll hear about that. And as he sat and tried to help his wife, he saw her life ebbing away." By the time Ranger Faherty arrived, Harold was "still hysterical," only to be told that his wife was dead and they would have to wait until morning to air-lift out her body.

"Apparently, they couldn't air-lift somebody in to help her, but they could air-lift her in the morning," said Truman, who seemed to suggest the Park Service shared some blame for Toni's death. "Mr. Henthorn said, I'm staying here with my wife. Ranger Faherty said, no, that's not permitted, not at all. You and I are going to hike out, we're going to hike out and the other two rangers are going to stay here and she'd be air-lifted out tomorrow."

Harold arranged for friends to drive him home because "he knew in his condition, he was in no shape to drive back to Denver, and he certainly didn't want to stay at the Stanley Hotel, where they started such a lovely anniversary weekend," said Truman. "Two days later Mr. Henthorn has had the opportunity to go home and to grieve his wife and to tell their young daughter that I need to tell you your mom is gone. I can't imagine what that was like. But he did it."

When Faherty arrived, he came with the map. "You'll hear about this map and see this map," said Truman. "And as you take a close look at it, you'll know what the map means and while there's a lot of discussion about X marks the spot, wait till you see the map. Wait till you see what it actually means." It was the first of several promises that Truman made that suggested the defense had evidence that conflicted with what the investigation uncovered, part of a defense whose theme was not everything was at it seemed.

"The government thinks lightning never strikes twice, that if you win the lottery twice, one is a celebration, one is an investigation, you remember that," he said. "And so they start looking into this [Toni's death]. And then the investigation begins, and it goes back to 1995. And in 1995, Miss Hazra talked with you a little bit about that. But let's talk about the rest of the story."

Taking the jury through the changing of the tire, Truman acknowledged that Harold's actions, including placing the boat jack under the axle, were reasonable only when viewed through the stress of the moment. "It's foolish, but you can see why a person would do it on a Saturday May night in 1995?" he asked. "Now, we don't know what happened. But I can tell you what evidence shows. The evidence shows that Lynn got down to retrieve one of those lug nuts. It will show that one of the jacks, in order to get the requisite height, had been put on a paver. . . . You know what happened? The paver broke."

That caused the Jeep to go down "leaving the vehicle to fall, not all the way, but onto Lynn Henthorn enough so that she was dreadfully injured," he said. "Now, that's the problem with this case for the Government. Because if Douglas County is an accident—and wait till you hear about that—then that's not lightning striking twice. That's an accident in Estes Park. If you take Douglas County away, if that's an accident—and I think, I submit, that that will be proven to you—then it will cause you to look at Estes Park, Rocky Mountain National Park, with new eyes."

The same was true for the injury at the cabin: an accident, he said, proven by the fact that Toni herself reported nothing differently. But the prosecution, he said, wrongly linked the prior events and came to an erroneous conclusion. "After Estes Park, after Rocky Mountain National Park, after the investigators hear about 1995 in Douglas and after they hear about this board incident, they say: My goodness, lightning doesn't strike twice, this is a plan, this is a black widow, this is a circumstance," he said.

"Wait to see the evidence," he continued. "For talk is cheap. I urge you to give some thought to what evidence there is that Harold Henthorn was involved criminally in the death of Lynn Henthorn. Once you hear how this unlikely and unusual turn of events caused her death, you'll know that Douglas County was an accident. Once you hear from Toni Henthorn, from beyond the grave, you'll know exactly what happened in Grand Lake. And then when you come to evaluate what the evidence shows, you'll know what happened in Rocky Mountain National Park. "

On one point, however, Truman acknowledged agreement with the prosecution. "Now, I need to tell you something," he said. "Harold is an unusual—Harold Henthorn is an unusual man. It is true that he didn't have a job. It is true that he told people he did and went to great lengths to have cards made and to talk BS." Making no effort to deny this, Truman said, "You'll hear about that. And for whatever reason, Mr. Henthorn, perhaps vanity, perhaps no self-esteem, had to make up these stories about what his job was. Those things are all true. He made them up. It's a lie."

But the lies stopped there, said Truman, suggesting Harold's inconsistent stories after the deaths of Lynn and Toni were "simply the product of a person in the course of grieving and trauma who doesn't get it all right every time."

To suggest otherwise, he insisted, was to come to the same wrong conclusion the prosecution did. "When you find that Douglas County is an accident and you hear what happened at Grand Lake, Mr. Maximon and I will ask you, based on the evidence, not character assassination, to find that Harold Henthorn did not kill his wife Toni Henthorn, who he loved very much, and we'll ask you to find this man not guilty."

Todd Bertolet now watched Harold more closely. "I'm thinking that he's thinking, like he always has, that this jury is going to believe him," says Todd. Most of Toni's immediate family was there—her two brothers and her father. Her mother had to stay away in the opening days because under court rules as a potential witness she wasn't allowed to watch the proceedings until after her testimony. "Harold never made eye contact with the gallery, would never look at anybody," said Todd. "I knew it bothered him, too, that we all were sitting in the gallery." The opening statements had the Bertolets feeling confident about the strength of the prosecution's case and the weakness of the defense's, knowing at trial anything could happen. "O.J. Simpson got off," said Todd.

The opening statements ended with plenty of court

day left, so the judge ordered testimony to begin. It started with the prosecution, which has the burden of proving guilt beyond a reasonable doubt, calling as its first witness Toni's brother, Barry Bertolet. Normally a relative comes to the stand to put a human face on the victim and the impact of her death, but in this case Barry had more substantial evidence to share. He spoke of how in the weeks after his sister's death Harold's stories changed at least four times and how Harold rebuffed Toni's family and had her cremated. Barry also analyzed the text messages from Harold from the mountain about Toni's vital signs: "I believe it to be inconsistent with her ultimate injuries."

Park Service personnel followed Barry to the stand, a dispatcher who had been on the line with Harold during the 911 call insisting, "I did not believe he was doing CPR." To try to back her up, the prosecution played parts of the call. Ranger Mark Faherty testified about interviewing Harold at his home, in which Harold said he was looking at the babysitter text when his wife fell— an account he'd later change. And Faherty spoke of confronting Harold with the X on the map. "When I showed him this, he hemmed and hawed before he gave an explanation," Faherty said. "He wasn't sure why there was an X roughly where Toni fell."

The second day of the trial brought home the horror of Toni's death plunge when the prosecution showed videos and photos of the area. Her father, Robert Bertolet, kept his head down and wiped tears as pictures of her body were displayed for the jury on large video monitors. The family had not seen the photos until now. "I didn't know how badly my sister had been injured," said her brother Todd. "I had wanted to see the photos, but as I sit here today I wished I hadn't seen them." Toni's father reacted the same way. "The one picture that was there that kind of caught me off guard was of Toni's body laying there with a cover over it," said her father. "I see her body and I wanted her to get up and say, 'Hi, daddy,' or something. But you know it's not going to happen."

Ranger Paul Larson sought to give the jury a sense of how remote and steep the final hike was to the cliff, saying that when another ranger tried to re-create the hike she at times had to get down on all fours and scoot along so she too wouldn't go over the edge.

Toni's fall, he said, was so violent that it knocked off both of her hiking boots, yet strangely her camera was found in good condition next to her body. The camera back was missing, otherwise it was intact.

As with other testimony, jurors in Judge Jackson's court were allowed to ask questions of the witness, a procedure seldom seen but allowable under the law. The questions were submitted in writing and the lawyers would privately work out with the judge at sidebar which ones could be answered.

"Was it strange," one juror asked, "[that] Toni's camera was found so close to her body?"

"I find it interesting the camera was that close," said Larson, adding he was surprised it wasn't farther from her body.

Park Ranger Paul Larson also brought to light an unusual development in the case, testifying that Toni was wearing her wedding ring set when she was hiking but that the diamond—worth $30,000—was missing by the time her body got to the morgue.

Other witnesses would speak further on this, but in the meantime another Park Service worker, Supervisory Ranger Mark Pita, answered the defense's question about why a Flight for Life helicopter wasn't dispatched the night Toni fell. He said that was because the area was too rugged to safely land after dark. It was, he said in response to a juror question, too rugged he thought for anyone to be hiking through. "To me it was surprising that someone would go down there," Pita said. "It was an unusual, rugged spot that was difficult to get to."

After a lunch break came the most tortuous testimony for Toni's family, that of Larimer County's forensic pathologist, James Wilkerson, who conducted the autopsy. Toni's father and Todd left the courtroom. "My brother Barry and my wife stayed," said Todd. "Barry's a doctor and my wife's a registered nurse. They're more capable of handling those photos." Those who stayed gasped and one woman uttered, "Oh, my God," when the first photos appeared on the monitors showing the extensive injuries to Toni's body. One of Toni's friends dropped to her knees and hid her face. Other members of her family dabbed tears as Wilkerson described close-up images.

The photos came with Wilkerson listing Toni's many injuries: punctured lungs, thirteen broken rips, a two-inch gash to her liver and the horrendous head injury that left her virtually scalped. But as difficult as the testimony and photos were, he said they revealed important information—and raised questions. The old scars on Toni's knees gave him pause to wonder why a woman with bad knees would have gone on such a difficult hike. The lack of injury to her breastbone and her perfectly applied lipstick cast doubt on whether Harold performed CPR for an hour as he'd claimed. And the extent of the bleeding would have put her into severe shock and become critical within thirty to forty-five minutes.

But there was one thing the injuries couldn't tell him: "I couldn't determine whether it was an accident or whether, with some of the unusual or suspicious circumstances, it was a homicide," Wilkerson told the jury. "You can't tell the difference between a fall and a push."

Another member of the medical examiner's staff, Deputy Coroner Jere Gunderson, recalled his conversation with Harold shortly after Toni's death. Harold delivered a "matter-of-fact" and unemotional account of her death fall, which Gunderson found odd. When asked about the missing diamond, Harold said it was worth $30,000, another strange comment under the circumstances, said Gunderson, who'd never heard a family member of a dead person speak of lost jewelry or its value.

Under cross-examination by Craig Truman, however, Gunderson acknowledged that Harold also said the ring's value didn't matter anymore.

The deputy coroner also elaborated on his direct testimony about receiving an anonymous letter revealing that Harold's first wife had also died under suspicious circumstances. That prompted Gunderson to contact the funeral home seeking the clothing that Toni had been wearing when she died, but the clothing had by then already been washed.

The cross-examination yielded little more information, the defense using its questioning of prosecution witnesses to clarify issues and raise the occasional point in Harold's favor, but scoring no knockouts. This meant the already brisk pace of the trial accelerated, and by day three, on Thursday, September 10, the prosecution's case was reaching its mid-point.

Daniel Jarvis, the lifelong family friend who considered Harold as an uncle, recounted how Harold would describe himself as a fundraising consultant working out of the basement of his house, when in fact, the prosecution showed through other evidence, there was no such employment. He talked about the day Harold said he was away on business instead of attending church, when in fact the cell phone records showed he was visiting Rocky Mountain National Park. He recalled how Harold told him a different account of Toni's fall, how he'd received a call from his daughter about her soccer game when Toni went over the cliff, when he'd told other people it was a text from the babysitter. Harold told Daniel that Toni had fallen about thirty feet, when in fact the plunge measured more than four times that. And he told Daniel that Toni had left $1 million in life insurance in a trust for Haley that Harold couldn't touch, when in fact there was $4.5 million in insurance, all coming to Harold.

But the most important part of Daniel's testimony centered on the map. He spoke of Harold telling him that a ranger was making a big deal out of a Park Service map found in his Jeep—a map that Harold claimed to Daniel showed only restaurants in Estes Park. Harold told Daniel nothing of the pink X marking the spot near where Toni died.

One of the jurors asked Daniel: "Had Mr. Henthorn ever given you a map before?"

"Yes," he said, "when I first moved to Denver, he printed a map that showed the highways to his cabin up in Grand Lake."

The judge asked, "Had he ever given you a map of hiking routes?"

"No," said Daniel.

Tamara Gordon, the photographer, testified about how Harold told her that Toni was taking a picture of him when he looked down and then she was gone. Tamara described her uncomfortable experience making the memorial slide show, with Harold having already picked out dozens of photos and the music, and how he didn't cry, even though Tamara did.

"He was talking about how blessed he was to be able to have Haley because his first wife was not able to have children," she said. "And at that point he started sharing with us how he had lost his first wife in a car accident."

"What did he say about that?" asked prosecutor Valeria Spencer.

"He said that they were—what I recall is that he said that they were on their way home from an event and it was at night and it was icy and that they slid into a tree. And I seem to remember him talking about headlights, maybe blinding them or something."

"So she was killed but he was okay?"

"He said she was killed instantly and that he was not hurt."

Once again, the defense did nothing to prolong the trial. Harold's attorney had no questions for cross-examination, but the jurors did, asking Tamara about the 2008 photo session in which Toni seemed fragile and Harold had orchestrated everything.

"When working with Mr. Henthorn did you feel that you had no control over the session? Was it his way or the highway?"

"I don't know if I would state it quite that extreme, but, yes, he was very controlling the entire process. From the minute he scheduled the shoot all the way through ordering the pictures, he wasn't happy with the pictures the first go-around. We had to go back and reprint the entire order. We helped him frame the pictures. We went to his home. We helped him hang the pictures. And so he decided when he was going to pay us and how much he was going to pay us. So, yeah, he controlled the entire thing."

The trial was now moving so quickly that the prosecution was caught off guard. "We will confess we didn't expect no cross of all these witnesses," said Suneeta Hazra. "So we don't have another witness. We tried to get another one here. She home-schools her children and can't find childcare. I apologize but we don't have anyone else. . . . We are way ahead of schedule, and I apologize. We just thought they would cross people more." Court adjourned for the afternoon until the prosecution could bring their next witness.

The next day, September 14, Dennis Dahl, a close friend of Harold's, testified he'd always thought Harold worked as an independent fundraiser for charities. It was only after Toni died that Harold admitted that he had been unemployed all those years. Harold explained he cooked up the fake job so that Toni's family wouldn't be unhappy with her moving from Mississippi to Colorado to be with him.

"He said it was Toni's idea," testified Dahl.

Like other witnesses, Dahl recounted how irritated Harold seemed about being under scrutiny in Toni's death. Harold felt the sting of insinuations he'd stolen Toni's diamond. "He said it was a horrible accusation," said Dahl—and at one point suggested rounding up his friends to go to National Park to look for it.

Next, twenty years after pulling over to the side of the road to help a couple with a flat tire, Patricia Montoya came to court to recall how they came upon more than they'd bargained for: a woman pinned under the Jeep and a man losing his grip, shouting, "Don't touch her! Leave her alone!"

"He was a little frantic." Montoya said of Harold. "He was very angry. We didn't understand why."

It was particularly puzzling since the man had flagged them down in the first place. Yet the man didn't seem to want anyone in Montoya's group to give his wife CPR, didn't offer to put his own coat on her—a "real nice jacket," she said—despite the cold, just kept pacing back and forth.

When the sirens approached, people in her group let out a cheer, but not the man. "I looked over and he had this really scared look on his face," she said.

For years, Patricia had nightmares about the lady under the Jeep. Seeking some understanding, she even went to the woman's funeral. "The whole thing was creepy, you remember things like that, it was one of the creepiest things that I had ever come upon in my life," she said. "They were married but he wouldn't do anything to help her."

During cross-examination, Truman took aim at why the Montoya group left before the paramedics got there. Patricia said the four adults had dispensed with a twelve-pack of beer. "Drinking had a little bit to do with leaving," she said, "but it wasn't enough beer to stop us from helping."

Testifying next, Dwight Devries said he suffered no nightmares, only a lingering sense of puzzlement over why the man changing a tire in the dark woods didn't want Devries' help. Devries described Harold's demeanor as brusque. "It just really felt strange."

By the time the next witness, Roxanne Burns, arrived on the scene with the rest of the paramedics, Harold "wasn't very upset." Strangest of all, though, was Harold revealing that his wife was changing the tire because he didn't know how to do it. "Odd," said Burns.

On cross-examination, Truman honed in on Burns' characterization of Harold's demeanor.

"You didn't smell any alcohol or anything?"

"No, I didn't."

"And if you had, of course, you would have reported that?"

"Yes."

"And you could imagine from his pacing that he was nervous?"

"I would imagine, yes."

"And he was concerned, having asked about his wife two or three times: Is she going to be okay?"

"Yes."

"And then later, you told him, in explanation: Here's what's going to happen. She's got a pulse now."

"Yes."

"And he went with her?"

"He did not go with her."

"He stayed at the scene?"

"Yes."

"Cooperated with other authorities?"

"At the time, I remember the detective asking him to sit in the back of the police car."

"And he complied?"

"Yes."

Jurors appeared particularly interested in Lynn's death. One asked in writing: "Could the EMTs tell where Lynn was crushed? Was it evident?"

"I could not answer that question because I wasn't the one that worked on her," said Burns. "And I didn't write the report."

Another asked: "Did she have any obvious head injuries?"

"I don't believe so," said Burns.

"In your professional experience as an EMT, how do loved ones of the injured typically react at the scene?" asked a juror.

"Usually they're crying, screaming. I've had people

punch me. I've had people grab me. Usually they're very upset and they're screaming."

"If a loved one is in shock, how do they typically act at the scene?" a juror asked.

"Again, usually during an accident people are usually crying, screaming, yelling, pacing, very upset."

This interest prompted the defense to go back to Burns and ask more questions.

"Miss Burns, had you ever seen Harold Henthorn before that night?" asked Truman.

"No," she said.

"Have you seen him before that time since 1995 and until this time?"

"I've seen him on the news."

"You don't know him?"

"No."

"You don't know how he reacts to shocking situations?"

"That's correct."

"And in your experience, you've seen people who scream and yell?"

"Yes."

"And some people, not most, but some shut down, don't they?"

"I've never seen someone shut down."

"And when they shut down, they don't say anything, and people have to pry information out of them?"

"I imagine so, but I've never had that experience. I've usually had people screaming and yelling at me to do something."

"So you've never seen anyone who's in shock and numb in all of your EMT experience?"

"I can honestly say I've never seen anybody shut down on an accident scene."

This busy court day also featured the testimony by

Toni's mother, Yvonne Bertolet, who recounted how Harold denigrated the Park Service ranger as an incompetent "Barney Fife." She also told the jury how Harold insisted on cremating Toni's remains against the wishes of the family, insisting that it was Toni's wish even though there was no evidence of that in her will. Yvonne's testimony meant that, for the first time since Harold had cut the family off, she could look him in the eye—and that's what she did, never taking her gaze off of him as she spoke. "I wanted him to know that I was strong enough to say what I needed to say and I didn't fear him," she said. "I think he wanted me to fear him. I just showed him that I didn't."

The next day, September 15, the trial continued to focus on Lynn's death with the testimony of the original investigators, including Jason Kennedy, who described Harold as "visibly shaken" after the Jeep crushed his wife. "His eyes were very wide," said Kennedy. "They were darting around surveying the scene."

Kennedy recalled taking pictures at the scene and when the photo of the shoeprint on the fender flashed on the monitor a woman in the courtroom gasped, "Oh, my God."

The photo also resonated with the jury, who asked about it.

"It would be hard to get a shoe that high on the vehicle," Kennedy said. "It was possibly a point of pushing off."

In the end, Kennedy said, he had his doubts about Lynn's death being an accident. "It was a suspicious incident," Kennedy said. "I had a feeling that there was more to what happened. I felt we needed additional investigation."

That extra investigation wouldn't happen for another two decades, testified Detective Dave Weaver, who described his reenactments on the look-a-like Jeep. He testified that no matter how hard they tried to get the Jeep to fall off the jack by tossing the tire, "We were unable to duplicate what was described by Mr. Henthorn in 1995." The only way he could do it was by pushing the Jeep off the jack by putting a foot roughly where the shoeprint was found and giving it "a lot of force."

Weaver endured the most strenuous cross-examination of the trial by Truman about his methodology, but acknowledged he couldn't replicate everything, including the exact conditions on the ground.

"Did you account for the vegetation being different?" Truman asked.

"I can't tell you if the exact vegetation was or if the rocks were the same," he said.

He also said he had not sent the shoeprint to the FBI or the Colorado Bureau of Investigation for testing, explaining that there was nothing to compare the photo against. The shoes Harold had worn that night were not available and the pictures taken of the bottom of his shoes were too blurry.

Grace Rishell came to testify about the aftermath of her former sister-in-law's death, how Harold said, "My bride is gone"—the same thing he texted her seventeen years later on the night of Toni's death.

Harold texted the same phrase to a close friend, Lee Hettick, around the same time, Hettick testified. When Hettick asked how Toni fell, Harold gave yet another version, saying he was trying to figure out how to work a new cell phone at the time and didn't see much, Hettick told the jury.

Hettick added that Harold never expressed any

responsibility after Lynn's death and appeared mostly annoyed at the Park Service after Toni's death, complaining, "I can't believe this has happened to me."

"He felt park rangers wanted to make a name for themselves," said Hettick, who quoted Harold as saying, "If Toni hadn't gotten herself killed in the park, I wouldn't have all these problems."

The prosecution wrapped up its presentation of evidence on the sixth day of trial with the testimony of one of those rangers, Beth Shott. Taking the stand on September 17, she gave the highlights of the investigation, noting that Harold was never out of official sights after Toni's death. She said a tracker had been placed on his car and that agents occasionally conducted surveillance by FBI teams.

As with all the cross-examinations, this one didn't go far and at one point took a strange turn when Craig Truman suggested that surveillance was even more extensive.

"There's also some drones?" he asked.

"No," she said, "well we did some drone footage that the jury saw"—the aerial video of the fall site—"but that was the only drones we had."

"There weren't any drones following Mr. Henthorn around?"

"No."

"No Uber Hawk drone that followed Mr. Henthorn's daily life?"

It wasn't clear what brought this on, though Harold had been under surveillance off and on for the last year.

"Not that I know of," she said, though she couldn't speak for what the FBI may have been doing.

Juror questions focused mostly on the circumstances of Toni's fall.

"At the fall spot," one asked, "what was the ground like? Was there room to lie down, how comfortable or uncomfortable would it be to do so?"

"If we're talking about the top of the cliff," she began, alluding to Harold's claims the couple had gone to a place for romantic time, "there's no place to lie down. It is an eroded top of a cliff. It's an outcropping of rock. It's not soft soil or anything like that. It's just an undulated, rocky, eroded top. There are places where you could sit, but it's not comfortable."

"And if the question were talking about the bottom of the fall?" asked the judge, referring to the area where Harold said he had to move Toni to a better place for CPR.

"The bottom of the fall is a small area," said Shott. "There is some soil. If you recall the photo of where Toni Henthorn's body lay, that would be the only place to lay down. It falls off, it continues to go down the slope pretty quickly past where the body was lying. So really that's the only place where you could lie down."

Another juror asked, "Did the computers contain anything pertaining to Harold's business?" This related to the computers taken from Harold's home by authorities, who under subpoena searched the hard drives.

"Yes, sort of," Shott said. "We saw a lot of business cards, files that were profiles of business cards for Resource Development Services and Development Services, which was the name of his alleged business. And then there was a fabricated card, you know, to be printed off for Development Services. But there were no client files, there were no financial files, there was nothing to indicate this was a real business."

"Next question," said the judge, reading the card. "Can you see a body from the cliff?"

"Well, depends on exactly where the body is. Looking down from the top of the cliff, you could actually see a person standing in that impact tree. And we know that her body fell through that impact tree and really there's nowhere else to go past that. So you would be able to see a body from the top of the cliff."

A juror asked, "Were binoculars recovered anywhere?" A photo taken by Harold showed Toni peering through binoculars.

"There were no binoculars ever recovered anywhere on the site. We did not look for them in the residence. But they were not ever recovered on the site."

What was recovered, Shott said, was the diamond missing from Toni's wedding ring set. During the initial search of the scene shortly after her death, nobody saw a diamond. But when rangers returned the following May—eight months later—there was the diamond on the ground.

A juror asked, "Do you have any explanation of how the diamond suddenly showed up?"

Shott said, "I do not." But when she searched Harold's computer, she did find invoices for diamond sales. "The defendant claimed to have a business selling and brokering diamonds. Whereas he did buy diamonds, sell them to friends and charged them tax, he never had a business that we were able to determine."

Shott was the last prosecution witness. After six swift days, the government rested its case.

The defense witness list, submitted before trial, was short. It amounted to five witnesses, none relating directly to Toni's death:

- Brock McCoy, the sergeant supervising the investigation into Lynn's death

- Wesley Riber, the former coroner investigator on the Lynn case
- Jeffery Schippel, the volunteer paramedic who gave CPR to Lynn.
- Tara Mendozza of the Colorado Brain and Spine Institute.
- Jennifer Moroye-Yong of Swedish Medical Center, to talk about Toni's injury from the deck incident.

It was a lean-enough presentation, all intended to address Lynn's death and Toni's injury at the cabin, until the defense sprung a surprise. Judge Jackson asked Truman how the defense planned to proceed after the prosecution rested. Truman said the defense also would rest. It wouldn't call any of those five witnesses. And it wouldn't call Harold.

NINETEEN

The courtroom was packed with family, friends, media, the public curious for summations in the case of the United States versus Harold Henthorn. Seats came at a premium. Outside, those who couldn't get in grumbled. Inside, tensions ran high. "Spectators were testy, some cussing because they had to squeeze in so close together," the *Denver Post* observed. "It was sweaty." Harold wore a gray dress shirt, with no tie. He appeared alternately impassive and tense.

It was 9 A.M. on September 18, 2015—two weeks shy of what would have been the Henthorns' fifteenth wedding anniversary.

"Ladies and gentlemen of the jury," began Assistant U.S. Attorney Suneeta Hazra, "on September 29, 2012, this defendant, Harold Henthorn, deliberately and intentionally pushed his wife off a 128-foot cliff. He murdered her in this brutal and violent manner to collect $4.7 million. The government has proved beyond a reasonable doubt the defendant committed first-degree murder when he shoved Toni Henthorn off that cliff, the cliff that he had scouted in advance with an X on the map."

After this introduction, Hazra took a brief side trip and brought jurors through the legal elements of the crime of murder—that it is conducted with malice aforethought and premeditated. She then went back to what the prosecution called the beginning: the death of Harold's first wife. "The government has not charged this defendant with Lynn Henthorn's death," she noted. "That's not the case before you. You don't need to decide that." She noted that under the law, jurors needed to only decide, by a preponderance of evidence—more likely than not—that Lynn Henthorn did not die by an accident. The legal distinction is narrow; the emotional one immense.

"There are many unanswered questions to what happened in 1995," she said. "And 20 years later, they may not all get answered." But, she insisted, the parallels to Toni Henthorn's death were clear: the remote location, the suspicious circumstances—"The tire was not even flat, yet he pulled over to change it"—the changing stories about what happened, his apparent callousness.

"We also know what he did that night in that he refused to help Lynn," she said. "He didn't cover her with his coat. He didn't pull her out from under the car, he didn't perform CPR on her, he did nothing to assist his wife as she lay dying."

What evidence remained, she said, didn't match his evolving stories. "There's a footprint on the wheel hub," she said. "There's the question of how could someone crawl that far under the car to get the lug nuts or flashlight or whatever story the defendant told." To reach those lug nuts required a tight squeeze under a car on a jack. "The defendant claims that Lynn just sort of scampered under there and he goes back and two seconds later, he doesn't see she's there. Whoops! That doesn't add up. Use your common sense, ladies and gentlemen."

Then afterward, he didn't reveal all about Lynn's life insurance. "You can use this evidence," said Hazra, "to form your determination of how he killed Toni Henthorn. The defendant learned from the death of Lynn. He learned many things. Most importantly, you can kill wives to get money. It worked well for him the first time. He learned that if you tell some sort of story to the cops, they will go away. It doesn't necessarily have to be the same story. You just need to come up with a version. And that's something the defendant is very good at doing."

The Good Samaritans, Devries and the Montoya group, nearly thwarted his plans, she said. "He knew his next stop for the next murder had to be farther, more remote, so help couldn't come," she said. "What he didn't count on, ladies and gentlemen, was that the location he picked for his next crime was in the park." A national park, not under the jurisdiction of local sheriff's deputies, who, she implied, had been too inexperienced to read into his shifting stories.

Showing a chart to the jury, Hazra traced the evolution of the insurance policies, not to suggest that Toni was unaware of some of them—she clearly was—but that Harold didn't reveal how the policies accumulated. He never told her that instead of canceling one and replacing it with another, the policies grew in number and size, eventually reaching $4.7 million. He paid for the policies secretly from bank accounts that only he controlled, the paperwork sent to a post office box that he used. "He was the one that got all the correspondence from the bank, he was the one that checked it, he's the only one that knew the checks were going out," said Hazra. He kept up those policies that she did not know about."

And in April 2011, just when the beneficiary of one policy is changed from their daughter to Harold, a piece of wood falls on Toni's head at their cabin in Grand Lake, the prosecutor said. "Here's the thing about the Grand Lake incident, ladies and gentlemen, it doesn't add up either," said the prosecutor. "It's another squirrely incident involving this defendant, in the evening, in a remote location, doing something that doesn't make sense."

In June 2012, Toni Henthorn opened her first solo bank account since their marriage at First Bank, the prosecutor said, citing the financial records. "She immediately diverts some money into that, as the defendant was well aware, since it came out of an account he knows about. After that we have nine trips to Rocky Mountain National Park." Nine trips by Harold Henthorn, backed up by cell phone records tracing his movements. The trips started on August 16 and ended Sept. 20. "Trips," she said, "looking for the best place to kill his wife."

Harold never told anyone about these trips. In his interview with Ranger Mark Faherty he said he'd taken maybe one, and that was to a different side of Deer Mountain, "the one that makes sense with the nice views of the meadow overlooking Longs Peak." He didn't admit that he'd gone to the north side, telling one friend only that he likes to scout hiking trails. "He never said anything about going nine times because he can't, because no one goes nine times to scout out trails unless you're looking for the best place to murder someone, a place remote enough and far enough away, but a place you can still plausibly somewhat sell as a reason to be there."

On September 9, 2012, he went to Rocky Mountain National Park for most of the day—a Sunday—and the next day Harold spoke to Toni's office manager, Tammi Abbruscato, about arranging the fake patient schedule so he could whisk her away for their anniversary. He went again on September 16, the day he told his close friend Daniel Jarvis that he had to skip church for a business meeting.

At some point, Harold found the location he wanted. "The X marks the spot," Hazra said. "He also, in one of these nine trips, probably plotted his coordinates, figured out in advance where his longitude and latitude would be so he could get back to this place."

On the weekend of their anniversary, he told people about going to the Stanley Hotel but didn't mention that he had a "rugged hiking trip" planned because "that wouldn't make sense" in light of Toni's age and bad knees. "This wasn't going to be some mountaineering trip. They were going to go to the Stanley, they were going to have a nice time, and as part of that they would maybe go do some gentle walking," she said, as Toni's backpack, stocked modestly, suggested.

After spending Friday night at the Stanley, where they took pictures of their hotel room and themselves on the grounds, they set out for the Deer Mountain hike, leaving at 1:30 P.M. "It's a moderately difficult hike," she said. "It's about 6 miles round trip. And you gain a significant amount of elevation. It's a decent hike."

They veered off the trail, Harold claimed, to get away from people so they could have private time, yet photos the couple took showed nobody was around that day. "It's actually fairly deserted," said Hazra. Showing the jury aerial and ground photos of the trail, Hazra traced the Henthorns' itinerary that led them off the path to the remote spot where they had lunch. Although Harold called it a "use trail," no such path existed. "Once you leave the established Deer Mountain Trail, you can't see where you're going, you don't know where to head back," said Hazra. "Pretty much once the Henthorns left this trail, Toni Henthorn was entirely dependent on the defendant to get back to the trail."

By the time they finished lunch, it was 3:50 P.M., with 7 P.M. dinner reservations set at an expensive restaurant. Showing one of the last photos of Toni, the prosecutor said, "Toni Henthorn, you can see from the pictures, does not look like the type of woman that wants to show up for a nice anniversary dinner in jeans and a sweaty pink T-shirt from hiking all day. She probably wanted a little bit of time to freshen up. But they don't head back at 3:59 P.M. in the afternoon. No," said the prosecutor. "Instead they go down this rocky scree to the spot where the defendant will eventually push Toni off that cliff."

Showing the jury GoPro video of the next leg of the hike taken by rangers, Hazra reminded them how steep it was to get to the spot where Toni plunged. "It's a hard spot for even experienced hikers," she said, "and it made no sense for a couple in their 50s." This flew in the face of Harold's explanation they went there to look for wild turkeys—no wildlife pictures were found on Toni's camera—or to catch a better view—the view got no better the lower they went, she said. Romantic time, his other explanation, seemed the most farfetched of all, the terrain so steep and rocky.

From here she fell 128 feet, an event for which Harold had a number of accounts, said the prosecutor. "In some she's walking behind him, in some she's walking rapidly around him," said Hazra. "He says she's fiddling with the camera or fiddling with the phone."

"Ladies and gentlemen," she continued, "the evidence proves that all these stories are lies, and you know they're lies." The camera, for instance, suffered little damage and was likely placed next to her body by Harold. She couldn't have been on her phone, since her cell-phone was in her office. He couldn't have been looking at the text from the babysitter since the times don't line up with the phone records. "It's just simply a lie that he's looking at the text," said Hazra.

From the phone records, she argued that Harold had turned off his phone less than an hour into the hike at 2:18 P.M. "to make sure that no one would bother him and no one would interfere with his plan to murder his wife." He snaps a photo of Toni at 3:24 P.M. from the lunch spot with the view behind her; another photo is taken at 3:52 P.M. from the same location, then at 4:44 P.M. a photo is taken from the top of the cliff, Harold posing in a white T-shirt, up there so long he put on a long-sleeved shirt. "In this one," she said, showing the jury the photo, "he's just looking back at Toni, standing on top of the ledge."

The text from the babysitter arrived at 5:54 P.M., and a minute later Harold called 911 from the bottom of the hill. "He pushed Toni at 5:10 P.M.," said Hazra—just ten minutes after the last photo was taken.

The prosecutor reminded the jury that Harold didn't call 911 from the top of the cliff. "He looks over, he could see her body in that impact tree, he doesn't call 911 then, he doesn't call them on the way down," she said. "Instead, he gathers up his backpack, gathers up her backpack and leisurely makes his way down. He then drags her out of the spot and only then calls 911."

Based on the testimony from the coroner, Toni lived from twenty minutes to an hour. "Here's the thing, la-dies and gentlemen, she's dead in 20 minutes. She's dead before he even calls 911," said Hazra. Toni was probably dead when he got to her at the bottom of the cliff, dead when he first called 911, and dead when Harold texted her brother her vital signs. By the time an officer coached Harold through CPR, Toni likely was dead for well over an hour. "He did not sound like someone that was doing CPR on his wife, and that's because she was already dead."

When he first reached her, he didn't act like somebody trying to save a severely wounded person, the prosecutor said. "He didn't cradle her body," Hazra said, showing a photo of the blood-spotted landing area. "She's bleeding out of her head, she's bleeding profusely, she's just fallen and severely injured. He doesn't cradle her body and try to gently move her. Instead he drags her down these rocks—boom, boom, boom—her head hitting them. It's not the way you treat a stranger, let alone a wife you supposedly loved."

In the 911 call, he downplayed the incident, saying she fell only about thirty feet and suffered a concussion, all the while seemingly more concerned about when he'll get picked up than for his wife's well-being. He rattled off the coordinates he already knew from scoping the location and texted her brother, never asking the cardiologist for medical advice, then texted friends, making arrangements to be picked up.

"Let's talk about what the defendant does after he's murdered Toni," said the prosecutor, shifting to the next key area of her argument. "He didn't say: I feel so bad, I can't believe I took her to this spot, none of it. He doesn't have any remorse—because he killed her."

He then spun a variety of stories about how she died. "It's because he can't actually say what happened, so he has to constantly give lies," said Hazra. "It's the lesson he learned from Lynn Henthorn's death in 1995." The prosecutor counted more than twenty versions Harold gave of Toni's death. In the immediate aftermath, he scrambled to get Toni's cellphone and to crack into her computer, then quickly filed the life insurance claims "because he needs to get his money." A fast cremation followed, just as he'd done with Lynn, "so there is no more physical evidence," then he cashed out Toni's bank account and tried to concoct a cover story for the X on the map by telling Daniel Jarvis that the map was made for him.

"He spent months, weeks, days, countless hours planning how to kill his wife," she said. "That evidence is what is called circumstantial. Yes, but as you know, circumstantial evidence is just as good as direct evidence. And look at how much you have here. Use your common sense, ladies and gentlemen, look at the inferences. What those two were doing on the side of Deer Mountain makes no sense unless you were there to kill your wife and get money."

In the end, said Hazra, "This defendant viewed Toni Henthorn, like Lynn before her, as a way to get rich. And on September 29, 2012, he took Toni Henthorn up there to cash in. The last human touch Toni Henthorn ever felt was not the loving caress from her spouse but, instead, a push from him, a push from this defendant, a push that shoved her, that sent her cascading over a cliff that's taller than the seventh floor of this courtroom, a push that broke her body and tore he scalp off and ended her life, a push that deprived Haley Henthorn of her mother and Yvonne and Bob Bertolet of their daughter."

After a fifteen-minute break to give the court reporter a respite, summations resumed with the defense.

"Ladies and gentlemen, the case here we're to consider is murder, and it's murder in Rocky Mountain National Park," began Craig Truman. "That's what we gathered together 10 days ago to present to you and to have you answer the questions framed by the instructions given to you by Judge Jackson: Has the government proven their case? Have they proven that Harold Henthorn murdered his wife Toni Henthorn with malice aforethought? Have they proven that?"

Coming to that conclusion, Truman suggested, would not be easy and he urged the jury to take time going over the evidence. "In the end, we believe and submit to you that this case is a difficult case," he said. "It is one you're going to have to spend a great deal of time on." It was a classic reasonable-doubt defense, constructed through the deconstruction of the prosecution's case.

Only there was one difference: a concession. Truman conceded that one thing will become clear about Harold Henthorn. "He had behaved in a foolish and reckless manner, and you will hear me go over that time and time again," said Truman. "Mr. Henthorn may not want to hear that, but you will hear it from us, for his character has been assassinated, and he has earned that by his actions."

It was a risky, but perhaps necessary move —one intended to win some credibility with a jury that had just heard a powerful story from Hazra linking lying to murder. In the absence of witnesses, it was Harold's lies that the prosecution sought to prove betrayed criminal intent, lies that when taken together in context held the power of a confession. This required the jury to draw an inference, an inference the defense suggested amounted to a logical leap too far. Truman sought to draw a distinction between what looked bad and what was truly and legally bad enough to convict. "We'll talk about, not speculation, not gee-it-must-have-been or could-have-been, but we're going to talk about evidence, what has been proven and what has not. So let's begin."

Starting with the anniversary weekend, Truman said

that Harold had planned the getaway "as he always does things, obsessive compulsively to try to get everything set up perfectly." This included creating the dummy patient list so that Toni would be surprised, scheduling a babysitter, even arranging for a friend to pick up Toni's car at the clinic. "It's not the first time that they had exotic, romantic interludes for their anniversary," he said, citing one witness who had babysat Haley for previous getaways.

"They go to the Stanley Hotel. They have a wonderful room. I don't understand these people that take pictures all the time, but it apparently happens quite a bit. They have a picture of their room that they Tweet out to their friends or send to their friends—text—I have no idea," said Truman. "But they take a picture of the room. They have a nice dinner, and the next morning they get up on their anniversary day, and they have a romantic breakfast. We know that. We know that they were going to take a hike."

Truman conceded that Toni had bad knees—"true enough"—but that didn't stop her from hiking. One witness, he pointed out, said the couple had hiked together, "not strenuous, but they had taken hikes." He called the Deer Lake Trail a "moderate hike," one that Toni was completely prepared for. "She has her boots and her backpack. She knows that there is going to be a hike. This is a family that has a cabin in Grand Lake. This is a family that goes to Rocky Mountain National Park like you and I go to City Park," he said. "They're there all the time. And so Toni Henthorn is ready, willing and able to take a hike."

Contrary to the prosecutor's suggestion, he said, "It's a crowded day at the park" because the government had waived the entrance fee for that day. "They take a hike, there are too many people, and they get off-trail," he said. "Now, thank goodness, unlike me who would never take pictures, but thank goodness, there's pictures not only of this hike, but there's pictures of them going off-trail. You've seen Toni Henthorn. You've seen her, she's not being taken in a hammerlock off the trail."

After lunch, also documented in photos, they hike farther down. "Now, why would somebody do that? How could that possibly be?" he asked. "Thank goodness there are the pictures because the pictures are evidence to show that Toni Henthorn went down there, one, willingly, and secondly: Who's taking the pictures of Mr. Henthorn standing up there looking out over the view? Who's taking the pictures? It's Toni Henthorn."

Whether this view is any better than one they could have had higher up "is in the eye of the beholder," he said. "You've heard the rangers say over and over again, it's a beautiful, fabulous spot. Both the lunch spot and the cliff. Now, perhaps it was a mistake going down there because the views were only just as good, but how are they to know?"

Describing Harold as a "fellow who plans everything," Truman acknowledged Harold had visited the Park "many times, stayed in the park, and went to Grand Lake" to their cabin. "The government says he's not planning a romantic anniversary weekend, he's planning murder. Well, let's see what the evidence of that is," said Truman. "Now, Sherlock Holmes tells us that any time there's a crime, not only is there something picked up by the perpetrator but there's something left behind. What do we have here?"

Truman suggested the only evidence they had was the existence of a cliff. "What is the evidence that she was pushed? Tell me one witness from the government's many that said they know she was pushed," he said. "In fact, the evidence is exactly the opposite." He cited the coroner's conclusion that there was no way to tell from her injuries whether she had been pushed or fell. "Is there any evidence of any scuffle on the ledge?" he asked. "Not a one."

As for the timing of Toni's death, Truman said the coroner again was "unable to tell any specific times" but that if there had been a helicopter sent to the scene "she was survivable." But Rocky Mountain National Park didn't send one. He mocked the Park policy as: "We don't use the helicopter because it's too difficult and it costs too much." Yet seventeen years earlier the volunteer fire department in Douglas County was able to get a Flight for Life helicopter to Lynn Henthorn in the middle of the night and actually got her going again."

"Now, Mr. Henthorn is down there. He's on the phone. Now, I have no idea why he's on the phone that much," said Truman, but he suggested that Harold did seek medical advice from Toni's brother when they discussed her vital signs and CPR.

Truman argued that by the time Toni's body was being autopsied, authorities "had signed it out essentially as an accident," releasing her clothes and her body to the mortuary. The dispatcher who coached Harold in CPR never voiced any suspicions at the time or expressed any fear he wasn't properly doing CPR.

"What caused that change?" he asked of the course of the investigation. "These anonymous letters. Holy smoke, Mr. Henthorn's first wife died, this is very suspicious, and that's what changed everything."

Going back to Lynn's death, Truman noted that at the time then-Investigator Robert McMahan—"now Captain McMahan," he reminded the jury—signed off on it as accidental and that no criminal charges were filed. "Now, how could that possibly be?" he asked sarcastically. "The government tries to tell us that that's because

Capt. McMahan is an idiot and a fool and he's so much of a rookie that he can't tell murder from accident. He didn't have any training.

"Imagine being a young detective with one of your first serious cases. It's a serious case, so serious that he calls his sergeant out in the middle of the night. And I can assure you that that's not appreciated for frivolous information. But the sergeant, an old-time, crusty cop named Brock McCoy, came along."

McMahan's investigation, said Truman, confirmed that the Jeep tire was "mushy" and not flat as Harold had said. McMahan did in fact follow up with Devries, leaving a message, but Devries "does not call him back," said Truman. "Now, should he have reached out to him? Maybe. But Detective McMahan was busy with other situations."

Turning to Detective Weaver's work, the evidence showed that it was completely possible for the Jeep to come off the jack the way it did. "When the paver broke, the bottle jack tipped, and the car came down enough, not crashing, but the car came down enough to pin Lynn Henthorn under that axle and causing her death," he said. It was, he said, an impossible murder to plan, requiring him to get her exactly under the Jeep at exactly the right spot exactly when the paver broke.

"Imagine how would that work," he said. "Imagine what would be the circumstances, throwing the lug nuts underneath there: 'Hey, Lynn, go get the lug nuts.' I can assure you that's unlikely." Further, there was no evidence she was forced under the Jeep—she suffered no bruises or scratches. "So how is it that she could have gotten under that car at that time? How is it that Mr. Henthorn, according to the government, is able to make up her mind, get under that car at exactly the time that the paver breaks?"

McMahan did in fact talk to Patricia Montoya at the time, and the account he had in his report left out much of her more colorful language, Truman said, noting the police report said nothing about the dirty plastic or putting the coat over Lynn. She even attended the funeral and was hugged by Harold. Her account only changed, he said, knowing that a second wife had died, according to Truman.

Ridiculing Detective Weaver's experiments with the Jeep, Truman said the investigator did not reach out to more qualified scientists with the FBI but decided to go on his own, using a different model of Jeep—a Loredo instead of a Cherokee—at a different time of day on different ground using different jacks, lifting up the Jeep at whatever random height he thought was best and "gets some sergeant . . . , to crawl underneath the vehicle to look for these lug nuts.

"Now, first of all, the test is ridiculous," he said. "Secondly, it shows us nothing. But third, if it does show us something, it shows us that Harold Henthorn was right with the two bottle jacks."

The critical error was that Weaver didn't use a paver—a paver that cracked into three pieces and caused the Jeep to lower, leaving the marks on Lynn's back that coroner Investigator Wesley Riber noted exactly matched the dimensions of the brake assembly. In the end, after all these years, the coroner's finding was changed only from accidental to undetermined.

Years later, the injury that Toni Henthorn suffered from the falling wood also was an accident, he said. The paramedics, trained in spotting domestic violence, rightly separated Toni and Harold to get their stories. "They examine her to see if there's any indication of any fight," said Truman. "There's not. It's just the knot on the back of her neck." Nobody at the hospital reported any suspicions of domestic violence, either, after talking to Harold.

"I submit to you that if there was a scintilla, a little bit, of evidence concerning domestic violence up at Grand Lake, that one of these professionals . . . would have reported it," he said.

That now brought up the thorniest part of the defense. "So let's talk a little bit about Mr. Henthorn," Truman said. "You have seen Mr. Henthorn tell many stories about many things. He is one of those guys that can't tell the same story twice. He says whatever comes to his head. Whether the story helps him or hurts him he just says it."

Harold, for instance, had told one person that he had left Toni behind to find the ranger, who was lost. Or that he told somebody else that a Flight for Life helicopter had been summoned. He texted some people that she was dead and others saying she's holding on and asking them to pray for her. "That doesn't help him. He just says those things, on text or in person. He just says them," said Truman. "And the biggest nonsense of all is this job stuff."

Truman acknowledged Harold didn't have the job he claimed to so many people for so long, that he was a stay-at-home father to Haley. "But it's not good enough for Mr. Henthorn to say, 'I'm a stay-at-home dad or not working.' He has to say, 'I'm a fundraiser, and not just a fundraiser for anything, I'm a fundraiser for big Christian things.'"

The statements, said Truman, are "just nonsense. But for whatever reasons he feels compelled to tell people that, not only tell them that, but he embellishes it with all sorts of details." He did the same when talking about his whereabouts, telling Agent Grusing he was in Salt Lake City working a big business deal when in fact he was somewhere else.

"Just nonsense," Truman said again. "He is incapable of telling the same story twice. And that's what got him in trouble in this particular situation. You can put up all the contradictions and we would be here another day. There are just so many of them, some are in his favor and some aren't. He just can't tell the same story twice. I have no idea why that it is. But that is the case."

While he may have been unable to keep his stories straight, there was no evidence Harold neglected to tell Toni about the insurance policies, that even though she was a physician herself and accustomed to dealing with such paperwork, that Harold somehow bamboozled her. Truman dismissed the testimony of Neal Creswell as nonsensical. "Forgive me, but I couldn't understand a word that Mr. Creswell said about the replacement insurance," he said. But if that was the case Harold could have gotten more insurance.

"If Mr. Henthorn, an avaricious, money-grubbing wife killer, decided that he was going to get the insurance money, why would he let one policy lapse, not $4.5 million but $6 million? Maybe the government will help you understand that when they get a chance to visit with you again."

In the end, he suggested, Toni was worth more to Harold alive than dead, from the money she had coming in as a partner at the eye clinic and potentially millions of dollars in inheritance when her parents died. "So under those circumstances, $4.5 million? Guys, that's chicken feed. That's chicken feed. And so Mr. Henthorn's motive that Miss Hazra talked with you about is suspect."

Wrapping up his summation, Truman reminded the jurors that this was his only chance to speak and that the prosecution would get a rebuttal. "I cannot say another word, and you may think that's unfair, but it's not," he said. "The reason it's not is because the government has the tremendous burden of proof. They have to convince each and every one of you beyond all reasonable doubt that they've proven their case of murder."

He advised them to listen carefully to the rebuttal argument from Assistant U.S. Attorney Valeria Spencer. "Perhaps she'll tell you where's the evidence that Toni Henthorn was pushed. I've been waiting for that this entire trial," he said. "Perhaps she'll tell you where the evidence is other than circumstantial evidence that Harold Henthorn can't tell the same story twice. Perhaps she'll tell you how it is that they think Lynn Henthorn was killed. Perhaps she'll tell you how the detective McMahan and the coroner Riber said this is an accident. Perhaps she'll tell you how come this Grand Lake deal, they didn't even call the cops. And not only that, but Toni Henthorn could have asked for help at any time. Maybe she'll tell you why that is. What did they bring you instead of these answers?"

He argued that the prosecution case amounted to character assassination, nothing more. "Ladies and gentlemen, when you have reviewed everything, you must find that the government has not met their burden. They have not proven by evidence—not speculation and character assassination—they have not proven that Toni Henthorn died as a result of homicide. They have not proven that Toni Henthorn died as a result of murder."

Spencer began her rebuttal by telling the jury what she did that morning at the courthouse. "I went down to the seventh floor," she said, "because Toni fell over 128 feet to her death when the defendant killed her. And that was the seventh floor of this courthouse. And I went and looked down, and I wondered what the story was going to be today. I wondered what the defense was going to say today about how that happened."

Harold Henthorn's defense, she asserted, amounted to "nothing." "He said to you: the defendant tells nonsense, whatever comes to his head, he can't tell the same story twice," said Spencer. "When you can't tell the truth, then you don't tell the same story twice. It's not called nonsense. It's called a lie. The defendant lied over and over and over again to everyone, from the 911 operators all the way through. . . . It was a lie the whole way through because he murdered Toni and he couldn't say that. He had to come up with a variety of stories."

The lies, she argued, stretched back to the night he told Roxanne Burns on the side of the road that he didn't know how to change a tire and reached to the tale he told from the side of Deer Mountain, what she mockingly called "a bad Roadrunner cartoon."

"Mr. Truman says: I'll be interested to hear what Miss Spencer is going to say about a push versus a fall," she said. "Here's what I have to say about a push versus a fall. I have a planner, I have an OCD man who is a planner who knows that there's no way to tell a push from a fall, and that's why he decides to shove her off a cliff to her death because he knows that there's not going to be a way to tell the difference."

But in telling his story, the details don't add up, she said. All he's left with are red herrings from his attorney to distract from the improbabilities. "He said Flight for Life was never called because the National Park said it would cost too much," said Spencer. "I'm sorry, what? Who said that? Nobody said it was a cost issue. What they said is the same thing that Roxanne Burns said, which is Flight for Life can only be called by EMS. Someone has to be on scene and say that's what is necessary. And, of course, if you pick a remote enough area where you can delay emergency response, that's not going to happen."

Spencer said Harold tossed out all sorts of red herrings. "I call them oops," she said. "He can make all sorts of oops." The call for the helicopter was only part of the plan—to sound frantic. Yet he still took the time to pick up the backpacks and trudged down the cliff. He talks about his cell phone dying then sends a bunch of text messages. He was supposedly a grieving husband but then complained the investigation was ruining his life.

"What? This is ruining your life? Your wife is dead. You murdered her, and it's ruining your life that these rangers are all over your back, that they want to know what happened up there?" she said. "So many missteps that he made."

Spencer disputed Truman's suggestion that the coroner was ready to wrap up Toni's death as an accident. "Mr. Wilkerson is the one who actually decides and he talked about the strangeness and he ultimately said because you can't differentiate a push from a fall, there is no way forensically and from the evidence to be able to tell that." The Park Service also never wrote off the case, bringing in both a special agent in Beth Shott and recruiting the services of the FBI

"He talks about CPR. There was no physical evidence of CPR. God bless her, she still had lipstick on. I'm a lipstick gal, so I'm probably not going to hike without mine," she said. "This is a woman who had her hair and makeup on to hike out there. This is not a woman without makeup for days, lipstick intact because the defendant did not do any breathing for her. He didn't do any CPR because she's dead."

As for Harold telling Toni's parents about dragging her across the rocks, it spoke volumes about Harold, said Spencer. "What kind of man tells the mother and father of his wife that he pulled her by her legs and her head bumped over rocks? That's a detail you probably don't need to share," she said. "But I'll tell you who says that: someone who's trying to cover up some evidence. Because the question is: How did he push her off? Did he bonk her on the back of the head and so he needed to make sure he covered that up by pulling her down? Look at that wound on the side of the head. Did he hit that rock on the side of her temple?"

That, she suggested, may be why he seemed to downplay her condition in the 911 call by saying she has a concussion. "That corn silk blonde, her hair was red with blood," said Spencer. "And he says she has a concussion? What? She is covered in bruises, she has broken almost all her ribs on the right side, her chest is smashed in, she has broken her shoulder, she has broken her neck, she has lacerated her liver, her ribs are now lacerating into the lungs and he just mentioned, well, I think she has a concussion. Talk about underplaying."

Another red herring, she said, was the insurance. A witness had reviewed five hundred checks on the Henthorn account and all were written by Harold. "Why, the defendant would have you believe that Toni was worth more alive than dead?" said Spencer. "I would tell you, with her parents sitting here alive in the courtroom, that's not true because he harped on and on about once her parents died she was going to be a wealthy woman. That's down the road, and that's if she stays with him after she's just opened her own bank account.

"Or he can kill her today," she said.

The case, she argued, amounted to so much more than character assassination. "It's not called character assassination. It's called evidence. That's what that is," she said. "It's about what he did. It's about behavior."

As for Lynn Henthorn's death, Spencer said she knew that Truman would beat up on Patricia Montoya. "I knew that was inevitable because that's what you do with a Good Samaritan who comes in here and tells you what she saw and what an impact it has had on her." But it was not Patricia's fault that Detective McMahan never followed up with her. "Suddenly, it's her fault that the interview was done so slipshod and poorly?"

She responded to Truman's argument that there was no evidence of a scuffle on top of the cliff. "A scuffle? He shoved her off a cliff," she said, her voice raising to a shout. "I don't think there was fighting going back and forth. There was a man who planned to kill his wife, not waiting until she was looking at him and saying I'm going to kill you now. I don't think there was any dramatic last words. He just shoved her off a cliff and sayonara to you." That last phrase boomed through the courtroom.

Harold's biggest error, she said, was that he killed Toni on federal land. Harold was "counting on the Douglas County response, a quick, couple-day turnaround," and didn't count on a more thorough professional response.

Then there was the missing diamond. "What did the defense call him? 'An avaricious, money-grubbing wife killer'? I agree with that," she said, drawing laughter in the courtroom. "Not only does he have $4.5 million in life insurance coming to him, not only does he change the beneficiary from his daughter to himself . . . but he gets the diamond, too.

"I would posit to you that the defendant saw that diamond sitting there loose, saw it sitting in the ring setting, but loose," she said. "And then he pockets it and then he's worried because the Park Service keeps asking him about it." So he put the diamond back. "Boy, is that interesting? Is that a red herring? It's a little bit, it has nothing to do with the evidence, but it's a fascinating

look into how this man thinks: If I can just get the diamond up there, this will all go away."

She concluded by reminding the jury of remarks
made in opening statements. "What defense counsel said
in his opening was wait until you hear the evidence," she
said. "What he said in his closing is there is not evidence.
Well, now you have the evidence. You've been charged
by the judge and you've heard us go on and on, there are
so many different nuggets here. Take that evidence back
with you, go through the instructions carefully, and do
what justice requires in this case and hold this man responsible for murdering his wife."

It was only 1 P.M., but the day seemed to have gone
on much longer and nerves were frayed. An alternate juror was thanked and told he was dismissed. Realizing
he wouldn't be involved in deliberations, he openly wept.
Eight women and four men retired to a private room
to decide Harold's fate. At 5 P.M., they broke for the
weekend.

Afterward, some of those close to Toni spoke outside
of the court. Tammi Abbruscato from the eye clinic
called the investigation and trial an ordeal. "It's very
difficult—very nervous, very emotional—[I'm] shaking
as we speak," she told 7NEWS in Denver. "It's been a
lot of up and down. We grieved, we settled with that
grief. We came to some rest in knowing what happened
and now we're grieving again." In the end, the case came
down to Harold Henthorn's attitude. "Typical, typical
Harold—it's his arrogance," Abbruscato said.

After listening to the evidence and the summations
Toni's brother Barry realized how little he really knew
about Harold: the many trips to the National Park to allegedly scout a murder location, the life insurance
money, the extent of Harold's manipulative and controlling personality. "I wanna say—I'm a smart guy—how

was I tricked, you know, by this person?" he told 7NEWS in Denver. "Was he really that good that we all got just so fooled and deceived in all that?" He now believed that Toni had seen it and had intended to leave Harold. "She was going to hang in there but she had probably reached her limit." The prosecution, he said, did a "good job" and he hoped for a guilty verdict.

Until then, he told CBS4 in Denver, he didn't want to hear the name Harold Henthorn. "The honest opinion is I want to beat his ass."

TWENTY

At 2:58 P.M. on Monday, September 21, 2015, after three days of deliberations, all rose for U.S. District Judge R. Brooke Jackson.

"Afternoon," he said. "Have a seat."

Prosecutors Valeria Spencer and Suneeta Hazra were there, as were defense attorneys Craig Truman and Josh Maximon sitting next to Harold.

"I understand the jury has a verdict," the judge said. "We will get the verdict in a just a minute."

He scanned the courtroom. Family members and friends of Lynn and Toni were there, as were reporters.

"I do want to say, however, in a case like this and with all the people that are involved," he said, then paused. "Up until this very moment, everybody has been extremely well behaved. Don't worry, I'm just teasing you. Everybody has done a great job of being behaved and observing courtroom decorum. I want that to continue. So no matter what the verdict is, no jumping up and down, screaming, yelling, applauding, criticizing, any of that. All right?

"Let's get the verdict," the judge said to his clerk, then told Harold that he could remain seated. "I talk to them for a couple of minutes before I take the verdict."

The jury was brought in.

"Have a seat," he told the panelists. "I understand you have a verdict." The jurors nodded and most said, "Yes."

"Would whomever the foreperson is please give the verdict form to the bailiff." A piece of paper was handed to the bailiff, who walked it over to the judge.

"Now, I haven't looked at it yet. It's all folded up," he said. "I'm going to leave it that way for a minute because there are a couple things I want to say to you 12. It's a tough job, isn't it? Very tough job. Of course, it's inconvenient having to give away ten days plus of your time. But it's really tough to listen to some of the evidence, to look at some of the evidence that you had to look at, and ultimately to make, really, a monumental decision. I'm so glad that we have juries so that this doesn't all fall on one person. Much better that we have 12 points of view.

"So I have nothing but respect for you. Truly, appreciation, respect, awe, really, for what jurors do, and I thank you for your service, truly public service."

The judge said that they would soon be free to talk about the case if they wanted to.

"There are a lot of people interested in your verdict. There are media, for example, here in the courthouse. When I walked in early this morning, there was a TV broadcast set up across the street. There are going to be people in the media and outside the media who would love to talk with you to find out what you thought and why you did whatever it is you did. If you would rather not talk about it, just tell anybody that contacts you that you would rather not talk about it, and that should be it.

If they insist, let me know, and I'll deal with that. You should not be criticized or complained about in any way. You have done a job that you were entrusted with."

The judge also said that he would be happy to meet with them "answer your questions, get to know you a little better, receive your criticism, anything you'd like to say, happy to do it. By the same token, once you're discharged, go through that door, you're free to go. You don't have to stay another second. That's entirely up to you."

He asked if they had any questions. They shook their heads no.

"All right, then, the court will announce the verdict in the United States vs. Harold Henthorn."

The judge unfolded the paper and read: "We, the jury, upon our oaths, unanimously find that the defendant, Harold Henthorn, in count one of the indictment is guilty. Signed by the foreperson. Madam foreperson, did I correctly read the verdict?"

The woman said, "Yes, you did."

Despite the judge's call for decorum, members of Toni's family members and her friends cried out and sobbed. Harold slowly shook his head.

The judge asked defense attorney Craig Truman if he wanted the jury polled. Truman said he did.

One by one, the judge asked each juror if that was their verdict.

"Is that your verdict, sir?"

"Yes, it is my verdict."

"Thank you," the judge said.

"Thank you," the juror responded.

Through the jury box the judge went, eleven more yeses to his question. Harold kept shaking his head.

"All right then," said the judge, "the jury has rendered its verdict. The court has polled each of the jurors indi-

vidually. Each of them has indicated that he or she as-
cribes to the verdict. The court accepts the verdict and
with this, ladies and gentlemen, you are discharged and
you are free to go. Thank you for your service."

"All rise for the jury," the bailiff said.

For the last time in the trial, attorneys, audience, and
Harold Henthorn rose for the jury as they filed out of the
courtroom, but not before one panelist, Dawn Roberts,
crossed the courtroom and hugged Toni Henthorn's
mother Yvonne. Then as all the jurors left, applause
broke out in the courtroom.

The judge took up the last of the scheduling matters.
A sentencing date was set for December. Then he had a
few words for the lawyers.

"I have mentioned several times to you, but I'll say
that one more time in public: Your professionalism on
both sides, counsel, was noticed and appreciated. Thank
you for that. We're in recess."

As Harold was handcuffed and led out of the courtroom, Lynn Henthorn's brother, Eric Rishell, shouted,
"Bye, Harold!" Then there was a cheer.

Deliberations had lasted for ten hours. On their first vote,
eleven of twelve jurors voted for conviction. Only one
juror held out. But this would not be a *12 Angry Men*
scenario with Henry Fonda triumphantly turning the
panelists one by one to acquittal. The decision was for-
gone, the delay only for due diligence by the juror who
wanted to spend time going through the evidence, to be
sure.

"The evidence was so clear," Dawn Roberts, a pre-
school director and the juror who had hugged Toni's
mother, told the *Denver Post*. (As for the hug: "From a
mom to a mom, I wanted to give her a hug. I felt so sorry
for the family and [Toni] was a wonderful woman who

didn't deserve to have her life end so horribly.") Harold's many lies doomed him as did his behavior after Toni's death. "He was very cold, very calculated," another juror, Jerry Taboada, said. "He didn't show anything. A person who loses their wife to something like that, you're going to break down sometime. He never did."

The jurors were challenged by the prosecution to connect the dots and use common sense and that, they said, they did. The evidence all "points to one thing," juror Christine Vogel told CBS4 in Denver. "It all added up. No way she could have just slipped off." The evidence of Lynn Henthorn's death, so much a point of contention before trial, played a role in their decision, but so, too, did something that many had shrugged off as a minor subplot. The disappearance and sudden reappearance of Toni's diamond weighed on jurors. Said Vogel: "He brought it back up there."

The U.S. Attorney for Denver, John Walsh, issued a statement thanking the prosecutors and investigators. "Toni Henthorn's family, especially her daughter and the entire Bertolet family, can now rest easier knowing that justice has been done," he said. "I also want to recognize the Rishell family, Henthorn's first wife, who has also experienced great pain. Finally, I would like to thank the jurors for their service. These individuals, who were asked to see graphic photos and listen to difficult testimony, should be recognized for their dedication to justice and their service as citizens of this great state."

Tom Ravenalle, special agent in charge of the FBI in Denver, reacted with more swagger. "Unfortunately for Mr. Henthorn, he met a team that was more detailed, more thorough and better prepared than he was despite them being late to the dance," he said.

Friends and family of the two Mrs. Henthorns faced the TV cameras to express relief. "We are overjoyed with the verdict and relieved this won't happen to any other lady," said Barry Bertolet. "We don't have to worry anymore." Looking back, Barry said, Harold viewed women as nothing but property. "I don't think he ever viewed them as people," he said. "And when he had gotten what he needed out of them, they were discarded." Toni's mother Yvonne Bertolet spoke briefly with jurors and described how she felt getting a hug from one of them. "I appreciated it very much," she said. "And she just said, 'As one mom to another, I feel your pain.'"

With the verdict in, Lynn's sister, Lisanne Bales, spoke out for the first time. "We do rejoice that this man is never going to murder anyone else, is never going to father another child who has to live in his shadow," she said, adding the family remained uncertain whether they'd want to endure another trial focusing on Lynn's death. "We think the perfect place for him is in a prison where he can continue to tell his stories and hang out with murderers, thieves and liars."

Grace Rishell said that "Harold Henthorn's love was lethal," and the jurors realized the same thing. "Lynn and Toni are gone," she said, "and I feel like it's not fair sometimes that I'm here because I do feel sometimes that I would have been next."

Harold's attorney, Craig Truman, declined to comment other than to say he'll likely appeal. The lone statement from Harold's side came from his brother, Robert Henthorn, who released a statement to CBS4 through an attorney saying, "While only Harold and Toni will ever really know exactly what happened on Deer Mountain, we respect the process that has considered enormous evidence and the verdict the jury has reached." Robert had his own problems: a future court date was set to deal with the $500,000 that Harold had allegedly transferred to him.

TWENTY-ONE

Lora Thomas had attended some of the trial and turned out for the sentencing hearing. For all the time and mental investment she had in the Lynn Henthorn case, she had never seen Harold Henthorn in person until she went to the court. "I had only seen videos of him," she said. "In the videos, he looks like a big man with dark hair. When I was sitting in the courtroom, I was trying to orient myself and figure out where the defense table was and which one he was. I was shocked. He was wearing a button-down shirt and pants like Dockers. The clothes were very baggy on him. I understand he lost a lot of weight in prison. He looked like a little creepy guy with gray hair."

The former Douglas County Coroner arrived in court on December 8, 2015, about a month after the verdict, to see Harold sentenced for murdering Toni. She sat among friends and family of the two Mrs. Henthorns. Because of the nature of mandated sentencing laws, the outcome was predetermined. But that didn't mean the sentencing hearing lacked for suspense. It's a peculiar aspect of sentencing hearings that they often deal with much more than the actual sentence. This was an occasion to explore deeper issues.

Craig Truman and the judge dispensed with routine matters. Truman said he was making a formal notice of an appeal. The defense would be challenging Jackson's ruling allowing the evidence of Lynn's death and the cabin injury to Toni. In hindsight, with the speed of the trial and the minimal defense, it seemed that the pretrial hearing had been the real legal battle as far as Harold's camp was concerned. The jury came to the conclusion that the defense had anticipated.

"Does Mr. Henthorn wish to make a statement this morning?" asked the judge.

"He does, Your Honor," said Truman.

"All right, sir, would you go to the podium, please."

"Your Honor, let me be brief this morning, just say a few words," began Harold. "Toni was a remarkable woman. And I loved her with all my heart. I did not kill Toni or anyone. With Toni's loss, there's been incredible pain in this case for everyone. Especially our remarkable and incredible little girl, Haley. I love Haley so much. I'll pray for her as she continues to go through this difficult time. As I go from here, I'll do the best I can under these difficult circumstances. Finally, I'm just so appreciative of my support and love I've had from my God, family, and friends.

"Thank you, Your Honor."

And that was it. Gone was the swagger from the dating site. Replaced by a quiet man in baggy clothes with little to say.

"Thank you, sir," said the judge. "Is there anyone in the courtroom who wishes to speak on behalf of Mr. Henthorn this morning?"

Nothing but silence.

"Apparently, there is not," said the judge. "Miss Hazra or Miss Spencer, do you wish to make an argument or statement this morning?"

"No, Your Honor. We would ask that the Court impose the statutory term of life, and we have no further argument to make."

"Is there anyone in the courtroom here this morning that would like to make a statement with respect to or on behalf of the victims?"

"Yes, Your Honor," said Hazra, "I believe there are six people here today that would like to speak on behalf of the victims."

While the guilty verdict is an occasion for reaction, a sentencing hearing is a catharsis.

"Good morning, Your Honor. My name is Barbara Cashman. I'm the guardian ad litem for Haley, and I am present today and speaking on Haley's behalf as her guardian ad litem.

"As the G.A.L. for Haley," Cashman continued. "I am the only person among the many who might have made or will make a statement today at this sentencing hearing whom Harold Henthorn did not betray. In my capacity representing Haley and specifically her best interests, I can say that Haley, in addition to her beloved mother, Toni's, tragic loss of life was the most deeply affected by Harold's numerous and consistent acts and words of betrayal over the first nine years of Haley's life. Harold's betrayal of Haley was not limited to the murder of the mother she loved and still loves. It went far beyond that. So let me tell you a little bit about who Haley was."

Tracing her involvement in the case back to March 2014, when she was appointed to represent Haley, Cashman recalled her first encounter with the "punctual and polite" little girl who was "understandably a bit wary of me." She spoke of Haley's little backpack filled obviously with items by Harold intended to impress and create a wrong impression. She spoke of those early "red flags" and her concerns about Haley's safety with her father, the disturbing comments from the other parents at Haley's school about Harold's behavior, Haley's compulsive hand-washing, and of Harold's lies. And she spoke of her relief when Harold was arrested.

"So everyone wants to know, how is Haley doing now?" Cashman said. "Free from Harold's insistence that everything is just fine, Haley has been allowed to grieve the death of her mother. Haley has also been encouraged to and allowed to make her own choices and decide for herself, something Harold never allowed her to do; that is, without some form of punishment, unless Harold approved of her choice in advance."

One manifestation of Haley's plight was that the child "used to hide a lot," said Cashman. "That was one of her many coping skills. She was a hurting and emotionally needy child, in need of nurturing. This was something that Harold was not capable of providing her. With the nurturing and love she has been receiving from caring people since Harold's incarceration, she has learned many new things, things that she wasn't familiar with before his arrest or was too scared to attempt on her own."

Cashman recounted a recent talk with Haley. "When I asked Haley if there was anything I could tell the Court in this statement, she reported two accomplishments that she felt were especially noteworthy," she said. "She has learned about telling the truth. And she has learned how to be independent, how to do things for herself and to help others. It seems counterintuitive that a child would be making huge emotional and developmental strides as a result of the incarceration of their surviving custodial parent, but this was the case with Haley."

Cashman referenced the April 2015 letter from Haley's principal observing "positive growth" at school since Harold's arrest and incarceration. "This positive growth is attributed to the stable home environment with her temporary guardians, who have provided her unconditional love," she said. More growth was seen in the statements from her temporary guardian. "Haley is doing well and thriving because she's no longer living with Harold and subject to his control and coercion," said Cashman. "Haley is now able to take responsibility for herself and her feelings and actions. She knows now that she has a choice about no longer being a victim of Harold's deception. She's currently taking stock of all behaviors that Harold modeled for her, the harsh punishments, the deception, the privation and cruelty, the lack of any empathy or compassion for others, along with Harold's use of manipulation control."

In the end, said Cashman, "Haley is afraid that she might grow up to be like her father. I have assured her that Harold's behavior is his choice and her behavior is her choice." By distancing herself from her father, she can now "behave like herself, without any interference or constraint from Harold. The more her father attempts to exert what little control over her he thinks he retains, he only serves to alienate her further and cause those near her to protect her more."

For a court session expected to be an anti-climax, the guardian ad litem's speech would leave the courtroom spellbound and set the stage for what came next. Since the day Brian Maass at Channel 4 blew open the story,

Barry Bertolet had been a constant media presence, providing a reminder that the case was about more than statutes and court filings, but about a woman with family and friends, surrounded by love and support, whose loss created a void. With more time and reflection, working off of a prepared text, this highly trained physician summoned all of his intellectual faculties and delivered a speech as profound and poetic as it was emotionally raw.

"Toni Bertolet Henthorn was blessed with a gift of intellectual brilliance, impeccable character, extraordinary talents, and a big heart. It's often said that when a brilliant mind, heart, and talent come together as one, one should expect a masterpiece. Toni Bertolet Henthorn's life was a masterpiece and a role model to those who are fortunate to be part of her life."

Reminding the courtroom of her accomplished life, a committed ophthalmologist to the patients she could help, and to those she ultimately couldn't. "Toni always carried the pain of the loss which you know those tragic moments taught her as a person. Every great doctor has seen loss, has seen suffering, has seen life struggles, but all had discovered a purpose in their own lives to rebound in the purpose of tragedy. Toni was a medical doctor that had had unique perspective on life, and those moments confirmed her compassionate care and concern for others."

One could sense the doctor as much as the brother in Barry Bertolet as he spoke. "There is no unique perspective or lesson to garner from the wrongful death and loss of Toni. It is what it is, a devastating loss," said Barry. "To the man who thought he needed a new prescription for glasses but was diagnosed by Toni with an aggressive brain tumor, requiring immediate intervention, Toni's life mattered. To the young man facing total blindness from an injury requiring the skilled hands of a surgeon, Toni's life mattered. To the young person contemplating suicide, in need of compassion and skillful guidance, Toni's life mattered. To the young medical physician in need of an accomplished mentor to guide a promising medical career, Toni's life mattered. To that little boy dying on the emergency room table that felt the healing hand of a wonderful physician but was in need of a guiding hand to heaven, Toni's life mattered."

It was a life that was cut short, he said, by Harold Henthorn, a name Barry didn't utter. He called him only "the defendant." This man, he said, finally was held accountable by "an attentive, intelligent, meticulous, and methodical jury that considered the facts and evidence in this case and reached the verdict of guilty of first-degree murder.

"This case," he continued, "has revealed more about the circumstances behind the wrongful death of Toni Bertolet Henthorn, but it also revealed the ugly truth of the extent of the deceitfulness of the defendant. The defendant is the evil that lurks in unthinkable places and manipulated his way into Toni's life as well as several others. The defendant preyed on women of faith in a Christian environment because, as with Toni, Christian women moved forward in their life with goodness in their heart."

There were no lies to Harold's detriment, as his attorney contended; only lies "to his direct benefit," said Barry. "The defendant proclaimed to be a Christian man when in fact he is an immoral man," he said. "The defendant claimed to have a career in business when in fact he had neither. The defendant claimed to be financially wealthy when in fact he had no fortune at all. The defendant claimed to be a provider when in fact he offered and gave nothing. The defendant claimed to be a family man when in fact he is a selfish man. The defendant's entire adult life was a lie and a scam to live his life and lifestyle while others paid the price. The defendant only made withdrawals and made no deposits in the lives of his wives and their family."

The contrast to Toni then was stark and severe. "While Toni lived her life to inspire people, the defendant lived his life to drain people," he said. "And he represents a human that can never be reimbursed." The defendant "created his own reality and everyone in it," he said, exhibiting "phony traits" that took precedent over family.

Barry, it seemed, was trying to analyze the vital signs of evil, to glean some meaning. It was an extensive search. He quoted Warren Buffett and he quoted the Bible. And it kept coming back to evil, the causes—linked somehow with narcissism—and its manifestations, its ramifications, particularly upon the innocents.

"To a child, evil and villains are supposed to be easily identifiable," he said. "The innocence of a child shouldn't be violated by evil and more importantly, evil within a trusted family unit. The bad guy is the defendant. And evil our children must now comprehend came from within the family in the form of a parent and an uncle. My child has now asked the appropriate questions of how do I know. How does she know that a trusted person is not lying to her? How does she know that the person that she chooses to love her is not just loving her for wealth and lifestyle? How does she know that a person of perceived trust would not cause her harm? How does she know that grief and sadness will not follow her at the hands of someone she trusted?"

While the family struggles, "the defendant" merely wanted to move on with his life, blaming everybody—the investigators, the media, the in-laws, the justice system, even the victim—but never himself, said

Barry, cloaked in a world all his own, all his making. "Of all the titles that the defendant has bestowed on himself without merit, the title of murderer bequeathed by the jury is the only title the defendant has earned."

Barry's father followed him and introduced another emotional element. "We never imagined that murder would enter into our lives like a thief in the night," said Tom Bertolet. "The Bertolets have always been a close-knit family, loving, helping, and protecting one another. We feel guilt that we failed to act on our suspicions concerning Toni's welfare and her marriage. We grieve that we were not at her side in her dying moments."

On an easel in their home, he said, is a framed photo of Toni and at the bottom it reads, "In loving memory, January 10, 1962—September 29, 2012." Toni, he told the judge, was born one day before her mother's birthday. "Yvonne always considered Toni the best birthday present she ever received," he said. "I am haunted by my wife's lament that, 'When Toni died, I died. I will never celebrate my birthday again.'"

"Yvonne and I won't ever hear again Toni say, 'Hi, mama, hi daddy, this is Toni,'" he continued. "We hear you, Sissy, in our hearts. We are hopeful that you have no more nights, no more pain, no more tears, with the heavenly father. But for us, there will be forever in this life the pain and tears, maybe not seen by others, but for our daughter, killed in a cruel, sadistic, senseless and cowardly act of violence."

There was still work to be done, he said. Alluding to a custody dispute with Harold over Haley, Toni's father said, "We wanted to provide a safe and loving environment for Haley, preferably with her mother's Mississippi family." That case was still pending in another court. "The sentencing today is the final act in completing a first goal and has opened the door to achieving our second," he said. "We take solace that prayers have been answered."

Guilt surfaced again in the statement from Kevin Rishell, Lynn's brother. "Words cannot describe the pain and the loss we all felt," he said of Lynn's death. "We were all traumatized by the event, but my parents were hit hardest of all and they were never the same afterwards. There is something unnatural when a parent has to bury their child." And added to that, he said, Harold denied Lynn's parents by going against their wishes and having her remains cremted.

"I don't know which is more monstrous—to drop a 4,000-pound jeep on your beloved or to push her off a cliff," he said. "The heartless, avariciousness of this defies my ability to grasp it. We grieve that we didn't see Harold for the monster that he is and didn't ask more questions or demand a better investigation. If we had, Toni might be alive today. It's just so very sad."

In hindsight, he said, the family should have seen through the lie, the absurdity of Harold's story about the Jeep. "It was a lie, and we are beyond sorry for not seeing through it. We pray for the Bertolets, that they will forgive us for our blindness to the truth. There is no doubt in my mind, this monster planned and coldheartedly dropped the Jeep on my sweet, gentle sister, with malice aforethought, and he pushed sweet, gentle Toni to her death as well. I think there is a special place in hell for someone like him."

His former wife Grace Rishell spoke of what could have been, the dangers that lurked with what she thought was this strong Christian man to whom she entrusted her daughters, her finances, and herself. "I now shared something with both women. All three of us had policies on us where Harold was both the owner and the sole beneficiary. What we didn't have in common was that I was still alive. I began to feel something akin to survivor's guilt. I also began to feel fear, something I had never experienced before with Harold.

"The pain he has put my daughters through is hard to forgive. My youngest suffered from nightmares that he was going to hurt me, and another daughter turned more and more to substance abuse to quell the pain and fear she felt from this. Harold was a man she looked up to and saw as a father figure. He put their father down for being a fraud and to now know the truth about him. My daughters and I now struggle to know how we will know when someone is lying to us and doesn't have our best interests in mind. It is not a good feeling to carry around."

One of those daughters, Laura Rishell, told the court how her life had been shaped by the case. "The impact he had on my life is represented in a truly painful, life-altering fashion," she said. "I have known Harold since I was born. This means this man has not only seen me grow up but had a direct influence on the process. This effect is through countless visit, letters, vision, and role far greater than a normal uncle would play out. He became a man I saw in a fatherly way. So when I look back to all my childhood memories that I remember all too vividly, I don't feel a sense of joy and gratitude as a loved one should feel. I instead have feelings of betrayal and distrust. These feelings have and always will play out in the life I will continue to lead and impose on others."

This was her "new normal," she called it, and she expressed little hope things would improve. Harold hurt her family and put her mother on a mission that consumed her. "I lived with a mother who spent every waking moment on a case to bring justice to two beautiful women taken away. I lost a mom, and I gained an investigator in the house." Her mother's pain became the family's pain, her fears their fears. "I saw the anxiety of a policy that he refused to cancel," she said. "I saw a police car every night circle our house to try and give some peace of mind. I saw what absolute life-altering actions it had on my mother's lives and my sisters.'"

All this robbed her of a healthy college experience. "I have missed classes due to court, family obligation, and to resolving night terrors in my bed over a man I feared would take my mom away from me. I have to accept that a man I thought loved me is a man who intended to cause me the most pain I have yet to encounter."

It was the bleakest of the statements, coming from one so young, and it served as the most dramatic reminder of the insidious reach of murder, how it kills more than a body. The autopsy reports on Lynn and Toni spoke of internal injuries, of hemorrhaging and broken bones, of organs crushed and sliced. But only in court could the other wounds be described for the first time.

At a little before 9:30 A.M., the judge then did what the statute told him to do. "With respect to the sentence, the Court now imposes the mandatory sentence as set by the statutes of the United States and the defendant is sentenced at this time to spend the rest of his life in prison, with no opportunity for release," he said. The lawyers having nothing else to say or do, the judge then said: "The Court at this time remands Mr. Henthorn to the custody of the marshals to be taken to the federal Bureau of Prisons to spend the rest of his life in prison."

Or not. Certainly, a pall fell over the sentencing hearing at points. There was the guilt felt by Tom Bertolet and Kevin Rishell over something a jury said Harold did, the fear and anxiety by Grace Rishell, the "new normal" of her daughter Laura. Lynn and Toni were dead, and nothing could be done about that. Harold remains but one appellate decision away from returning to court, with a new trial and a new jury, one that may never hear about a woman crushed in the night or the falling wood flung from a deck. The Brides in the Bath case would be resurrected, though, examined anew, applied again to the circumstances at hand, a sobering testament to how little things have changed.

It would all have seemed hopeless but for one thing: the resilience of a child.

"So how is Haley doing?" Cashman had asked in her speech, a speech that left the courtroom spellbound. "In one word, she's thriving. She's now able to do things that other ten-year-old girls are doing. She went trick-or-treating for the very first time this past Halloween. And she's looking forward to starting her new life. A life far away from her father. This new life includes love, kindness, and caring for others, which are explicit rejection of Harold's fear-based us versus them way of relating to others."

Cashman did not miss the cruel and perverse irony that the deaths of two women, Toni and Lynn Henthorn, at the hands of Harold should result in the "freeing" of Haley. But, she said, it has, in the most dramatic way. "Haley does not wish to refer to Harold any longer as her father but rather simply as Mr. Henthorn," said Cashman, concluding: "She does not wish for him to remind her of anything. This is her choice. It is a healthy and life-affirming choice for a ten-year-old girl, and I support it. The only thing that Mr. Henthorn has going for him right now are Haley's prayers for him."

Kevin Rishell wanted a special place in hell for Harold Henthorn. This may be it.

TWENTY-TWO

In late 2015, the Douglas County Sheriff's Office informed the family of Lynn Henthorn of the suspension of the investigation into her 1995 death. "We're not going to be filing immediate criminal charges," Sheriff Tony Spurlock told CBS4 in Denver. "We're going to keep it static." The decision, he said, was made "in the best interest of justice." He claimed the department had sufficient evidence for charges but wanted to wait until Harold exhausts all his appeals in Toni's death before deciding on whether to seek additional charges to avoid causing any interference in the legal process. This could take years. The detective looking into her death has been taken off the case and given other assignments. In all likelihood, no charges will ever be filed, Lynn's family having to be satisfied that her death at least helped send Harold to prison for the death of Toni. Media reports described her family as disappointed but understanding of the sheriff's position.

Another piece of unfinished business was also resolved. Minutes after the jury had announced its verdict
against Harold, a process server handed his brother, Rob
Henthorn, papers compelling him to appear in probate
court to answer for the $500,000 that Harold allegedly
had transferred to him. This money, discussed in the pretrial hearing about the state of Harold's finances, had the
judge wondering aloud whether Harold was trying to
hide assets around the time of his arrest. Administrators
for Toni's estate wanted these funds to benefit Harold and
Toni's daughter Haley, not Harold or his brother. Within
days, an agreement was reached: Rob agreed to give all
the money to the estate.

More good news would follow. Just before Christmas 2015, the family court in Colorado named Toni's
brother Barry the permanent guardian for Haley. The
child moved to live with him and his family, including
his wife and daughter, in Mississippi. She now goes to
school. She sings in the choir. She has friends and a
loving home and extended family, including aunts and
uncle and cousins and grandparents, who all love her
completely and unconditionally. "She's finally allowed to
be a ten-year-old," old says Barry's brother Todd.

In early 2016, Harold was transferred from the federal
lockup in Englewood, Colorado, to the FTC Oklahoma
City, a prison holding 1,400 male and female inmates,
with another transfer likely as the Oklahoma facility is
a holding center for inmates awaiting final destinations.
From behind bars, he filed court papers seeking to set
aside the guardianship decision, according to the Bertolets. "Harold doesn't seem to want to let that go," said
Todd. The Bertolets think Harold is motivated in part
by money. Toni's life insurance policies still meant a
payout potentially in the millions. "In a practical matter,
if Haley died, all that wealth would go to Harold," said

Toni's father. "That's just horrible. I'm not talking about the wealth. I'm talking about the fact that she died for that money."

Toni's family believes it's about more for Harold. "I think it all goes back to his controlling issues," said Todd. "He realizes obviously that he's lost everything. The one thing that he still has out there is his parental rights over my sister's daughter. That's his last bargaining chip. He wants to push that as far as he can go. Everything has been a fight from day one."

If it's a fight he wants, the Bertolets are prepared to give it to him for as long as it takes. Despite Harold's conviction, several legal matters lingered, including Harold's appeal in the murder case, the dispensation of the life insurance money, the dissolution of Toni's trust, and the parental rights for Haley. "One of the things that helped us in the grief process was doing everything that we could to be Toni's voice," he said. "We're still pretty much involved and busy."

Harold has visitation privileges; Haley has declined to see him. She also won't open his cards and letters sent to her uncle's house. She asks to use the last name of Bertolet instead of Henthorn. "She doesn't want anything to do with her father, doesn't recognize him," said Todd. "That's in the past with her. She doesn't want to go down that path." She calls Barry "dad" and his wife, Paula "mom." The Bertolets say Haley seems more and more like her mom every day. She even has shown an interest in science and medicine, just like her mother. Haley went one day with her guardian uncle Barry to his hospital, where the nurse told Haley about how Barry is a hero because he saves lives. Haley called him a "superhero."

Haley's own healing will take time, maybe a lifetime. For a long time, she didn't want to talk about her mother at all. The Bertolets believe that was because Haley's memories of her mother were scrambled with the things Harold said—often terrible things, according to the Bertolets, who are just now learning what they are. After Toni's death, Harold removed all signs of her from the house—photos, clothes, personal items. And when the house was sold after his conviction, friends found cards, letters, and gifts to Haley from the Bertolet family, all hidden and unopened. "There was a gift that I had sent to her way back," said Toni's mother Yvonne. "It was under the bed, still wrapped in the gift paper."

Toni's family has been reintroducing Haley to her mother. "Her mother was a very well respected, smart, intelligent lady," says Todd. "We felt like it was important for Haley to be able to grieve for her mother and talk about her mother and always remember exactly who her mother was. In Mississippi, people knew her mother, knew the person that Haley should know her as and not the person Harold wants her to know her as."

The Bertolets are under no illusions about how long and difficult it will be for the child.

"At different times in her life she's going to have episodes," said Toni's father. "She's never going to escape this. I just hate that the child has to live with this, to lose a mama and a daddy." But every day brings encouraging signs. At a choir performance at Haley's school, her grandparents saw her turn to a classmate, point to the audience, and say, "That's my family." Said her grandfather, "We've got to show her that there are people who love her unconditionally."

In memory of Toni, her parents established an endowment at the University of Mississippi Medical Center to train future generations of ophthmalogists. To make a donation, go to www.umc.edu/tonibertoletendowment.